ADVANCED
DEER HUNTING

ADVANCED DEER HUNTING

New strategies based on the latest studies
of whitetail behavior.

JOHN WEISS

Drawings by Robert Ritter

Published by Outdoor Life Books
Distributed to the trade by Stackpole Books

Published by
Outdoor Life Books
Grolier Book Clubs, Inc.
380 Madison Avenue
New York, NY 10017

Distributed to the trade by
Stackpole Books
Cameron & Kelker Sts.
Harrisburg, PA 17105

Library of Congress Cataloging-in-Publication Data
Weiss, John, 1944–
  Advanced deer hunting : new strategies based on the latest
  studies of whitetail biology and behavior / John Weiss.
    p. cm.
  Includes index.
  ISBN 1-55654-014-0
  1. Deer hunting. I. Title.
SK301.W357 1987
799.2'77357--dc19   87-17615

Manufactured in the United States of America

Dedication

◆◆◆◆◆◆◆◆◆◆◆◆◆◆◆◆◆◆◆◆◆◆◆◆

For deer hunters everywhere
and of all persuasions
who want to be better
than just good.

Contents

◆◆

Acknowledgments

◆◆◆

Book publishers have a tough job dealing with authors. Writers, by their very nature, tend to be slightly neurotic, unreasonably demanding, and consistently unpredictable. If a book is to be successful, the balance must therefore be tipped in the other direction, and this requires that an editor be firm, insightful, compassionate, fair, and sometimes even clairvoyant. My editor, Henry Gross, who has laboriously guided me through the birth of four other books with unwavering professionalism, has been all of these things, and more.

I'd also like to thank Clare Conley, editor of *Outdoor Life,* Tom Paugh, editor of *Sports Afield,* Duncan Barnes, editor of *Field & Stream,* and Lamar Underwood, editor of Harris Publications, for allowing me to include in this book updated and expanded versions of my articles that were previously printed in those periodicals.

Introduction

◆◆

The book you are about to read is different from others that deal with the subject of hunting the whitetail deer. There are dozens of deer hunting books presently on the market, reflecting the continually growing preoccupation of millions of sportsmen with whitetails. In my home library are twenty-one books on deer hunting which have been published in just the last ten years. Most are well written and a couple are magnificently illustrated. Yet the overwhelming majority are quite disappointing in content, for the one thing they all have in common is that they are directed to an audience of apparently rank amateurs who have yet to embark upon their first whitetail hunt.

The authors of these books cover at length such rudimentary subjects as how to choose an adequate deer rifle, how to sight-in a rifle, how to select a proper knife for field-dressing, and the proper clothing for cold or wet weather. The aspiring hunter is next led into the field where he is taught what foods deer like to eat, how to recognize trails and things called "scrapes" that may be randomly chanced upon and, last but not least, where to aim at a deer should one pass by.

Such deer hunting books serve a valid need. Every year, throngs of men and women, young and old alike, decide to take up deer hunting. Like all beginners, they have to learn the basics.

However, these newcomers to the sport are vastly outnumbered by millions of others who have spent plenty of time afield. Their gun cabinets are filled with a wide selection of firearms, and they'll eagerly talk ballistics into the wee hours of the night. Although they may not succeed in taking a buck every year, they wish they were able to do so, and their den walls already display several racks of modest dimensions, with one special empty place reserved for the trophy of a lifetime they hope to collect.

They are veterans of more annual hunting camps than they can remember and have both the curiosity and background knowledge to discuss with any wildlife biologist the peak rutting times in their locales, the trace minerals responsible for antler development, whether spike bucks are genetically inferior, and why harvesting of does translates into an overall more healthy deer population.

In driving down any given backcountry road, it is impossible for them to pass a towering oak tree without instantly speculating what the mast crop will be like later that fall and how either an absence or plentitude of acorns will affect the movement of deer along the forested ridges. And although they may occasionally forget birthdays and anniversaries, the opening dates of their state's bowhunting, muzzleloading, and rifle seasons are etched in their minds.

In short, they live for deer hunting, never quenching their thirst for new information that will allow them to deepen their insight and hone their abilities in the hopes they'll become more proficient in their favorite sport.

It is for *these* millions of dedicated and diligent students of whitetail deer hunting that *Advanced Deer Hunting* has been compiled. Consequently, in glancing through the table of contents, you'll immediately notice a distinct absence of chapters dealing with subjects most deer hunters consider elementary because I'm taking for granted you're already familiar with the basics.

Although I've attempted to arrange the chapters with as much continuity as possible, don't feel compelled to begin with the first one and progress through the book in sequence. Each chapter focuses on a specific aspect of advanced deer hunting as comprehensively as is practical within the space limitations allowed. As a result, if as you are reading this your state presently is having one of the warmest deer seasons ever recorded and you're just not seeing any deer in their customary haunts, go straight to Chapter 19 and harbor no apprehension that you've missed something critically important by skipping the many preceding chapters. Or if your state's deer season recently came to a close, Chapter 6 deals with the new technique of *post-season* scouting, which will help you to peg the routine of a big buck you'd like to level your sights on when the season reopens next year.

I wish you the best of success in your whitetail hunting, but more important, I wish you the happiest of memories afield.

JOHN WEISS
Chesterhill, Ohio

ADVANCED DEER HUNTING

PART I

THE
SENSORY WORLD
OF
WHITETAILS

1

Reading a Deer's Body Language

◆◆◆

The bottom had just about dropped out of my deer hunting. After diligently scouting an area in southeastern Ohio where there was plenty of fresh sign, and after patiently sitting on stand for five days, I had seen absolutely nothing other than squirrels and songbirds. It was the final day of the season and the last minutes of daylight were rapidly fading when a big doe came loping in my direction. My remaining spark of hope suddenly turned into a glowing ember. Very slowly, I raised my slug-loaded shotgun and began settling the crosshairs on the deer's lung region. There would be no antlers to hang on the wall this year, I thought, but I'd get my winter's supply of venison. If you're an ardent game cook, that is success in itself.

Then I noticed that the doe was holding her tail off to one side at a sharp angle. I knew what that meant and took my finger off the trigger. The doe moved on and eventually vanished in a tangled thicket of brush and honeysuckle.

My insight paid off. Several minutes later, a handsome buck came down the very same trail. I raised my gun a second time and, in addition to collecting my deer meat, received a fine eight-point rack as a bonus.

Even though I had done my scouting well and had spent close to fifty hours sitting in a tree, I got that buck only because I could interpret whitetail body language. Otherwise, I'd have settled for the doe without remotely suspecting that a buck was following her.

If you learn to interpret the body language of whitetails and the sounds they make, you'll be a better hunter. In this particular case, the doe's tail was cocked to one side—the common signal that female deer use to let bucks

3

By observing and interpreting a deer's body language, a hunter can often predict its next move. The way this doe is holding her tail as she walks along indicates normal, unafraid behavior, and the position of her ears tells you she's probably alone.

This doe's tail is lifted slightly and cocked to one side, her ears are cupped toward the rear. She's keeping track of a buck following her and indicating that she's interested in his attentions.

Although this is a handsome buck, he's exhibiting subordinate posture. The tell-tale signs are a slightly hunched back, tail clamped between the legs, and a stiff-legged gait. These mannerisms indicate there's a larger, dominant buck in the area.

Dominant bucks intimidate lesser bucks by such signs as holding their heads high and extending their tails straight back.

know that they're in estrus and receptive to being bred. If you ever see a doe exhibiting this behavior, freeze! Within the next several minutes, you'll almost surely get a shot at a buck so preoccupied with a doe that he'll have no idea you're there.

Bucks communicate with their tails, too. In prime habitat, several bucks may have overlapping home ranges. The largest, dominant buck commonly saunters around with his head held high and his tail slightly lifted and extended straight back. This is a threatening posture that proclaims to lesser bucks not to mess with him. Bucks with lower rankings in the pecking order acknowledge the status of the superior deer by walking timidly in a stiff-legged gait with their tails tucked between their legs.

The value of knowing these signals comes into play when a hunter is patiently watching a major deer runway. If a six-pointer comes along with his tail tightly clamped against his hindquarters, an enterprising hunter might elect to let the deer go about his business. Although the six-pointer may be a quite acceptable trophy, his tail is telling all the world that he's low on the totem pole and that a much larger buck is on the prowl nearby.

At the other end of a whitetail's anatomy, head-holding mannerisms can be equally revealing. A whitetail employs head-bobbing when it senses danger and wants to drum up some further activity to confirm its suspicions. The deer begins to lower its head toward the ground as if to feed but then quickly jerks its head back up. This sudden, unexpected movement can cause a predator or hunter to flinch and reveal his presence. Often, this head-bobbing ruse is accompanied by the animal stamping its front feet. If you fall for either trick, you'll probably be left, at best, with a difficult shot at a departing animal.

If, on the other hand, the deer lowers its head and actually begins to nibble upon this or that, you can go ahead and slowly raise your rifle. The deer is mistakenly sure that there is nothing nearby posing an immediate threat.

When a deer employs the head-bob, it uses its eyes to detect danger. Other head movements are geared to the use of other senses. For example, when a whitetail holds its head high and tilted back and the upper lip is curled back so that the gums show, the animal is smelling something it considers pleasing and would like to find the source of the scent. Biologists refer to this lip-curling behavior as the "Flehman response," named after the scientist who first identified and explained the behavior. The Flehman posture is most commonly displayed when a rutting buck catches a whiff of a doe in heat. However, does and bucks also assume the Flehman posture as a favorable reaction to many other odors. These include any number of commercial deer scents used by hunters, which we'll look at in greater detail in another chapter.

Conversely, when a deer lowers its head to about knee-level and its tongue protrudes laterally out of the side of its mouth, the animal has smelled something that has triggered alarm. Most often, it is either human scent or a nearby deer's release of metatarsal gland scent—a warning signal of impending danger. But such "tonguing" behavior can also be triggered by a commercial deer scent that is not appropriate to the time of year or locale. This could be a rutting scent used during the non-mating season, or an apple scent used in country where there are no apple trees.

Insightful hunters can use this knowledge to determine both the placement of stands and the best scents to use for the particular region or the time of year. When whitetail body language tells you that deer smell something alarming, note the wind direction and relocate your stand or blind if you suspect that the animals are catching your body odor. It may also be your chosen deer scent that is causing the animals to panic, and you should experiment with other potions.

An angry, aggressive buck often displays a sidling gait, his head bobbing and lowered. There's probably another buck nearby competing for available does.

When a deer is alerted by a sound, it cups both ears and points them in the direction from which the sound came, hoping for follow-up sounds that will tell it what made the initial noise. Many times I've seen deer do this, and then turn and bolt for no apparent reason. Five or ten minutes later, some other hunter or a dog usually comes poking along.

Just as often, deer swivel their ears in different directions. They can point one ear forward and the other directly to the rear. This is nature's way of allowing them to monitor their whereabouts simultaneously in different directions. When a hunter observes this kind of body language, he should know that there's something else making noises that interest the deer. That something may be another hunter or several hunters participating in a drive.

In other instances, particularly if the deer is a doe, watching the animal's ear movements can help to put antlers on the wall. If a doe has one ear cupped forward and the other pointed backward as she minces along, she's checking for anything that might be up ahead along her intended route or behind on her backtrail. Early in the hunting season, she's probably keeping track of twin fawns following somewhat behind, but during the months of November and December, a rutting buck is undoubtedly following her. Don't alert the doe. Let her pass unaware of your presence and rivet your attention on her backtrail.

Some of the most revealing body language whitetails exhibit is in the ways they hold their ears. With ears cupped forward, this doe is intently concentrating on something up ahead.

This doe is listening for sounds up ahead and at the same time monitoring her backtrail

This deer is alarmed and in brief seconds will probably flee. The tell-tale signs of her fear are her folded-back ears.

If a deer suddenly lays its ears back, the jig is up. You've blown your cover and the deer knows you're there. The insides of a whitetail's ears are very sensitive and the animals fold them back just before fleeing so they won't be stung when bounding through brush and briers. When you see this behavior in its earliest stages, it's often wise to take the best available shot because the deer will be gone in seconds.

This body language provides the hunter with vital information that can tilt the odds in his favor. Whitetails are gregarious and maintain a community awareness. They use body language both consciously and unconsciously to keep tabs on each other and on other creatures. Consequently, an astute onlooker can determine a deer's state of mind and what the animal will usually do next by interpreting its body language.

Most hunters are well aware that spooked deer usually run with their tails held high and waving from side to side. Actually, this behavior is more characteristic of does than of bucks. Because the brown coloration of deer blends well with their surroundings, it would be easy for a mature doe in flight to quickly lose her offspring, making them vulnerable to predators. The doe's waving white flag is like a neon sign to young fawns. It guides the fawns when they follow the doe through dense and dark cover as she quickly dodges left or right or bounds over obstacles.

Because bucks do not take any responsibility for rearing their offspring, they do not instinctively "flag" while running. When they do raise and wave their tails, it is merely a happenstance. There's valuable insight here for hunters. When several deer are routed from their beds or feeding grounds and are bounding away, it's often quite difficult for a hunter to pick out a buck. Try to focus your attention on the animal that has *not* lofted a waving white flag. Then look for antlers. In many cases, your sights will settle on the only buck in the group.

When deer are not fleeing but are going about their everyday activities, the ways in which they hold their tails can tell you many other things. For instance, hunters on stand often conclude that they have been spotted when a deer stares at them. Thereupon, the hunter begins raising his rifle and the motion does indeed reveal the hunter's presence, causing the deer to bound away. If the hunter had remained motionless and had watched the deer's tail, he might have filled his tag. Scientific studies have shown that deer are quite adept at spotting the slightest movement. But if a hunter remains as still as a statue, a deer usually cannot distinguish him from a stump or a tree trunk.

On countless occasions, deer have looked straight at me from as close as 20 yards, craning their heads from side to side to change their visual perspective. Yet they did not really "see" me. Provided there is no revealing scent or sound to arouse other senses, the deer eventually decide that whatever I am, I pose no worry, and they very shortly return to unalarmed

Running with tail held high is usually more characteristic of does than of bucks, as shown in this photo. Does raise their tails to signal their fawns of danger.

behavior. Moments later, when the head is turned away or their view of me is blocked by screening cover, I'm able to raise my rifle or bow.

Getting a shot here, though, all depends on how the deer is holding its tail. If the tail remains down, and perhaps swishes occasionally from side to side, you can be confident that the deer is not suspicious of danger and doesn't know what you are. It's smart to play the waiting game for however long it takes. On the other hand, if the deer raises its tail so that it is horizontal and pointing straight to the rear, you might as well take the best shot you can make. The animal is spooked and will almost always make a quick exit. But you must temper such interpretations with good judgment and react according to the circumstances. I've often seen deer coming

Two good examples of running bucks with lowered tails. When you see a group of running deer, look for the animal whose tail is not aloft—it's usually a buck.

toward me, holding their tails straight back. The deer were actually moving away from other hunters or fleeing from them. The animals did not know that I was there. Remember, too, that bucks commonly extend their tails straight back in a threatening posture to intimidate subordinate bucks.

Whitetails also use a variety of vocal noises. Fawns commonly make mewing sounds when they are temporarily separated from their mothers. If you hear them, a doe is almost always nearby. No fair-minded hunter would knowingly shoot a doe still tending her offspring, but that's not the point. If you know she is there, you'll want to make every effort not to cough, reposition your feet, or make any other sound or movement. To do so would almost surely alert the doe and would probably cause her to flee in panic, thus alarming any bucks also in the area.

The most common vocalization made by whitetails is a deep, raspy snort or wheezing noise created when the animal quickly exhales a large volume of air. It's a universal fear response, most often elicited by the deer smelling something alarming. These snorts can be triggered by visual and auditory cues, as well.

Of course, if a deer has pegged your location and snorts as it bounds away, there's not much hope of getting a shot at that particular animal that day. But if you're sitting on stand or stillhunting, be alert for deer snorts coming from some distance. Likely as not, the deer is hastily retreating from another hunter. By listening to the intermittent snorts the animal makes as it moves, you can often get a "fix" on the deer's route. This allows you to get your gun up and pointed in the right direction.

Several years ago, I used deer snorts to tag one of the biggest bucks I've ever taken. I was hunting from a tree stand in Sumter National Forest in South Carolina. I heard a deer snort several hundred yards to my left and knew it was not registering alarm to my presence. Because the deer snorted every few seconds, I could tell where it was going. The distance was so great and the cover so thick that it was unlikely I'd spot the animal from my chosen stand site.

On nothing more than a gamble, I quickly abandoned my stand and jogged about 300 yards to my right toward a 10-acre clearcut. I had scarcely positioned myself behind a gum tree when a buck stepped out of the dark forest and tried to cross the opening. His impressive headgear now hangs on my office wall as a continual reminder that when deer are "talking" to you, it's wise to listen to what they're saying.

There is yet another kind of deer talk. It's a low, guttural, grunting noise and is made when bucks in rut are following the scent trails of does in estrus. The sound is quite reminiscent of the noises a hog makes when it is rooting around in a full feeding trough. If you hear this sound while sitting on stand, don't even blink! Momentarily, you'll probably spot a buck zigzagging along very rapidly with his nose tight to the ground like a bird dog working a scent.

He's trying to catch up with a ready doe. The buck's mind is fully occupied and the shot is usually an easy one.

We know that a human being's body language and tone of voice often speak more clearly than mere words. Much the same applies to whitetails, but you must be able to accurately interpret what they're trying to tell you.

2

How Deer See You

◆◆◆

"Deer are completely color-blind. They live in a world of black, grays, and white."

That is typical of the declarations about deer vision that have found their way into sportsmen's magazines and books for the past fifty years. We have recently learned it is not true, and constitutes still another myth about deer that has been passed down among generations of hunters. A whitetail deer's eyes do indeed contain functioning color-sensitive cones, and the discovery is being heralded as one of the major advances in animal biology.

Of course, how deer see and how they interpret what they see have long been the bases for heated arguments in hunting camps. Are tree stands effective because deer don't expect danger from above, or is there some other reason? Are deer inactive on moonless nights because they can't see in pitch darkness?

Perhaps more important is the question of colors of garments that sportsmen should wear, especially the proved safety color variously known as hunter orange, fluorescent orange, and the pigment's trade name Blaze Orange. This color makes hunters far more visible to each other, but does it also make them more noticeable to the deer?

I've always encouraged the use of hunter orange, but I've had many very different experiences in which deer seemed to exhibit definite reactions to it and other colors. At other times the critters seemed entirely unaware or unconcerned with color.

Minnesota's 1979 deer season is a prime example. I was sitting in a tree stand, so a deer would not be as likely to see me unless it looked directly up, and I was careful not to make any noise. A light breeze was blowing directly into my face, so any deer that approached along the trail I was watching wasn't going to detect my scent. I was wearing a fluorescent orange coat and hat, black gloves, gray trousers, and brown boots.

About midmorning an eight-point buck stepped from a thicket of birch whips into a clearing. He was scuffling the leaves in search of the season's last remnants of green clover. With each step he briefly raised his head to ensure that the route ahead wasn't dangerous. The buck was about 60 yards away when he looked squarely in my direction. It wasn't that the animal looked up. He was far enough away to have me in his field of vision when he looked forward.

I remained like a statue, confident my outline was well broken by the branches surrounding my stand. Nevertheless, the deer snapped to attention and craned his head from one side to the other. His body language told me he obviously *was* seeing something alarming. He snorted, about-faced, and loped away in the direction from which he had just come. I was lucky. Thirty yards of open ground separated the deer from the birch tangles behind him, and I dropped him with a single shot from my .30/06.

When several other members of our party gathered to help drag the deer out, I performed a casual experiment. I asked one of my pals to put on my coat and hat and climb into my tree stand. Then I stood where the deer had been. Because of the irregular swatches of cover around the stand, the various body features of the hunter in the tree blended so well they were almost indistinguishable. Yet two large chunks of safety orange (the coat and hat) could easily be seen, and their bright, glowing appearance did not fit in with the surroundings.

Two weeks later I was deer hunting on my family's farm near Chesterhill, Ohio. The events were exactly the opposite.

I was sitting silent and motionless in a tree stand, wearing the same safety-orange coat and hat. A slight wisp of wind was blowing in my face. I was keeping tabs on the intersection of two major runways. Only minutes after it was light enough to see, a doe and two fawns approached. Several times they looked toward me, just as the Minnesota buck had done, and apparently detected nothing amiss. Eventually, they came close, walked right beneath my tree, and slowly evaporated into the distance.

Moments later a forkhorn buck stepped into view, and I decided to try for him as soon as he came within range.

The slowpoke buck seemed intent upon savoring every morsel of food he chanced upon before advancing another step. But, like every whitetail I've seen, he was suspicious and alert. Between bites he repeatedly jerked his head up in typical head-bobbing fashion to pan the landscape. For long minutes he dawdled around, and looked straight in my direction no less than a dozen times. Finally the buck turned his head away, and that is when I slowly raised my 12-gauge and squeezed the trigger. The deer went down in a heap.

Every hunter can describe similar contradictory experiences. They add to the debate about how deer see the world around them, but startling break-throughs have given scientists more insight. Research is still in progress, but after reviewing the latest studies I am convinced deer can see, or at least distinguish, various colors—with one major qualification. It seems that the context within which colors are seen, and the time of day, play important roles in determining whether a deer will register alarm or ignore colors that obviously clash with the natural surroundings.

For the most part, deer are shy and secretive. Although they may be up and around any time of day or night, most of their feeding and other activities that take place in relatively open meadows and along forest edges are done in the dim light of dawn and dusk. Scientists have confirmed that deer are well adapted to low light levels. A deer's eyes, in proportion to its head, are quite large, a characteristic shared by many night-oriented crea-tures: owls, bats, rabbits, flying squirrels, opossums, raccoons, and some fish such as walleyes.

Eyes are situated so that an animal sees best what it needs to see most. Humans, like all mammalian predators, have eyes directly in the front of their skulls. This provides straight-ahead, binocular (two-eye) vision. Our lateral (side-to-side) vision is very poor, but that is inconsequential because we don't have great need for lateral vision. When we need to see far to one side, our flexible necks easily allow our heads to swivel.

By comparison, deer have relatively rigid necks. The ability to crane their necks would really be something of a disadvantage because frequent move-ment would reveal their presence to predators. It is better for deer to have good side vision. Frontal and wide lateral vision are provided by eyes well to the sides of the skull. This gives deer fairly good straight-ahead, binocular vision, but their eyes can also work independently of each other (monocular vision) to see to either side without head movement.

The comparatively rigid neck is the main reason a deer seldom looks up at a sharp angle. You've heard that deer never look up because they have no reason to expect danger from above. In fact, deer *do* look up from time to time, as any tree-stand hunter will tell you. But anatomy makes it some-what difficult and uncomfortable, so they don't do it often. To demonstrate this, get onto your hands and knees and move around like a four-legged animal. Notice the discomfort you experience in trying to look straight up at the ceiling.

It's obvious that the most effective tree stands are well above the ground, at least 12 and preferably 15 to 18 feet. In states where laws affect tree stand height (in Minnesota, for example, stands may be no more than 10 feet above the ground) it is imperative to achieve additional elevation by putting your stand in a tree on ground a good deal higher than surrounding terrain.

If you hunt from a ground-level blind, try to place it on high ground such as a knoll or ridge. Tree stands have never been popular among mule-deer hunters in the Rocky Mountain states because the real estate is nearly vertical, and hunters can ambush deer without climbing trees. But in flat terrain, many mule-deer hunters rely on tree stands.

Placement isn't the only thing about deer's eyes that adapts them to engaging in activities in low light levels. The eyes of deer—and other animals, many of which are exclusively nocturnal—contain millions of specialized nerve endings known as rods, which are very efficient at gathering light and detecting movement. This explains why deer can move about when most humans, who have fewer rods in their eyes, find it too dark to see their boots. It also explains why motionless tree stand hunters are more successful than stillhunters, trackers, or stalkers.

While rods are extremely efficient at gathering light, they aren't color-sensitive. This is the function of the color-receptive cones. We know how these cones work in human eyes, but their function in the eyes of other animals has not been studied much. Scientists once believed that deer had no cone cells in their eyes. Lately, though, there has been a small but important surge of interest in animals' color vision. Researchers have been able to respond to anglers' and tackle manufacturers' questions about feeding and striking responses in fish, for example, and this has produced some surprising information about deer.

This is not to say that there has been an entire lack of information about color vision in grazing and browsing animals. As early as 1902 a Dr. Zurn described the color perception abilities of sheep and goats. His studies were confirmed in 1928 by a Dr. Menner. In 1952, a Dr. Hoffman reported upon the color vision of cows, camels, and giraffes, and a Dr. Grzimek revealed the color vision abilities of horses. In 1958 a Dr. Backhaus did a study of hooved mammals such as pigs, cows, and horses. In 1977, Drs. Riese and Sambraus experimented again with the color vision of sheep. Evidence of color perception was found in many of these studies.

If members of certain animal families have some color vision, one would think close relatives should have a similar ability. If a domestic sheep or goat has the ability to perceive certain colors, then so should wild sheep, wild goats, and perhaps even pronghorn antelope (which actually are goats, not true antelope). And if European red deer can see certain colors, they why not also closely related species like whitetails and mule deer?

All the scientists I mentioned are German. Most of their studies were conducted in Europe, with European and Asian animals, and this leaves some question as to any presumptions we might make about North American species. So most of what we've come to believe about how deer see has fallen into the category of folk wisdom.

Several years ago I wrote a magazine article about whitetails and, again, like my colleagues, parroted the same unsubstantiated information about

A whitetail's eyes are located for straight-ahead, binocular vision. Its eyes can also work independently of each other so it can see to the side without moving its head. This is called monocular vision.

deer being color-blind. I promptly received a response from the eminent scientist A.B. Bubenik, project leader of the Ontario Ministry of Natural Resources Wildlife Research Station near Maple.

"I have to say it is a pity that most editors and writers for hunting magazines in America are so vastly misinformed and do not have consultants among wildlife biologists," he wrote. "At least one highly respected study that was concluded in 1980 in your country will show you that North American deer are *not* color-blind."

I thoroughly investigated the matter and not only did the study blow my mind, but I was also privileged to be the first writer to share the information with hunters nationwide. That exclusive report appeared in the March, 1981 issue of *Outdoor Life* magazine.

The study was conducted by Drs. Witzel, Springer, and Mollenhauer at the U.S. Department of Agriculture's veterinary toxicology and entomology research laboratory in College Station, Texas, where many theories concerning whitetail vision were disproved.

The researchers live-trapped deer at the Aransas National Wildlife Refuge at Austwell, Texas. In the laboratory they studied the deer's eyes with high-powered electronmicroscopes, using new chemical staining techniques. The first battery of tests confirmed what was already known: Whitetails have rods in the retinas of their eyes. However, the second battery of tests provided proof positive that deer also possess an average of 10,000 color-sensitive cones per square millimeter of retinal tissue!

They have the visual equipment, so shouldn't deer also have at least some degree of color perception?

"We decided to find out," Mollenhauer told me, "by conducting electroretinographic tests. Under highly controlled conditions, the rods and cones are separately stimulated to determine whether they respond to various cues. We began by capturing more live deer at the Aransas refuge, and then we mildly tranquilized them so they would be easy to handle."

First, the deer were light-adapted to simulate their daytime responses to visual cues. Later they were dark-adapted to simulate their responses during the night hours. They were tested with individual flashes of white, blue, and red light. (Blue is a short-wavelength color, red is a long-wavelength color, and white is a neutral noncolor; therefore, these three colors represent the entire color spectrum, from one wavelength extreme to the other.)

Both rod and cone activity were detected in the eyes of the test whitetails. As in the human eye, the rods came into greatest use when the deer's eyes were dark-adapted and at presentation of the white light. When the deer were light-adapted, their cones responded to red and blue light flashes. As is the case with humans, the deer did not respond to color flashes in total darkness.

"As a result of our deer studies," Dr. Witzel told me, "we now know for

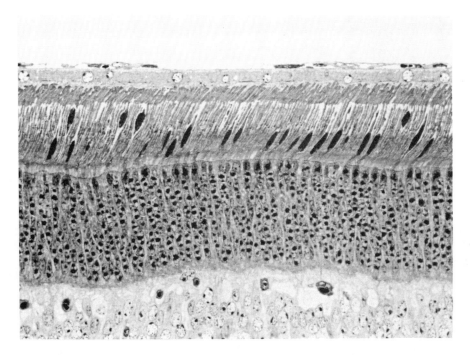

Initial evidence that deer might have color vision came when Texas biologists took microscopic photographs of their retinas and found color-receptive cones, shown here as long, black cylinders.

sure that whitetails have cones in their eyes. Those cones function in a manner almost identical to ours, and they respond to color cues!"

How sophisticated are a deer's retinal cones? How clearly do deer see colors? Do their brains receive and interpret the color cues the same way ours do? Scientists are not yet sure about the answers to those questions.

"The fact that there are 10,000 cones per square millimeter of retinal tissue is very strong evidence that deer can see colors," Dr. Earl Smith, laboratory chief of the College of Optometry at the University of Houston, told me. "But keep in mind the human eye has a far larger number of cones in the retina. So even if deer have color vision, and I definitely believe they do, there is the likelihood it is not nearly as well developed as ours."

Larry Marchington, an animal biologist at the University of Georgia whose research regularly appears in scientific journals, expressed a similar view.

"Whether you're talking about human beings or wildlife species, there are wide extremes in the abilities of individual animals to distinguish various colors," he says. "Some humans, for example, are quite adept at distinguishing between very subtle shades of just one color, other humans are mildly color-blind, and still others with congenital defects to their cones can't see any colors worth a hoot. The same is probably true with different wildlife species as well as specific individuals within each species.

"The Blaze Orange subject is really a controversy. I have a biologist friend who, like me, also is a serious hunter. He is color-blind and absolutely cannot distinguish between red and green, but he can easily see fluorescent orange. However, it is not the same orange you and I see. The way he describes it, the color is very bright and highly reflective in vivid contrast with its surroundings. If we apply a little logical deduction, deer should also be able to see Blaze Orange . . . as something bright and not belonging, much as my biologist friend sees it."

Whether deer have good color perception, are mildly color-blind, or are completely color-blind, bright hues that boldly contrast with their surroundings should be readily detectable by whitetails.

What scientists need to perform next, Marchington suggested, are some of the same types of experiments that have been done with fish.

"You've probably read about them," he said. "Fish are given either food or mild shocks associated with certain colors." The fish soon learn to seek out the colors associated with food and avoid those associated with shocks. Scientists concluded that not only can fish see colors, but they can also distinguish between even the most subtle hues.

"We could easily do the same thing with deer in fenced enclosures," Marchington said, "but it would take a good deal of time, and some foundation or another would have to cough up a hefty grant."

Well, as it happened, the money was indeed found. The results have impacted upon the hunting community like a bombshell.

It was in mid-1985 that Dr. James Zacks of Michigan State University and biologist Wayne Budde of the Michigan Department of Natural Resources presented their findings gleaned from studies undertaken at Michigan's Rose Lake Wildlife Experiment Station. Their startling paper, titled "Photopic Spectral Sensitivity of the White-Tailed Deer," was showcased at the Association for Research in Vision and Ophthalmology in Sarasota, Florida.

"Although it was proved in Texas that whitetails do have color-sensitive cones, this didn't really tell us conclusively that deer actually make regular use of that specific visual apparatus," Zacks said. "As an analogy, some bird species don't fly even though they have wings. Therefore, the only appropriate data to conclude whether deer use the color vision capability they have must be behavioral, not physiological.

"Basically, the detailed procedures and measurements we used for determining whether deer use their color vision boiled down to a simple variation of standard operant conditioning techniques, in which penned deer were taught to make responses to different colors.

"Our research showed whitetails are fully capable of seeing and responding to long-wavelength lights, particularly red and orange; correct responses occurred as high as 95 percent of the time.

"Now the question is to refine our understanding of the precise kind of
color vision the animals use. Are they trichromats (normal humans are),
dichromats (capable of seeing most colors but incapable of discerning certain others), or might they have even better color vision than humans and
be, for example, tetrachromats? We know that some animals, such as the
pigeon, have better color vision than humans. There are also many different
kinds of di- and trichromats that are possible. I am trying to undertake
behavioral experiments to begin to answer some of these questions."

Where does all this leave the hunter who always is striving to advance his
skills? Well, we are still concerned with only two basic things: being as nearly
invisible to deer as possible to avoid being detected, and at the opposite
extreme, being highly visible to other hunters.

Both goals can be achieved.

First, during the firearm season, wear an ample quantity of fluorescent
orange because it has been proven to both reduce accidents and save lives.
But you should also be aware that there are many different ways to use the
color to make yourself a good deal less visible to deer.

Going back to 1979 and my Minnesota and Ohio deer hunting experiences, for example, I have a good idea why one buck readily detected my
fluorescent orange clothing and spooked, and why the other deer paid me
little mind. The key, I'm convinced, had to do with time of day.

I encountered that Minnesota buck during mid-morning when the terrain
was brightly illuminated. That deer's eyes were light-adapted, meaning the
color-sensitive cones were fully operational. Therefore he responded readily to safety orange.

But the Ohio deer came by my stand just at the crack of dawn, when much
of the landscape was still in deep shadows. These deer were almost surely
still in a dark-adapted state. As a result, they were still relying heavily upon
rod function, and their color-sensing cones, in their retracted state (deer
involuntarily push them forward to the front of the retina or pull them back
in accordance with varying light intensities) were therefore unable to respond to the orange of my clothing.

It seems to follow, then, that hunters who wrap themselves in a cocoon
of fluorescent orange for stillhunting, stalking, or tracking should make a
special effort to hunt in the early morning or at dusk. During these low-light
times, deer are dark-adapted and much less likely to see the hunter's fluorescent orange.

Conversely, when deer are light-adapted, hunters wearing fluorescent-
orange clothing are better off waiting on stands. As we'll see in a later
chapter, it's entirely possible to see deer moving during midday periods. But
because deer also frequently bed during the middle of the day, the effort

may be aided by staging drives as well. Fluorescent orange is not a disadvantage to a driver who is only trying to push a deer to a stander and does not intend to shoot the animal himself. The safety orange that stand-hunters wear in this case may still be detected occasionally by deer, but at least the hunters are not adding to this disadvantage by combining high visibility with frequent movements.

Whether you hunt on the move or take a stand, consider other solutions as well. One alternative is to wear fluorescent orange in small units—a vest, hat, and gloves—so long as the total area satisfies minimum legal safety requirements, if any, set by the state. This makes a hunter highly visible to other hunters, but because the garments are small and differently shaped, and because they are separated on the body by garments of other colors, your entire form will not stand out so starkly against the background.

Still another solution would be to wear safety-orange clothing with a camouflage pattern of dull tans and greens printed on it. The glowing orange would be highly visible to hunters, but the floral camouflage would break up the orange and make it less startling to deer.

Many companies now have garments on the market that they claim are a combination of safety orange and camouflage patterns, when in fact they are not and it can be quite difficult for the hunter to tell the difference between bright red or bright orange and true fluorescent orange. This is particularly true when the fabric is dirty or seen under artificial light. To be absolutely sure, look at the fabric in very dim natural light, so dim that you can hardly distinguish objects. True safety orange (Blaze Orange pigment as manufactured by Day-Glo Color Corporation) *glows* in dim light. Ordinary bright pigments do not. This occurs because the safety color has fluorescence, which is, by Webster's description, "the emission of or the property of emitting electromagnetic radiation usually as visible light resulting from and occurring only during the absorption of radiation from some other source." Quite simply, true Blaze Orange glows with unnatural brightness in dim natural light. If your garment does not do this, the bright color is ordinary red or orange. Another test is to examine the garment in dim light and compare it to a known sample of true fluorescent orange.

Increasing knowledge of how deer and other animals perceive colors is sure to revolutionize big game hunting. To date, we've only scratched the surface, but when the guys at the hunting club are once more talking about deer being color-blind, you'll know better.

3

The Craft of Camouflage

◆◆◆

Mention the word "camouflage" in any deer camp and the discussion predictably turns to bowhunters dressed in mottled clothing and wearing grease paint on their faces.

But that's only part of the total camo picture. Deer hunters of all persuasions can take measures to lessen the chances of being seen by their quarry. I've already described how deer react to colors in varying intensities of light, and suggested several hunting techniques and clothing options. Other tactics are worth mentioning, too. I'm reminded in particular of what happened during last year's firearm season in Kentucky.

There were four hunters in our party. By the end of the second day, all of us except Tom Moriwicz had filled our tags. Tom's chosen stand just wasn't paying off, so we decided to begin making drives.

On a topographical map, we showed Tom exactly where he was supposed to go, the direction we would make the first drive, and where he would most likely see deer approach. After all this planning, and then executing the rather lengthy drive, we were understandably exasperated—maybe even mildly angry—to discover that Tom was not at his assigned post.

"Doesn't this just beat all," Benny Williamson groaned with obvious frustration in his voice. "Moriwicz really fouled up and cost us a lot of valuable time. He must have misunderstood where we wanted him to wait and wandered away onto some other ridge."

"Hey, you numbskulls, I'm right here where I'm supposed to be," we heard, followed by a laugh.

It was Moriwicz! He wasn't more than 20 yards away, and although he was

25

Camouflage isn't important only to bowhunters. If I waited on stand during a drive dressed this way, I'd be readily detected by any deer pushed toward me.

This photo is of the same scene, but notice how I've effectively "disappeared" by merely thumbtacking a few yards of camouflage netting material between two saplings, then tied several dead branches in place.

Consistently taking nice bucks almost always requires spotting your quarry before it sees you. Here, hunting partner Ed Wolter poses with my 200-pound whitetail.

wearing a fluorescent orange coat and hat, we couldn't see him. After he had chosen his vantage point to best watch the area, he then used an old but still effective camo technique I had long forgotten about. He had merely taken a couple of yards of lightweight camouflage fabric out of his pocket, thumbtacked it between two saplings to create a makeshift blind, and then strategically placed a few dead branches around him to break up his outline further.

As a postscript, the next drive we made also proved unsuccessful. But on the third and final push that day, Tom collected a nice six-pointer.

"The deer had no idea I was anywhere around," Tom later mused. "In fact, when it finally did see me, it was only a few feet away."

That is the essence of camouflage: spotting your quarry before it spots you. Accomplish this and you can almost begin thinking about which favorite venison recipe you'd like to try first.

A whitetail's ability to distinguish colors is being heralded as one of the most revealing discoveries of the decade, but until we can teach deer to talk, we can't conclusively know how they interpret what they see. Undoubtedly, the outline or shape of what they may be looking at is just as important—maybe more so—than the color of the object, because throughout the animal kingdom some silhouettes are fear-producing while others are not. Moreover, any outline or silhouette that is moving, rather than remaining perfectly stationary, aids still further in its rapid classification, which in turn may trigger an alarm response.

This explains why gun hunters who are dressed in the garb that is typically worn during the firearm season, and especially those who prowl around, seldom have any close-range shots at deer. It has been estimated that for every buck a moving gun hunter sees afield, five other bucks see him first and manage either to hide or sneak away unnoticed.

Conversely, bowhunters who are perched in tree stands see virtually every deer that approaches, and they commonly have shots as close as 10 feet. Many ingredients contribute to their success, but high on the list is the clothing they may legally (and safely) wear to escape a whitetail's visual recognition.

The traditional, mottled camouflage design worn by so many bowhunters is effective because in the outdoors, seldom do large swatches or blocks of anything of singular uniformity exist. Rather, the irregularity of the ground terrain itself, the changing light intensities that play across equally irregular cover as clouds scud by, and even the changing angle of the sun as the day wears on present everything to the eye as a hodgepodge of widely varied and disintegrated colors and tonal values. Consequently, when a hunter wears mottled camouflage clothing, he "fits in" with his surroundings, usually to the extent that a deer doesn't recognize him for what he is but catalogs him as just another bush or leafy tree branch.

Therefore, one essential of proper camouflage is to present a mixture of light and dark to allow the bowhunter to blend with the existing cover.

However, not all bowhunters are as successful in their efforts as they'd like to be, in which case it becomes necessary to fine-tune their approach to the use of camouflage clothing. This can involve a bit of mental gymnastics because the outdoors is generally more brightly illuminated during midday than during the hours of dawn and dusk (although an approaching storm front can change the picture in minutes). Further, the color and density of the cover itself changes dramatically as fall yields to winter. But "color" is really only a combination of different wavelengths of light, so the matter is easily resolved by utilizing slightly different camo techniques in accordance with the prevailing type of cover or time of year.

One method is to acquire several camouflage suits; either one-piece affairs you slip into like coveralls or two-piece jacket and pants ensembles. The most common color combinations of these are green/yellow, green/brown, yellow/brown, red/black, and orange/green/brown (in the last example, the "orange" is not fluorescent). They're also available in a myriad of designs such as the traditional World War II mottled pattern, Viet Nam, floral print, tiger stripe, and tree bark.

As a result, an early-season bowhunter who wants to sit in a tree stand deep in the forest might select a dark green/brown color combination in a tree bark pattern. In later weeks, when colorful autumn foliage appears, he'd be smart to switch to orange/green/brown or red/black in a floral or mottled pattern. His partner, stationed in a ground-level blind at the edge of a cornfield, might simultaneously be wearing a yellow/brown, tiger stripe presentation. In many instances, you can even stretch your dollars by buying reversible camouflage clothing that presents one color combination on one side, then when turned inside-out allows you to use something entirely different.

The key words to keep in mind are flexibility and adaptability. The hunter who uses the same and only camo approach all season, in all types of cover, is likely to claim unimpressive results.

However, simply donning an appropriate camo outfit is not enough. To be effective in fooling the eyes of deer, a total camouflage system must be employed, which means hiding your face, neck, and hands. Then, you'll want to ensure no shiny objects can alert deer, such as glare from your bow or tree stand. On several occasions I've easily detected the presence of hunters, despite their camouflage clothing.

Once, a hunter inadvertently gave himself away by the metal band of his wristwatch. It glared in the morning sun like a neon sign. Another time, the unpainted aluminum framework of a portable tree stand was the culprit. But most often, it's a hunter's white face and hands that boldly stand out and trip the spook alarm in deer.

Some hunters swear by camouflage grease paints, and others swear at them. They come in small squeeze tubes in brown, green, and black colors and have a cold-cream base so they are easily washed off at the end of the

The essence of camouflage is to present a hodgepodge of colors and tonal values that matches your surrounding cover in different lights. This bowhunter has done a perfect job.

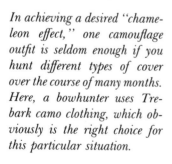

In achieving a desired "chameleon effect," one camouflage outfit is seldom enough if you hunt different types of cover over the course of many months. Here, a bowhunter uses Trebark camo clothing, which obviously is the right choice for this particular situation.

For this ground-level blind in thick honeysuckle, a traditional World War II mottled pattern is more appropriate. To economize, try to buy reversible outfits. Note the facial greasepaint, gloves, and camo tape on the bow.

In yet another situation, this tiger stripe camo pattern does a splendid job of blending with pine boughs. The hunter who learns to melt into his environment dramatically increases his chances of getting close shots.

day. Since most bowhunting is done in relatively warm weather, I like those paints that have an insect repellent added to them. The main disadvantage of grease paints is the time it takes to properly apply them, and the fact that they can make your face feel like you're sitting in a sauna.

Other hunters prefer to rub their faces and hands with a piece of charcoal or burnt cork. The advantage of these is that they're inexpensive and can be applied in just a few seconds. The disadvantage is that in very hot weather you may begin perspiring, which will cause beads of sweat to dribble down your face and leave long white streaks. If you have to sit through a brief rain storm, the stuff may wash off altogether.

With either paints or charcoal, begin by applying a soft, dull color to your entire face. Use the green grease paint, or simply rub the charcoal on very lightly. Then go over your face a second time with the dark brown or black paint, or rub the charcoal more firmly against your skin. As you make this second application, create short, irregularly shaped bars and splotches to help break up the oval shape of your face. Give special attention to your forehead, chin, upper lip region, cheekbones, and the bridge and sides of your nose, as these areas are the most likely to shine when beads of perspiration appear.

Remember to do your eyelids! Otherwise, everytime you blink, your eyes will look like waving white semaphore flags, and if a deer is staring intently at you from close range it will have no difficulty pegging you for what you really are. Remember that deer have an exceptionally high number of rods in the retinas of their eyes, their two-fold function being to allow the animals to see well in dim light and to detect the smallest of movements.

Now apply grease paint in a similar manner to your ears, neck, and hands. Extend the camo well up your wrists, which will be exposed by your jacket sleeves sliding back somewhat when you raise and draw your bow.

Hunters who slip out for only an hour or two, perhaps to sit on an evening stand, and who don't want to go to a lot of trouble applying grease paints or charcoal, should consider using a contoured camo face mask. When used along with camo gloves, the combination is perfect for cold-weather hunting. When the mercury soars, use a lightweight camo headnet and lighter-weight gloves.

Regarding other equipment, every effort must be made to eliminate the glaring shine emitted by fiberglass or laminated wood bows. Many proficient hunters like to make use of slide-on bow socks made of camouflage material, which stay in place because of elastic bands sewn into the tube-like affairs. Others like camo tape, available in any archery-supply store, that can be wrapped around the limbs of the bow and just as easily removed. But I prefer to spray-paint my bows olive drab and flat black. First I apply a base coat in one color, then create splotches and other irregular designs with the other. Incidentally, I use the same paints to completely camouflage my portable tree stands.

When using a ground-level blind, various types of camouflage netting or fabric can be used effectively. I've found that a mottled pattern in light green and dark green colors is best early in the season. But later I switch to another fabric with predominantly darker grays and browns. The Baker Manufacturing Company, long known as the firm that pioneered portable tree stands, offers an excellent ground blind. The lightweight camo fabric is rolled around five aluminum rods and tied securely for ease of carrying to your hunting location. The rods are then pressed into the ground, and when standing upright in whatever configuration you prefer, the netting is attached via grommets.

Whatever type of ground-level blind is employed, however, it's wise to gather dead branches, brush, pine boughs, or other native materials and strategically tie them to the blind with monofilament fishing line. Doing so will further break up the outline of the blind and the hunter hiding behind it.

One option for camouflage clothing for gun hunters is the venerable red-and-black-checked jacket. This garment, sometimes used in combination with checked trousers, has been quite popular among generations of hunters plying their trade in northwoods regions where hunting pressure is relatively light. Usually made of wool, these garments make hunters less obvious to deer. With such jackets being a checkerboard of light red, dark red, and black squares, the hunter simply does not stand out as starkly as one who might be wearing a solid-colored jacket.

Facial camouflage is imperative because nothing alarms deer more than a bright, human face. Greasepaints with a cold-cream base wash off easily.

Some hunters prefer to use charcoal or burnt cork (above). Pay particular attention to your forehead, chin, and the bridge and sides of your nose as these areas are most likely to shine as beads of perspiration appear.

Of all types of facial camouflage, I favor some type of headnet or mask. This porous, loose-weave design is ideal for warm weather.

As the weather turns colder, a fabric hood provides not only facial camouflage but also keeps your face and ears warm.

In below-freezing weather, consider a contoured, insulated face mask to keep you warm.

Gun hunters and bowhunters alike should remember that total camouflage means not only doing everything possible to avoid visual detection but also eliminating noises or odors that might alert a deer's other senses.

A variation of this pattern is the green-and-black-checked jacket. This has become the hallmark of the famous Benoit deer hunters, who have taken countless trophies in New Hampshire, Maine, and Vermont. However, this color combination blends so well with the environment, particularly conifer forests, that it can be risky to use in heavily hunted regions, in which case I strongly recommend wearing a sleeveless, fluorescent orange vest over the top of the jacket.

A few other random tips are sure to benefit both bowhunters and gun hunters striving to melt into deer habitat. When selecting any type of deer hunting clothing, whether of camouflage material or not, stick with either wool or cotton, or a combination of the two. Both fabrics are durable, provide warmth, and lend themselves well to most hunting applications.

More important, cotton and wool are classified as "soft" fabrics, which is a two-pronged advantage: They are relatively noiseless, and they absorb bright sunlight and therefore take on a somewhat subdued form. Conversely, nylon, polyester, denim, and duck are "hard" fabrics. Not only do they produce loud rasping noises when briers and brambles grate across them, but they have a distinct sheen to them in bright light that can make hunters stand out like billboards.

Carefully examine your duds for other shiny items that may cause glare and alert deer, such as bright plastic buttons, polished aluminum or bronze zippers, and even rubber or chrome-tanned boots that have not been worn enough to become weathered.

Of course, you'll want to remove from your person your wristwatch (buy a pocketwatch for field work), ID bracelet, shiny belt buckle, or anything else that may give you away.

Leave spare change behind so it won't jingle in your pocket. And always have a short strip of masking tape attached to your bow or gunstock; when you leave your parked car, your keys can be taped together so they won't

Crafty whitetails seldom step into open, brightly illuminated places; they like to remain inside cover edges where there is shade. Keep this in mind when selecting your own stand. Stay back in the shadows, as I did when photographing this buck, and you'll have a better chance of being undetected.

clink in your pocket. Gun hunters may want to consider having elastic cartridge loops sewn inside their coat pockets, so loose bullets don't rattle.

You might have already guessed that total camouflage means not only hiding your body from a deer's visual apparatus, but also eliminating any possible noises that might alert its sense of hearing. We might even say the use of various scents to hide one's body odor falls into the category of camouflage, but that is a subject that deserves its own entire report and can be found in the next chapter.

Finally, keep in mind that any camo effort always is more successful when the hunter situates himself in a stand or blind bathed in shadows. When a hunter is in the open, sunlight will magnify even the slightest hint of movement.

Therefore, whether you're a bowhunter, muzzleloading enthusiast, or strictly a rifle hunter, successful camouflage hinges upon first evaluating the coloration and tonal values of the area you're hunting at that particular time of year. Then, use specific garments and other aids that will permit you to blend with those features rather than contrast with them. Do it right, and you'll nearly disappear in your favorite deer hunting cover, and when you reappear chances are good you'll be dragging your buck behind you.

Scents and Nonsense

◆◆

It was probably because I was getting desperate that I decided to buy the deer scent. I figured there was nothing to lose. That day had been a dismal disappointment, just like all the others. It began with a mile-long trek in pre-dawn darkness across crunchy, frosted ground to a stand I had in Ohio's Wayne National Forest.

I knew where the buck lived and how he moved, and I wanted him. The big deer obviously was rutting like a herd bull. I had seen him chasing after does on several occasions. Each time his tongue was wagging from his open mouth, his neck was swollen, and there was a seemingly drunken swagger to his gait. But it is all too common for such bucks to vanish when opening day arrives.

The night before the last day of the season, I stopped at a sporting-goods store for flashlight batteries. While I was waiting at the cash register, I saw a display of deer scent.

"Secret Indian Formula!" the add on the display placard read. "Made from the scent glands of a doe in heat and guaranteed to attract lovesick bucks to your stand!"

Ordinarily, I'm not very gullible. But as I said, I was getting desperate, and several minutes later I walked out of the store with a bottle of the stuff. My hopes began to climb.

The eight-pointer finally came to me on the last morning of the season—the morning I used the scent—and when I squeezed the trigger he went down like a sack of potatoes.

That buck reeked, reminding me of a courthouse bathroom. But had the scent really been responsible for the kill? Or had I merely been lucky enough to be in the right place at the right time? I didn't have the answer, so I decided to investigate. It was a bigger project than I suspected. Since then, my study of deer scents has spanned almost twelve years. It began when I contacted every known manufacturer of deer scents for as much information as they would reveal, which wasn't much because of industry competition and the secrecy surrounding the recipes for these potions. Then came numerous in-field experiments, interviews with chemical ecologists (those who study odors and olfactory communication among various animal species), and the publishing of the very first report on the use of deer scents in the October 1977 issue of *Outdoor Life.*

Ever since the appearance of my report, and a follow-up article in the November 1978 issue of *Outdoor Life,* writers nationwide have penned tens of thousands of words for other publications. The deer-scent manufacturing industry has likewise proliferated. Today, more than fifty companies make a combined total of more than 200 scents and are raking in an estimated $57 million a year.

Because I have never made a deer scent and have never been on the payroll of any company that makes scents, I'm in the enviable position of being able to call the shots as I see them. So I'll begin right off by saying that some deer scents work all the time, some work some of the time, and for reasons I'll explain later, some of them never work and are a big rip-off.

But these strong declarations must be tempered somewhat with a few qualifications, because we simply don't know everything there is to know about the whitetail deer's physiology as it relates to their thought processes and subsequent behavior mannerisms. Exactly how their complex olfactory mechanisms are able to continually absorb millions of molecules of different odors, transmit them through sophisticated neural channels to the brain, catalog them in their respective niches, then sort through those of greatest importance to the moment so an appropriate response may be elicited—all within a split-second—is one of nature's facinating mysteries.

That deer do indeed rely strongly upon their noses is clearly evident by the wide variety of scents each particular animal is capable of emitting, in order to relay messages to another individual of its own species about its behavioral and physiological states, as well as its intentions. As a broad category, scientists refer to these scents as *pheromones.* By definition, a pheromone is any chemical substance secreted to the outside of the body by an individual, to be received olfactorily by a second individual, in order to elicit a specific response such as species identification, membership in a specific social unit, sexual attraction, aggression, or fear.

With the exceptions of urine and fecal matter, the molecular structure of these secretions are very complex, and they are released only in very minute quantities. In many cases they are secreted only at certain times of year.

Until about 1960, no sophisticated equipment existed for the extraction of these scents so that they could be "played back" to deer under highly controlled conditions to observe their reactions. Then came the development of a highly sensitive microchemical analysis technique known as gas liquid chromatography that eliminated these obstacles. Our knowledge of olfactory and glandular activity in mammals has progressed in leaps and bounds ever since.

One of the things we've learned is that five basic kinds of scents play important roles in the social lives of deer.

Tarsal scent is released from the tarsal glands. These are located on the inside of the ankle and consist of specialized oil and sweat glands. Tarsal scent is used by whitetails for the mutual recognition of their kind, and also indicates the sex and age of individual deer.

Metatarsal scent is released from the metatarsal glands on the hind feet. This is an alarm pheromone that deer spontaneously release when they are afraid, when they suspect danger and want to warn other nearby deer.

Forehead scent is secreted by rubbing the forehead on twigs and branches. It serves as a self-informing reference so that a deer knows the boundaries of its home range.

Interdigital scent is a waxy substance secreted from glands between the lobes of the deer's cloven hoofs as it runs or walks. It provides the animals with an ongoing reference or catalog of its own trails within the home range, and also indicates the routes taken by other deer that may be sharing the range.

Urine and fecal matter also serve scent purposes. During the non-mating period (about eleven months every year), the odors of urine and pellets serve to reinforce each deer's knowledge of its home range, its previous movements, and the presence of other deer using the same territory. During the mating season, tests have established that the level of steroid hormones in the urine are reliable indicators of the reproductive status of an individual deer. These steroids have distinct, pungent odors that even the human nose can detect. This odor also allows male deer to detect the onset of estrus in does.

As the rutting period begins and the body chemistry and hormonal secretions of all deer change, tarsal scent generally is released along with urine to aid in deer's mutual recognition and their state of "readiness." Both bucks and does assume an unusual "rub-urinating" posture, in which their backs are hunched up and all four feet are placed close together so that the released urine runs down the hind legs and over the tarsal tufts on the hind legs to carry the scent combination to the ground.

But with most mammals, whitetails included, various reproductive stages are undeniably under multisensory control. Bucks, for example, do not rely upon information from a single stimulus for the initiation of mating. Rather, a sequence of highly-ordered stimuli—including postures, sounds, visual cues, and odors—must be fitted together in a definite order before copulation is attempted.

Also, all the scents or secretions described above are close-contact phero-

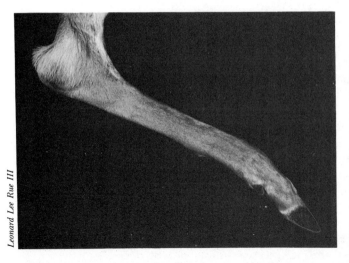

The tarsal glands, located on the inner surface of the deer's hind legs at the hock, release scent for mutual recognition and also indicate the sex and age of the individual. The metatarsal gland, located on the outer surface of the hind legs near the foot, releases a scent when a deer suspects danger.

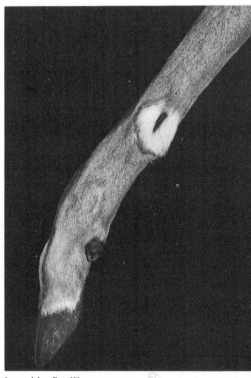

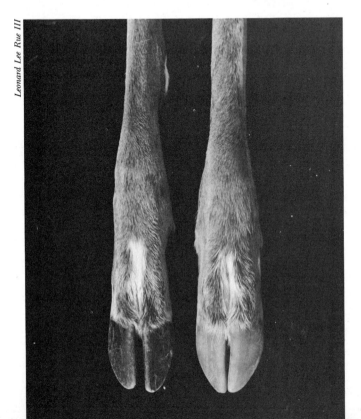

The interdigital gland, located between the hoofs, releases a scent when a deer walks and serves as a reference to its own trails and those traveled by other deer.

Deer rub their forehead glands and those at the corners of the their eyes on twigs and branches to mark their home range.

This deer is urinating on its tarsal gland during the rutting season to signal its presence and readiness. Note the "rub-urinating" posture: back hunched, feet together.

mones, except one. A deer's ability to detect odors is highly refined, but it works best and is used most often at very close range.

According to the research reports I have studied, tarsal scent, forehead scent, interdigital scent, the scent of urine and fecal matter, and the combination scent consisting of urine/tarsal secretions are usually detected by deer only when the animals happen to bring their muzzles very close to the scent deposit. One report went so far as to say that beyond a distance of only 3 yards, a buck will *not* be aware of the tarsal scent of a doe. It also stated that does are only able to detect male tarsal scent from a distance of 5 yards or less.

These two pieces of information disprove other studies noting that bucks, during daylight hours, often scent-check their scrapes from 50 to 75 yards downwind, to avoid exposing themselves in open places where scrapes typically are made. It also shows that, contrary to the claims of many scent manufacturers in their advertising campaigns, you cannot expect to splash some type of scent on the ground and have deer funnel themselves in your direction from all over the county.

The one scent category that both does and bucks can detect from greater distances includes metatarsal scent and other fear-inducing odors that trigger the secretion of this alarm pheromone.

But the exact distance that deer can detect fear-inducing odors is questionable, because these odors move in the air and are affected by many environmental variables, such as the geography of the terrain, humidity, wind direction, and wind velocity. The intensity or degree of concentration of the odor also determines whether or not there will be a response reaction. Most literature suggests that under most conditions, metatarsal scent recognition is limited to about 40 yards.

When it comes to encounters with human beings, the distances at which they rely upon their noses becomes even greater. But don't believe a word of what you hear about whitetails registering alarm at human odor from half a mile away. If that was possible, consider the consequences.

Whitetails live within very close proximity of humans. Farmers and field-hands continually tread the same ground as deer, as do rural road crews, loggers, utility-line workers, surveyors, trappers, fishermen, hikers, cross-country skiers, and, of course, hunters. As a result, if deer spooked and bolted everytime they detected a faint whiff of man-odor from half a mile away, they'd be running themselves to a frazzle twenty-four hours a day, 365 days a year.

Biologists claim that beyond 100 to 150 yards, which constitutes a whitetail's so-called "security zone," deer are not likely to react to *any* odor carried by the wind. "React" is the key word here. By the time the odor has carried that distance, its molecular structure has become so diluted it is not capable of triggering the animal's olfactory chemoreceptors, which must be stimulated in order for some behavior response or another to follow.

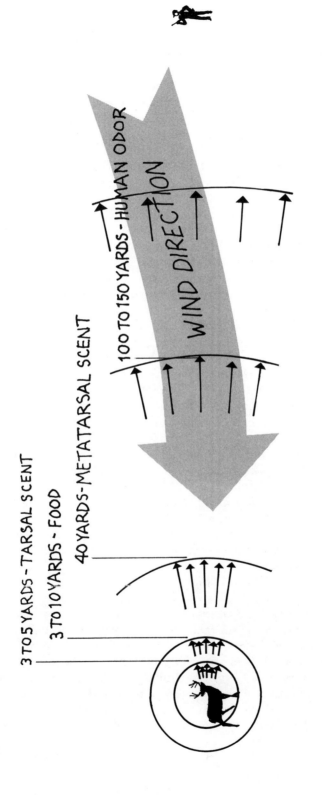

3 TO 5 YARDS - TARSAL SCENT

3 TO 10 YARDS - FOOD

40 YARDS - METATARSAL SCENT

100 TO 150 YARDS - HUMAN ODOR

WIND DIRECTION

A whitetail's response to various odors is mostly a close-range recognition process. Don't believe the stories about deer registering alarm at human odor from half mile away.

I've proven this to myself many times during the course of performing experiments on stand when I've seen deer placidly feeding downwind on the opposite side of a meadow, perhaps 200 or 300 yards away. I've eaten a salami sandwich, puffed on a cigar, and even urinated on the ground, with the breeze obviously carrying these and other related man-odors directly toward the animals. And yet they seemed oblivious to my presence. But when the animals are closer, say within 75 yards, it's a different story!

All of this compels me to note something that every deer-scent manufacturer will dread seeing in print. After many years of intensive research and experimentation with deer scents under every conceivable condition, I firmly believe that in most instances riflehunters are wasting their money when they buy deer scents (there are several exceptions to this, to be discussed later, such as when using the technique known as "mock-scraping.") With their chosen firearms, rifle hunters can reach out several hundred yards to down a buck. In fact, it's the rule, not the exception, for rifle hunters to select vantage points that give them wide-ranging coverage across ravines, from atop high ridges, along lengthy forest edges, and across wide meadows.

On the other hand, if you're a rifle hunter and take a stand in tight cover where the average shooting distance is less than 100 yards, or if you live in a state where only shotgun hunting is legal, and especially if you're a muzzleloader hunter or bowhunter, then various scents may indeed help tilt the odds in your favor.

Let's examine these scents individually and the best ways to use them.

First, there is the broad category of masking agents, made of concentrated oils, lotions, or extracts. The purpose of a masking agent is not, or should not be, to arouse the curiosity of a deer, but rather to overpower a hunter's human odor, and camouflage his ever-radiating human scent so as not to alarm deer at close range.

Some common masking agents are oil of wintergreen, pine oil, cedar oil, skunk scent, and fox urine. Even trained biologists heatedly debate the effectiveness of these scents, so hunters are left with the rather shallow and subjective matter of merely making first-hand observations of how deer react in the presence of such odors. In many cases, plain down-home logic may help us understand how deer live and operate within their environments.

Take skunk scent as an example, which I refuse to use anymore because common sense and past experience tells me it actually decreases a hunter's chances of seeing deer. Contrary to the claims made by manufacturers, skunk scent is *not* a common woodland odor that deer encounter regularly and automatically accept as a natural component of their habitat.

I live and work in a rural area: right in the middle of southern Ohio's best whitetail country. Seldom does a day pass that I don't see deer going about their usual business. We also have plenty of skunks, yet it's a relatively rare

This is a representative sample of just a few deer scents on the market. They all fall into one of three basic categories: masking agents, food scents, or sex lures.

experience to actually smell their spray. Once or twice a year at most we'll detect skunk odor in the air, and because it's so pungently uncharacteristic, we take notice. Surely, that sudden odor-oddity draws the notice of deer as well.

Therefore, it seems to me that a hunter who douses his clothing with skunk scent before heading to his stand is clearly not becoming an unobtrusive part of the deer woods. He is standing out just as boldly as if he turned on sirens and flashing lights to pinpoint his location.

More down-home logic proves this insight. Every creature in the animal kingdom has a method of exhibiting a fear response, and skunks are no exception. When a skunk sprays its repellent as a means of self-defense, it is telling all the world that it is alarmed. The reason could be a pack of marauding dogs, a wolf or cougar in wilderness regions, or even a human that unexpectedly happened upon the animal at close range. In any event, these potential threats to skunks are the very same ones that deer have learned to avoid since they were fawns. They even may have had close calls in which the air suddenly was filled with rank skunk odor and moments later dogs came bounding through the woodlands.

The point is that skunks release their odor as a self-defense mechanism,

One of the biggest mistakes hunters make is dousing their garments with a scent. The last thing you want to do is become the source of an odor that a deer is trying to locate, as that invites detection. Instead, place the scent on bushes, branches, and treetrunks away from your stand but still within shooting range.

so there is no way for a deer to make any kind of positive association with the scent. There is no way it can be recognized, interpreted, or accepted as "normal." On the contrary, if a whitetail detects skunk odor, its previous conditioning dictates that its response must be a negative reaction.

So do you really want skunk scent on your clothing and sprinkled around your stand, even if a manufacturer's claim that it hides human odor is true?

Perhaps we could even say the same thing about fox urine, another potion touted as an effective masking agent. Like skunk scent, fox urine may indeed disguise human odor, but if it is so uncharacteristic of the natural environment that it draws attention to itself, then what is gained?

The survival of every whitetail depends on the deer's ability to detect anything that is not a customary part of the environment. So there's little value in hiding your odor if you simply replace it with something that is equally out of place.

I likewise question the effectiveness of other masking agents, such as the vegetable extracts (pine oil, cedar, etc.). While some may indeed camouflage human odor and not simultaneously alarm deer, things can go awry if the hunter is not careful. First, such scents should always be used within the proper context. For example, a pine-oil scent used in the brush country of south Texas, where there are no pine trees, is certain to be out of place. Similarly, when a deer is working its way through a plum thicket and suddenly gets a whiff of concentrated oil of wintergreen, it may not wait around to ascertain why that unusual odor is there.

Secondly, use such scents properly. One of the greatest myths surrounding the use of masking agents is that they should be sprinkled on boot soles and on either clothing, felt headbands, or pads that can be pinned onto a jacket. Hunters who use this approach will doubtlessly be disappointed with the results, and I believe it's again due to the fact that they are making themselves conspicuously stand out from their surroundings.

To avoid leaving a trail of human scent as you stillhunt or hike to your stand, professional deer hunter Tink Nathan came up with an ingenious product called a Master Scent Pad (available from Safariland Hunting Corp., Box NN, McLean, VA 22101). It's a rubber pad with an absorbent insert.

To cover your scent as you walk, don't place deer scent on your boot soles. Use one of Tink Nathan's Master Scent Pads so that when you arrive at your stand you can remove the scent from your person.

Simply squirt several drops of the masking scent of your choice onto the insert, then wear the pad on the bottom of your boot, held in place by the pad's elastic band. When you reach your stand, take the pad off and leave it 20 or 30 yards upwind of your location. You may wish to sprinkle a bit more scent on brush or vegetation near where you've left your pads. In this manner, an invisible cloud of scent molecules will drift by your station and overpower your human scent being carried by the wind. More important, you will not be the source of some odor that may alarm an approaching deer.

Finally, do not hesitate to experiment with different brands of masking agents if an approaching deer, through its body language, tells you it is alarmed by something it smells.

The confidence many hunters have in deer scents often is rooted in the knowledge that early Indians and our later pioneer ancestors were known to rub their bodies with berries and animal tallow prior to embarking upon their hunts. But remember that these early hunters seldom bathed or washed their clothing. Therefore, anything that helped to cover their strong body odors was sure to be beneficial.

Modern man, however, is much more concerned about his personal hygiene. As a result, a growing number of expert hunters believe the best scent in the world is no scent at all. The theory is that if you don't do anything to arouse a deer's sense of smell, the animal will have no reason whatever to even suspect your presence.

I take some measures to abolish scent, although admittedly I do not as religiously adhere to them when rifle hunting as when bowhunting. One hour before hunting I bathe with Phisoderm, a skin cleanser used in hospitals and sold in drugstores that is not a soap and leaves no residual, perfume-like odor. It is the best product I know of for removing odor-producing bacteria and leaving you virtually scent-free for at least a while. Remember to wash all body hair as thoroughly as possible, including the hair on your head and, if you have one, your beard.

During the course of the day, I occasionally "dust" myself with baking soda carried in my pocket in a small plastic bag, paying particular attention to the most odor-producing areas of the body (underarms, groin, small of the back, and upper chest). Baking soda temporarily neutralizes odor, so it's wise to sprinkle a bit into your hunting boots now and then, as well as inside your hat.

Outer hunting garments should be washed very frequently to remove household odors that may otherwise cling to them interminably. After the clothing has been washed once in your favorite detergent, wash it again a second time using no detergent at all, followed by a double rinse cycle. Then, hang your duds outdoors to air-dry. If I am going to be hunting several days in a row, I leave the clothing hanging outside at the end of each day.

Many expert hunters even like to store their clothing year-round in large plastic garbage bags partially filled with several pine boughs, pine bark, cedar branches, sassafras leaves, or other natural-smelling items.

Inner clothing—trousers, shirts, underwear, and socks—should be changed frequently. When it is convenient, as when bowhunting on my farm, I sometimes change clothes three times a day.

Obviously, after you've gone through all this trouble to reduce your body scent, don't defeat your efforts by wearing cologne, after-shave lotion or hair tonic. Women should not use cosmetics.

Beginning three days before a scheduled hunt, try to avoid spicy, pungent, aromatic foods such as garlic, onions, highly seasoned meats such as pastrami and salami, certain cheeses, or any other strong-smelling foods. Bowhunting expert Tink Nathan even goes to the extent of avoiding smoke-filled taverns (and never smokes on bowhunting stand) as well as greasy-spoon diners where the odors of frying bacon and hamburgers may cling to his garments. And he does not patronize self-service filling stations where getting out of his vehicle may have him inadvertantly picking up traces of motor oil on his boots, not to mention gasoline fumes on his hands and clothing.

This brings us to the second category of deer scents, which are those that smell like foods that whitetails are fond of such as apples, grapes, and acorns. In my opinion, these food scents are of little value to hunters. Because most of them are synthetic compounds—in other words, chemically created—I doubt that the sophisticated noses of deer are fooled by them one bit.

Have you ever compared the smell and taste of fresh grapes, for example, to artificially-flavored grape soda? The difference between the real thing and the imitation is striking, even to our comparatively dulled human senses. Believing that deer, with their far more refined sensory apparatus, can't do the same thing simply doesn't give the animals their just credit.

In fact, I once performed an experiment to prove the point. On our farm is a crabapple thicket in a saddle where deer regularly cross between two ridges. From a camouflaged blind, I photograph quite a lot of whitetails there. By late fall, most of the crabapples have already been eaten, and so to prevent deer from passing too quickly through the saddle, I regularly scatter a peck of apples on the ground, each apple sliced in half to exude as much aroma as possible.

I've never seen deer exhibit any awareness of the apples until they were within mere *feet* of the food, and then they always unhesitatingly walked over and began munching upon them. This tells me, and confirms what was said earlier about deer's responses to other odors, that when they are using their noses in conjunction with finding food, it's strictly a close-range identification process. Hunters reading between the lines might therefore realize the futility of using a food scent to attract deer from afar.

However, the particularly revealing part of this experiment is that one time I didn't put out real apples. Instead, I scattered on the ground a number of apple-size rocks and then sprinkled them with an imitation apple deer scent.

This time, the reaction was entirely different. The deer apparently detected the artificial apple scent from much farther away (about 20 yards) because they were very reluctant to come any closer. With heads held low, they suspiciously skirted the bogus apples from downwind and eventually slinked out of sight. Several days later I repeated the experiment with real apples and the deer wasted no time coming in to enjoy the free hand-out. Several days later, I doctored more rocks with an apple scent, this time by a different manufacturer, and the deer again revealed nervous behavior and an unwillingness to come close.

Although I haven't tested every food scent on the market, these casual experiments have convinced me that whitetails can readily differentiate between purely natural aromas and those that consist of chemicals blended in a laboratory.

I suppose some food scents might have some value as masking agents to hide a hunter's odor, but only if they are used in the right context: an apple

In my opinion, food scents are of little value to hunters because they are synthetically derived from chemical compounds. I photographed this deer picking up a real apple after avoiding apple-sized rocks sprinkled with imitation apple deer scent.

scent in an apple orchard, an acorn scent on an oak ridge, and so on. My only advice in this regard, if you are so inclined, is to experiment with several potions made by different companies and observe the results first-hand. Personally, I no longer fool around with them.

Now we come to the most intriguing aspect of deer scents: the use of sex lures. I cannot honestly say what they may consist of, although manufacturers claim there are glandular secretions from does in estrus, along with other "secret" ingredients in them. By their smell, I suspect they also are laced heavily with urine.

Remember that odor released from the metatarsal gland is an alarm pheromone deer use to warn others nearby of impending danger. This glandular odor has a distinct garlic smell to it, and studies with penned blacktail deer have shown that if a few drops of metatarsal scent were added to their water troughs or feed bins, they would come nowhere near the food or water. Although it's not very scientific to stereotype animal behavior, even between very similar species, I presume whitetails would react in the same manner. Unfortunately, some manufacturers of deer scent, which haven't consulted with biologists, continue to use in their scents the secretions of *all* of a deer's glands, and thereby, inadvertently, include metatarsal scent. The way to avoid these scents is to simply smell them before buying them. This can be impossible in some cases, because of wax-sealed caps or bottles enclosed in plastic blister-pacs. If the scent in question has a distinct garlic odor to it, place it back on the shelf or return it to the dealer.

There are two things a hunter should never forget about when using sex lures. First, contrary to what you may have heard or read, you don't have to restrict the use of sex lures to the whitetail's rutting period. Bucks are capable of impregnating does whenever they're sporting hard antlers. They may attempt to mount does any other time of year as well, but simply not be successful at impregnating them. For many years, hunting literature has wrongly referred to a specific time of year "when bucks go into rut," when in fact it is the does alone that have a specific time in which they can and will allow successful copulation to take place. Because bucks are always ready to mount a doe, you can use a sex lure at any time.

A sex lure, like any other scent, should never be placed on your clothing or at your immediate stand location. The purpose of a sex lure is to fool a buck into thinking he is hot on the trail of a doe ready to be serviced. Because he wants to find the precise source of the scent—the doe—he may home in upon your specific hiding place. That's the last thing you want to happen, because you'd almost certainly be detected.

I generally begin a day's hunting by sprinkling some sex scent onto a Master Scent Pad strapped to the bottom of one of my boots, thus leaving a scent trail when hiking to my chosen stand location. If the ground is wet with dew, recent rainfall, or snow, I stop and add more scent to the pad about every 200 yards. If a buck, during the course of his wanderings, crosses the trail, he will waste no time attempting to eventually rendezvous with the supposed doe. It is not unusual for a hunter who performs these steps to take his stand, and in time see a buck following right in his boot tracks.

Once you reach your stand, remove the scent pad from your boot and place it on the ground some distance away to create a "scent post." The exact yardage, of course, will depend upon the type of sporting equipment you're using. When bowhunting, and thereby requiring a relatively close shot, I establish my scent post about 20 yards away. The scent post can be farther when using a shotgun or rifle, but not more than 50 or 60 yards.

In addition to this scent post, I like to make use of what Tink Nathan calls a "scent bomb," especially when I'm bowhunting. A so-called "bomb" conserves the use of the sex lure, which otherwise can be quite expensive if you merely dribble it on brush and vegetation in the vicinity of your stand. You can make such a bomb by taking a plastic 35 mm film canister with a snap-top lid, thoroughly washing it out, then filling it with a wad of cotton. Next, saturate the cotton with the sex lure and replace the cap.

At your stand location, remove the cap from the canister, pull the cotton out about an inch to serve as a wick, and set the affair on the ground. (Actually, it's best to use eight at a time.) When you're ready to leave, merely push the wick back into the canister, put the lid on, and slip the works into your pocket. One word of caution: Never touch the scent-saturated wick with your bare hands—wear rubber gloves or use a stick to pull it out and push it back in.

This is what a so-called "scent bomb" looks like. It is nothing more than scent-saturated cotton stored in a 35mm film canister.

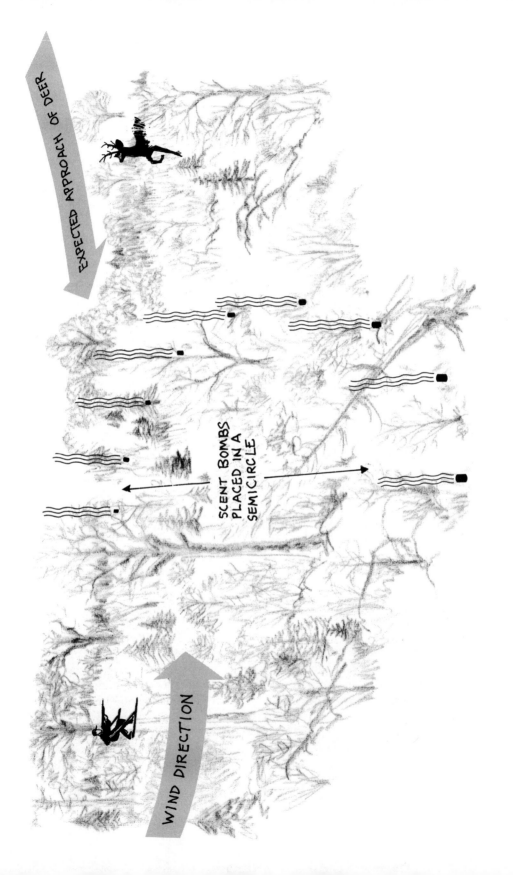

EXPECTED APPROACH OF DEER

SCENT BOMBS PLACED IN A SEMICIRCLE

WIND DIRECTION

The best placement of scent bombs is in a semicircle downwind from your stand.

The best placement of these bombs is in a semi-circle, about 15 to 25 yards downwind from your stand.

The purpose of a scent post and the scent bombs is to simulate a place where a doe in estrus has momentarily paused to urinate. A buck traveling through the area will detect the odor in the air and eventually find its source.

A sex lure can also be placed in scrapes. Or, you can dribble a few drops on a trail known to be used by a buck, evidenced by the presence of rubbed saplings adjacent to the trail. In both cases, the idea is again the same: to simulate a doe in heat and thereby cause a buck to want to investigate, and as he is doing so to divert his attention from your location as you wait for just the right shooting opportunity.

Another type of deer scent that is extremely popular among "advanced" hunters doesn't fall into any of the previous categories discussed so far.

It is called Deer Formula, and it is the brainchild of Dr. David Bethshears, a pharmacist who founded the Keeper Bait Company (Box 95, Bruceton, TN 38317). Deer Formula is based upon the well-documented knowledge that deer like to keep company with their own kind. Although Bethshears obviously won't divulge his unique formula, I'm of the opinion it probably contains a good deal of tarsal and interdigital gland secretions, which we noted earlier are the pheromones whitetails use in the mutual recognition of each other's presence and their sexes, ages, and trails they are using.

Deer Formula attracts does and bucks alike and is effective any time of year. It's recommended to be applied on scent pads attached to your boots. Take a roundabout way to your stand, in order to leave as long a scent trail as possible. Upon arriving at your stand, remove the boot pads and set up a "scent post" some distance away. Your scent trail smells like there is a new whitetail in the area, and if a buck or doe happens to cross the trail, it will want to investigate. Besides, if the newcomer is destined to become accepted into the local herd population, there is a necessary pecking order to sort out. It's this simple principle, of deer very commonly taking up each other's scent trails, upon which Deer Formula is based. It is an excellent addition to any hunter's repertoire of tactics.

I use deer scent on absolutely every whitetail hunt, the exact type of scent depending upon the conditions I expect to encounter. In short, I believe in scents.

But keep in mind that deer scents are after-the-fact aids that can never take the place of first acquiring an intimate knowledge of how whitetails live and operate within their environments, and then embarking upon extensive scouting missions to find out exactly where they are engaging in their many different activities. The novice who is looking for a short-cut to success and who randomly plunks himself down somewhere, then splashes some supposedly magic buck lure on his clothing, is fooling himself. Deer scents are neither cure-alls nor substitutes for hunting know-how.

How Deer Hear You

In most hunting and fishing magazines these days, it's rare to find an article dealing with a whitetail's sense of hearing. Most of them continually seem to focus upon either deer's visual abilities or the use of bottled potions to fool their highly refined sense of smell.

Consequently, many hunters assume that if they simply avoid crashing through the woodlands, giving any further consideration to a whitetail's auditory capabilities warrants little more than lip service.

Yet this can be a big mistake because a whitetail's ears are indeed formidable defense mechanisms that can easily spell a hunter's undoing. The key element in using this insight is understanding that there is a tremendous difference between what a deer is capable of hearing and what a deer hears that is likely to warn or frighten it.

This point was driven home more than twenty years ago when I was an infantryman at Ft. Benning, Georgia. Like most fenced-in military installations where hunting is restricted or altogether prohibited, the terrain contained too many whitetails. During maneuvers, we'd see them grazing by the dozens like cattle. But the significance of the situation, to me anyway, was what regularly happened on the artillery range.

I had two MOS (military occupation specialty) designations: a range-plotter on a mortar crew and a loader on a two-man bazooka team. And it was more than just a little awe-inspiring to take our turn on the firing line and lob rounds down-range, where they absolutely annihilated derelict tanks and armored personnel carriers with outrageous explosive sounds and flames that leapt skyward.

But it was a relatively common experience to see groups of whitetails placidly feeding on distant hillsides, seemingly oblivious to the deafening noises created by our arsenal of weaponry. Occasionally a deer would briefly look up, but then very shortly it would return to the more important matter of eating.

Unquestionably, generations of deer living on that particular military base had long since become quite used to all manner of loud explosive sounds and related fireworks. And because those goings-on never posed any threat to them, they simply paid them little mind.

Scene II: Many years have passed. I've long since been discharged from the Army and I'm hosting a party of deer hunters on my farm in southern Ohio. There is one special tree stand where I want my good friend Al Wolter to station himself on opening day, but he is apprehensive about sitting there. On this particular morning, the wind is a bit stronger than usual and the stand's wooden platform is making creaking noises. Understandably, Al is certain any bucks in the vicinity will avoid the area.

At first, I agree that perhaps the stand is not a wise choice this morning, but then I have a flashback of Ft. Benning.

"Al, I wouldn't worry about the stand making so much noise," I explain. "From the very day I nailed down the first board, that stand has creaked and groaned whenever there is the slightest breeze. Multiply that daily occurrence by the ten years the stand has been in existence. I'm sure the local deer no longer pay any attention to it. That stand has long since become a natural part of the forest's woodwork, so to speak."

Two hours later, Al climbs down from the stand in the old beech, hikes 40 yards, kneels, and with a wide smile on his face attaches his tag to a splendid eleven-pointer.

Exactly how acute is a whitetail's hearing? Moreover, how does it compare with our own hearing? Of critical concern, how do deer catalog specific sounds as harmless, while others are instantly perceived as potentially threatening?

To begin with, deer are particularly adept at distinguishing high-pitched sounds extending to 30,000 cycles per second. The significance of this readily comes to light when you consider that an average human's hearing range extends to only 16,000 cycles per second.

Even more noteworthy is the enormous reflective surface of a whitetail's ears, each of which encompasses approximately 24 square inches and can be instantly swiveled 180°. When compared to a human's ear, which encompasses only about 3½ square inches of sound-catching surface and cannot be swiveled, it's no wonder deer are able to so keenly detect even the faintest sounds over surprisingly long distances.

Yet there is much more to understanding a whitetail's sense of hearing than simply respecting their ability to detect sounds. The animals actually engage in a three-step hearing process of recognition, classification, and response. (Depending upon the nature of the first two elements, the third item—response—may entail no behavioral reaction whatever.) Moreover, the influence of the so-called Doppler Effect primarily determines the varying distances at which deer are capable of detecting those particular sounds most likely to elicit responses from them.

As an analogy, consider the pitch of a locomotive's whistle as it approaches and then passes you. As the train draws nearer and nearer, the pitch of the whistle seems to rise. When the locomotive passes, the pitch deceptively begins dropping, until eventually you cannot hear it at all.

What has really happened is called the Doppler Effect. As the locomotive was approaching, the whistle's sound waves became compressed or crowded close together, causing a type of upheaval in the number of cycles per second of vibration reaching your ear, which became translated into a higher pitch. After the locomotive passed, the sound waves became stretched out or gradually spaced wider and wider apart, with fewer and fewer cycles per second of vibration reaching your ear with a resulting lower pitch. Actually, the pitch of the whistle never changed at all, only your interpretation of that pitch in accordance with the varying distances at which the sound was heard.

From an anatomical standpoint, whitetails "hear" in the same manner as humans. But because the neural channels linking their ears to their brains are attuned to much higher-pitched sounds than we are capable of discerning, they tend to overreact to those noises occurring closest to them, which may not necessarily be "loud" noises but are characterized by higher numbers of cycles per second. Those closest noises are the ones most likely to influence both their immediate safety and the effectiveness with which members of the same species are able to communicate with each other.

You may be watching a doe, for example, and notice with surprise that she doesn't react at all to the thud of a distant gunshot—a sound that immediately drew *your* notice—but she'll instantly turn her head in the direction of her nearby fawn at its faintest soprano-like mewing for attention. In performing casual experiments, I've also seen a buck reveal no alarm reaction whatever to the clearly audible voices of two hunters on a distant ridge, but at the barely discernable "clink" of my cigarette lighter from 10 feet away, almost turn himself inside-out trying to leave the area.

Of special curiosity to scientists is trying to understand the function, if any, behind a whitetail's ability to hear those especially high-pitched sounds that are far beyond the frequency level that humans can hear.

I've seen this occur many times during photographic outings, when I often use a "silent" dog whistle to cause otherwise placid deer to suddenly reveal a tense, alert posture that enhances any picture. Why they respond to this sound is open to speculation. Bats make very high-pitched twittering noises we cannot hear, which they use as a type of radar to avoid flying into objects in the dark. One theory is that eons ago, certain species of night-flying dinosaur birds may have likewise made similar sounds and deer subsequently developed the ability to hear them to avoid being preyed upon. If this is the case, then perhaps a whitetail's ability to detect exceptionally high-pitched sounds bears no importance to today's hunter, but is merely a trait the animals have carried over from earlier times. We just don't know.

We do know, however, that whitetails seldom rely upon any one of their senses exclusive of all others. Although each sensory capability obviously has its own assigned task, any input or stimuli received by a particular sense generally must receive confirmation from at least one of the other senses before the deer reacts.

Because it may be difficult for a deer to pinpoint the exact location of a sudden, brief sound in the forest, the animal is not likely to flee immediately because it knows instinctively that to do so might cause it inadvertently to blunder into whatever made the sound. Instead, a deer's customary reaction will be to freeze and cup its ears in the direction the sound came from, hoping to detect additional noises, while its nose and eyes try to locate the source of the sound.

Studies involving the presentation of various types of stimuli to penned deer have shown that the animals possess sensory attention spans of various lengths. Incidents of the moment that trigger their senses of vision or smell may cause whitetails to remain alert for quite a while, especially when associated with a human or suspected predator. And when these two senses are alerted simultaneously, or when one quickly follows the other, the animal predictably shifts into high gear to leave the area as quickly as possible.

But when it comes to a deer's sense of hearing and the detection of sounds in the absence of confirmation from the other senses, the chink in a whitetail's armor is a very short memory. Scientists say it's limited to about three minutes.

This insight is of tremendous value to hunters, even those who perch themselves in tree stands or hide in ground-level blinds and occasionally cough or make some other sound. It is of even greater importance to those hunters who enjoy sneak-hunting, stillhunting, and stalking, because we now know it's not necessary to worry too much about the sounds you periodically create. Not only are they inevitable but in typical whitetail habitat they also constitute only a miniscule percentage of the sundry other sound-stimuli that constantly bombard deer.

When you do indeed snap a twig or crunch upon dry leaves, stop instantly and don't even blink an eyelid for at least four or five minutes. Then you can begin slowly advancing once again, with the confidence that any deer in the vicinity that heard your initial sound have long since forgotten it and turned their attention to other matters.

I had the rare opportunity to witness this axiom first-hand on a hunt in South Carolina's Francis Marion National Forest. I was skulking through a lowland swamp when I spotted a buck with a modest six-point rack about 150 yards ahead of me. As I began raising my rifle, my jacket sleeve grated against the rough bark of a cypress branch and the deer immediately turned and looked squarely in my direction. I almost stopped breathing.

Long minutes later, the deer continued ambling along, browsing upon branch tips drooping from willow saplings. I took only one step forward in an attempt to improve my shooting position and then silently cursed when my boot made a loud sucking noise as I pulled it out of the swamp muck. Again the deer wheeled around and gave me the once-over, craning his head from one side to the other. Fortunately, the wind was in my favor and surrounding brush adequately broke up my outline. Finally, the deer again went back to concentrating upon the tender willow twigs. This time I successfully managed to center my crosshairs on his shoulder and drop him.

Regarding their ability to catalog various types of sounds, it's worth repeating that whitetails become intimately familiar with the unique goings-s-on that characterize their own particular home ranges. A clear, although admittedly extreme example of this was evident at the Ft. Benning firing line. Yet I've constantly observed deer elsewhere and noticed their lack of concern over noises they've become quite accustomed to hearing over long periods of time.

Near where we used to live in southern Florida, armadillos were as thick as flies. They would root around noisily in dense stands of palmetto, with nearby deer almost totally ignoring them. In the brush country of south Texas, I've often sat in elevated tower blinds and watched javelinas bickering among themselves as they rustled around in thick mesquite. I could see them although nearby deer couldn't, and yet the deer seemed to register no alarm whatever.

In other areas, the sounds of falling nuts, the crash of a dead branch to the forest floor, the rubbing of tree limbs against each other in the wind, and the scurrying activities of squirrels and other wildlife seem to be within the context of what deer accept as "normal." In other instances, the loud chainsaws used by logging crews or the use of farm machinery in agricultural regions may not bother deer. In all of these situations, the key is that such sounds are not alien to their environment but something the local deer have almost come to expect to hear on a regular basis.

But one must never lose sight of the fact that whitetails everywhere exhibit spontaneous and entirely unpredictable behavior.

One cold dawn, while waiting in a tree stand in northern Minnesota, I watched a ruffed grouse drop down from its nighttime roost in a nearby spruce. As it was pecking around on the ground, about 25 yards away, a whitetail doe trotted into view. Neither was aware of the other's presence or of mine, but when the deer approached just a bit too close the grouse whirred from the cover, sending a shower of leaves flying in all directions amidst a frenzy of beating wings. This had the effect of sending the deer over the next ridge like she'd just been turpentined. The puzzling thing is that this occurred near the small town of Hinckley where grouse numbers are exceedingly high, and one would think the local deer would have long since become quite used to the birds' explosive flushing antics.

Another time, also in Minnesota, a small buck approached my stand where I'd been amusing myself watching a chipmunk scurrying around an old log. The deer spotted the movement of the ground squirrel, apparently recognized it as familiar and harmless, and then went back to feeding. For a full five minutes, the buck and chipmunk each went about their own business within scant yards of each other. Then, suddenly and unexpectedly, the chipmunk squeaked. Without even taking a moment to look up, the deer was in full flight.

Although I have no evidence to support this idea, perhaps the chipmunk had become uneasy with my presence and its squeak was some sort of alarm signal the deer recognized. After all, not only do whitetails have their own ways of communicating danger (throwing their tails aloft, stamping their feet, snorting, and releasing metatarsal scent), but they also seem to be similarly attentive to potential danger when they hear the alarm calls of other creatures. Just a few examples are the scolding bark of gray and fox squirrels, the shrill scream of the jay, and the raucous warning call of the crow.

The smart hunter, therefore, doesn't concern himself solely with how or what nearby deer may hear but goes to great pains to make sure he does not alert or spook other creatures as well, which may turn on their own warning sirens.

But whitetails also seem to possess an innate curiosity about sounds they've obviously never heard before. One time I was reading a book on small-game hunting in which the author recommended loudly kissing the back of your hand to bring shy squirrels out of hiding. On my next bushytail outing I tried it and an eight-point buck sneaked into view, apparently trying to find the source of the sound.

Another time, in the typically inept way in which I accomplish such things, I tried to handcraft a turkey call I'd read about. The project entailed cutting a coconut shell in half, scooping out the meat, then inserting an alder stick through a hole drilled in the shell. If you rubbed the stick on a small piece of slate, the instructions said, the gizmo would produce a realistic gobbling sound and the hollowed-out shell would serve as a resonance chamber to send your enticing call through the woodlands. As it happened, however, the noise was absolutely horrible and sounded nothing like any turkey I'd ever heard—sort of a high-pitched squeal—and yet to my total amazement, two does that seemed mesmerized by the bizarre noise came closer and closer until eventually they detected my presence and took off into the distance.

Then there are the sounds that draw no curiosity whatsoever from deer, instead having the opposite effect of making them flee. The specific nature of the sound doesn't seem nearly as important to whitetails as its cadence. A steady, rhythmic sound, for example, such as a hunter walking along with no occasional pause in his footfalls, strikes terror in the hearts of deer. In this type of situation, the animal needs no additional confirmation from its eyes or nose, because the repeated auditory stimuli is enough for the deer to make an appropriate response.

This brings us back to once again emphasizing the need to move slowly— which all hunters are already aware of—but also to vary the pattern of your footfalls. When you do inadvertently clink rocks or scuffle dry leaves, instantly come to a halt for that recommended four to five-minute period described earlier.

Even the times when and the places where certain sounds naturally or unnaturally occur can have a telling influence upon a whitetail's reactions to them.

It stands to reason that a windy or stormy day makes whitetails extremely nervous and jumpy. Not only does the constantly swaying brush, grass, and tree branches make it difficult to classify things seen, but the wind also homogenizes the air currents to make identifying intruders by smell an equally futile endeavor. Add to this the noises of clacking limbs and howling winds, which severely impairs their hearing, and it's no wonder they dive into cover and hide until the weather calms.

For the same reasons, whitetails seldom dawdle around loudly gurgling streams or rivers. They'll come to drink and then leave, or they may cross and continue on their way, but dilly-dallying increases their vulnerability simply because the noise of the rushing water competes with a deer's ability to hear other sounds.

Another interesting point has to do with the way whitetails classify sounds they hear in forested regions. I find it somewhat laughable that, for years, some hunters have been labeled "softies" for even considering sneaking along on hiker's pathways, fire trails, and old logging roads looking for their game. "Be tough and get into the brush!" the self-styled critics admonish.

But a hunter moving along at a snail's pace on such beaten trails and paths, with long pauses between each forward advance, actually has an excellent chance of getting very close to unsuspecting deer. Staying right on deer trails themselves is another good bet.

The reason is that such well-established routes are generally tamped down and thereby offer silent footing. Also, and perhaps more important, deer themselves use these trails religiously, wending their way along with a minimum of effort and few obstructions to contend with as they travel between feeding, watering, and bedding locations. Consequently, deer actually come to "expect" to hear various sounds on such trails, perhaps attributing them to other members of the local deer population as they engage in their own activities. It's the off-trail sounds that are most likely to send them high-tailing for the next ridge.

With whitetails possessing so many highly-refined defense mechanisms, they obviously are never easy quarry under any conditions. But understanding how their sense of hearing works, and how it is continually used in conjunction with their other senses to monitor their surroundings, is sure to help any hunter increase his chances for success.

PART
II

HOME
ON A
SMALL RANGE

Advanced Scouting Techniques

Because the definition of scouting is "to find by conducting a search," the deer hunter who does not religiously make use of maps cannot possibly hope to take home big bucks on a regular basis.

One exception to this rule is an acquaintance of mine by the name of Mule Morris, who lives in central Tennessee. Morris, pushing sixty-five years old, has taken a nice buck every year he has hunted. The reason for his success is that he hunts exclusively upon the 520-acre homestead farm where he was born and has lived all his life. It probably would not be stretching the truth to say that Morris knows more about every feature of the terrain than the animals that live there. As a result, if you know him well, and are able to gain permission to hunt his acreage, there's no need to do any scouting. Mule will simply point out any number of places where you can go sit on opening morning, and no matter which place you select, he'll bet a dollar your buck will be hanging in his barn by sundown. To the best of my knowledge, he has never had to reach for his wallet.

In virtually every other circumstance, however, maps are vital to a hunter's success.

Various types of maps and charts have served mankind ever since early Indians carved or painted pictographs on stone walls to convey hunting information to others who would later pass the same way. Thousands of years later, astronauts studied detailed photographic maps of the lunar surface before stepping foot upon the moon. Weather forecasting, oil and coal exploration, and travel by sea and air would never be attempted without the use of maps. And how many of us would even think of driving cross-

"Scouting" means to find by conducting a search. The hunter who combines reconnoitering with the use of maps is on his way to collecting a good buck.

country without a road map? It is, therefore, strange indeed that every year legions of hunters attempt to scout new terrain they may never before have stepped foot upon without consulting maps.

The three types of maps that are the most valuable to hunters are plat maps, topographical maps, and aerial photographs. I highly recommend using all three together. In fact, when planning a hunt in an unfamiliar region, my very first scouting mission takes place in the comfort of my den with my assortment of maps and photos laid out on a large table.

County plat maps are created for the purpose of assessing property taxes and are available at minimal cost from your county engineer's office, usually located in the courthouse at the county seat. Such maps show who owns every parcel of land within the county, the exact amount of acreage contained within each tract, and its exact configuration. Therefore, although a plat map probably has limited value to the hunter working several thousand acres of public land, such as a national forest, it can be an extremely important tool if the tract is smaller (50 to 500 acres) and is under private ownership.

With a plat map, not only are you able to size up your intended hunting grounds at a glance, but you can also quickly familiarize yourself with prominent landmarks such as rivers, streams, county and township roads, and in some cases even buildings. This enables you to orient yourself well enough so it's difficult to get lost.

One time, I became preoccupied following deer tracks in a light skiff of snow when I suddenly realized I didn't know where camp was. Being lost can produce a few moments of gut-wrenching anxiety in anyone, and I am no exception. So I sat down and smoked a pipe. Then I dug out my plat map. I knew the name of the landowner who had given me permission to hunt, of course, and was therefore able to locate that particular tract of acreage on my plat map. I also remembered that when I left camp I began hiking in a northerly direction. In examining the map, I saw that County Road 61 paralleled the entire length of the huge farm along its eastern border. Because plat maps are accurately drawn to scale and show distances in feet, I made an educated guess that if I followed my compass due east, I'd reach the road in about forty-five minutes.

As it happened, I had to take off my boots to wade across a knee-deep stream, then go almost on my hands and knees to pick my way through several acres of jungle-like honeysuckle, but in one hour I peeked over the crest of a ridge and there below lay County Road 61. It took me still another hour to follow the road back to camp, but when I arrived I had a new-found sense of confidence toward traipsing around in unfamiliar territory—something that destines most hunters who don't use maps to staying close to roads and trails and thereby not doing a thorough job of scouting the terrain.

Another thing I like about plat maps is that property boundary lines are so well delineated that there's little chance of inadvertently trespassing onto another's land and getting involved in a steamy altercation. In fact, knowing the names of neighboring landowners, and how their property is laid out, can be quite helpful in securing permission to hunt upon adjoining lands or perhaps even when trailing a wounded deer that crosses a boundary line.

The second category of maps that are beneficial to deer hunters are U.S. Geological Survey topographical maps, or *topo* maps. They are unquestionably as essential to the hunter as his rifle and knife, but they must be purchased from an agency of the federal government so it's wise to order them well in advance of a scheduled hunt.

For purposes of distributing topo maps, the U.S. Geological Survey has divided the country in half, the Mississippi River being the dividing line. If you're interested in a map of an area somewhere east of the Mississippi, write to the U.S. Geological Survey, Map Distribution Center, 1200 South Eads Street, Arlington, VA 22202. For maps of areas west of the Mississippi, write to the U.S. Geological Survey, Federal Center, Denver, CO 80225.

Whichever office you contact, send no money at first. Topo maps have to be ordered by quadrangle number, and either of the two USGS offices will send you a free index listing maps available for the region you request, along with an order form and price list.

At first glance, a topo map may seem quite complex, but with a bit of

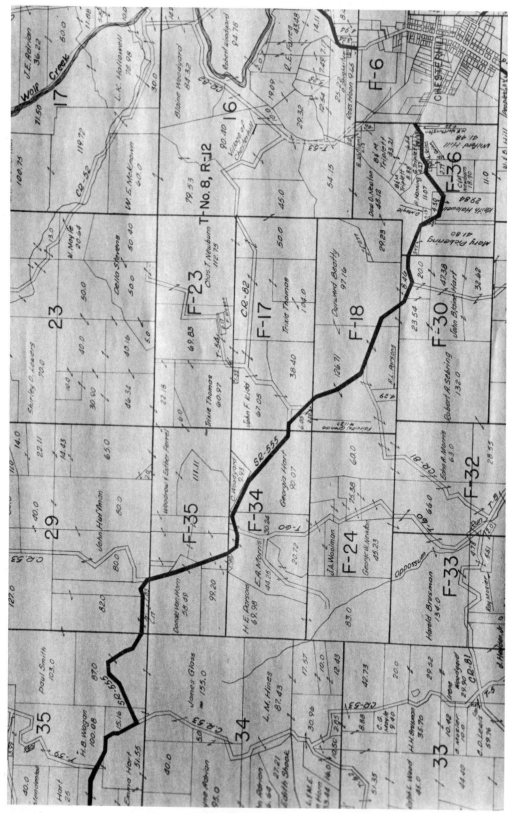

County plat maps reveal who owns every parcel of land, its acreage and exact dimensions.

practice you can become as intimately familiar with an area as Mule Morris is with his Tennessee homestead, even though you've never stepped foot upon it. By using contour lines, cartographers are able to portray land elevations in feet (generally, 20-foot intervals), thereby enabling you to identify ridges, valleys, and everything in between. If the individual contour lines are spaced very close together, it means the terrain is quite steep there. Wider-spaced contour lines indicate gradual slopes. No contour lines at all in a particular region means flat ground.

Topo maps also depict the nature of the existing cover in specific regions through the use of different colors. Generally, green is used to represent forestland, blue to indicate some type of water such as a pond or stream, and white to represent open ground (fields, clearings, meadows, or croplands).

Other features commonly represented on topo maps are public roads, jeep trails, railroad tracks, county and township boundary lines, buildings, quarries, mines, swamps, and even locally familiar names of certain pieces of topography such as "Scatter Ridge," "Wolf Hollow," or "Simpson Run."

The great value derived from studying a topo map is, in effect, actually being able to "see" what the intended hunting area looks like prior to ever leaving home. Coupling this with one's acquired knowledge of whitetail behavior, it's quite easy to determine probable bedding regions, feeding areas, and security zones the animals may move into when hunting pressure begins to mount.

Just as important, by studying the configurations of fingerlike projections of forestlands, narrow corridors of cover separating croplands, saddles connecting ridges, woodland edges bordering meadows, side gulleys running perpendicular to long hollows, and even natural barriers such as sheer rock walls or steep cliffs dropping off into deep canyons, one can predict with a surprising level of accuracy the travel routes that deer will logically use during the course of their daily activities. This greatly narrows the search because, by knowing in advance key areas worth later exploring, you can hike directly to them to confirm what your topo map has already taught you.

Aerial photographs are another type of "map" that few hunters use, but they can further help piece together still more vital clues that will add to a hunter's insight.

There are two types, unidimensional and two-dimensional. The one-dimensional looks just like an ordinary black-and-white print, and everything about the topography has a somewhat "flat" appearance. Two-dimensional aerial photos, however, look blurry to the naked eye and one must obtain two photos of the same terrain, place them side by side, then view them through a small stereoscope (available through any company that sells field equipment to engineers and surveyors). It is like donning a pair of special glasses to watch a 3-D movie in which certain features seem to jump into the foreground, giving you a bas-relief look at the terrain. You can

easily distinguish between the high ridges and deep valleys, just as though you were actually in the plane overhead taking the pictures yourself.

The most ready source of aerial photos are local agencies of the United States Department of Agriculture, such as the Soil Conservation Service and Forest Service. Although USDA aerial photos do not show as much detail as topo maps, they do tell the deer hunter many valuable things a topo map doesn't reveal.

Two-dimensional photos (above) look blurry to the naked eye and must be viewed in pairs through an optical device known as a stereoscope.

One type of aerial photo (left) is one-dimensional. In the top-center of this photo, the patch of open ground is an area recently clear-cut. When regenerative vegetation appears, this will be a prime food plot that will act like a magnet to deer living in the surrounding, mature woodlands.

For example, because aerial photos are updated more frequently than topo maps, they may show clear-cuts where timber has been logged off, or clearings where recent forest fires have left certain portions of a mountain range denuded.

Moreover, with an aerial photo, it's quite easy to evaluate the characteristics of the flora covering the landscape. Large, mature trees will show up as large dots, while immature trees will be depicted as small dots. If those large dots are relatively light colored, they are hardwoods that should be producing a varied mast crop, possibly with acorn-bearing oaks among them. This tells you in advance where a prime food source may be located that the animals are regularly visiting. But such mature trees create a high canopy overhead that prevents sunlight from bathing the ground, so there shouldn't be much ground-level cover for the animals to hide or bed in.

Conversely, small dots thickly saturating a given area are immature trees not yet bearing an annual mast crop, so deer may bed here but have to travel elsewhere to feed. By plugging into this equation the data that can be gleaned from a topo map, it is amazing how one can know beforehand almost exactly where deer are likely to be feeding, bedding, and the connecting trails they'll probably be using as they trade back and forth.

Similarly, on aerial photos, large dark-colored dots represent mature conifer species. Because pines, firs, spruces, and other evergreens constitute only starvation rations for deer when they cannot find more desirable food types, and because such trees will likewise have high crowns shading out the understory, whitetails are not likely to use these areas for much of anything. But if those dark-colored dots are small, you know it's an immature conifer plantation with individual trees having dense whorls of branches close to the ground. This makes for an ideal bedding location for deer, plus a retreat for hiding in when the pressure is on, providing splendid opportunities for staging drives.

After using various types of photos and charts to begin mapping out a game plan comes the matter of actually scouring the terrain to confirm what you already suspect. However, a big mistake made by many hunters is getting out too early in the season, because the landscape undergoes many radical changes as fall yields to winter. Sometimes you can notice this face-lift occurring almost on a daily basis as the temperature begins plummeting and hard frosts sparkle the terrain.

Farmers begin harvesting crops such as corn and soybeans. This not only eliminates a prime food source the deer may have been regularly visiting, but also leaves a barren field where previously they had a refuge for hiding. Succulent grasses and other vegetation begins turning brown and eventually dies, eliminating still another food the animals relied upon. Now, they have no choice but to switch from grazing to browsing upon branch tips and buds, which means their feeding location may now be a significant distance away from where it was just a week or two earlier.

Here, expert deer hunter Al Wolter studies two-dimensional aerial photos. It's like looking at a 3-D movie through special glasses in which terrain features literally jump out at you for careful scrutiny.

As the vegetation wilts and falls to the ground, leaving nothing but branches and tree trunks, the animals also begin using entirely different trails and bedding locations because they no longer have an abundance of lush edge cover to conceal their movements. In weeks to come, mating behavior will markedly influence travel patterns as well.

Consequently, the hunter who has the best chance of scoring is not the one who gets out early. Knowing where the deer are and what they're doing in October is not a reliable indicator of where they'll be or what they'll be doing in late November or early December. So wait until about three or four days before the season opens and then cram as much scouting time as possible into those days in an attempt to dope out the routines the animals are adhering to then.

Of course, seasonal changes are not nearly as abrupt throughout the southern states as they are in the northerly latitudes. Also, the above advice presumes the hunter is strictly an autumn bowhunter, a late-fall rifle hunter, or an early-winter muzzleloading enthusiast. If, on the other hand, you pursue whitetails over the course of many months, simply exchanging one type of sporting equipment for another as required by law, scouting will necessarily have to be a continually ongoing affair. And you'll likely find yourself making periodic adjustments in your hunting strategies; the stand you sit in during the muzzleloading season, for example, may well be a mile or so away from the bowhunting stand you occupied three months earlier.

Many hunters make the mistake of doing their scouting too far in advance of the hunting season. By then, radical changes in the cover and food availability have caused related changes in the animals' behavior patterns. Wait until three or four days before the season opens, then cram in as much scouting time as possible.

In any event, let's say it's just prior to opening day of the gun-hunting season and now you're ready, with maps and photos in hand, to begin taking a first-hand look at the terrain you'll be hunting.

A study conducted by the Wisconsin Department of Natural Resources demonstrated how easy it is for a hunter to estimate the number of deer in any given region. It simply has to do with locating deer trails and then performing some basic arithmetic.

Begin along a lengthy, well-defined edge of a large tract of forestland or other potential deer habitat. Using your compass, hike into the cover in a straight direction for about 450 yards. Note on a scrap of paper the number of deer trails you crossed. Because whitetails also use human trails such as logging roads, firebreaks, and hiker's paths, include those in your count as well, but only if they reveal evidence of deer use.

After you've traveled about 450 yards, turn right and hike 200 yards. Now, turn right again and pace back in the opposite direction another 450 yards, again counting all the trails you cross; eventually you'll return to the forest edge where you started. Continue down that forest edge for 200 yards, enter the forest and make another "run" as you did before. Make as many of these "trips" as you have time for or until the cover peters out.

Now comes the math. To determine how many deer are in the immediate vicinity, it's necessary to first arrive at an index number. You can find this by dividing the number of trips you made into the number of deer trails you crossed (disregard the fact that several of the trails were undoubtedly crossed more than once). If you counted twenty trails, for example, and made four trips, your population index number is five. According to a statistical analysis computed by the Wisconsin DNR, an index number of five can be translated into approximately ten deer per square mile. This figure is pretty good and indicates the terrain is worth a closer examination. I consider five deer per square mile the minimum I'll settle for, and if my math doesn't reveal at least that many, I'll start over in an entirely different location. Sometimes you'll really strike it lucky and chance upon a locale having fifteen to twenty-five deer per square mile, and in some regions whitetails may number as high as forty per square mile!

It can be seen from the above research that two hunters with comparable skills may nevertheless have vastly different success rates in accordance with *where* they've chosen to apply those skills.

The next order of business, and I cannot emphasize this strongly enough, is to keep in mind that outwitting other hunters who will likewise be in the immediate vicinity is as crucial to your success as outsmarting the animals themselves. This sudden surge of human activity, which will be evident even upon most privately-owned lands, can be counted upon to disrupt the deer's otherwise normal routines and push them back into remote parts of their home ranges. Here's a slick trick most experts are now using to counteract the influx of hunters.

On your topo map, use a felt marker containing a see-through ink (such as yellow or light blue; the type students use to highlight important sentences in their textbooks) to color in all the terrain laying within 1,500 feet of either side of every road and trail a vehicle can be driven upon. On standard 7.5-minute series topo maps, ¾-inch equals approximately 1,500 feet. You can now entirely eliminate this ground from any further consideration because the chances of taking a nice buck there are quite slim.

Studies of hunter pressure on deer have shown that the vast majority of deer hunters do not venture farther than 1,500 feet (approximately one-quarter of a mile) from some type of road. Some are simply lazy, but most of the others don't make use of maps and undoubtedly fear becoming lost. Consequently, these zones will constitute a hub of activity the deer just won't tolerate for very long, and if you are therefore working somewhat farther back in the hinterland, you'll actually double your chances of seeing deer. Not only will you encounter the undisturbed resident deer whose

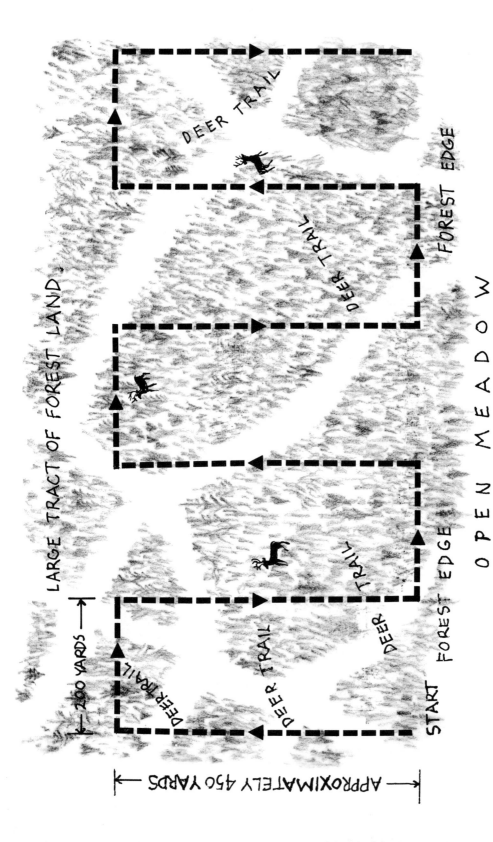

By using the Wisconsin DNR "trail counting method," you can determine while scouting which particular areas have the highest deer populations.

routines you've pegged, but in time you should also begin seeing immigrants that have retreated from the 3,000-foot-wide hunter influence zones bordering the roads.

It seems logical that locating deer sign would primarily entail little more than leaving plenty of boot tracks across the landscape until you chance upon tracks, scrapes, and so on. But next it is imperative to sift through these clues to evaluate how the animals are using the topography in their travels. The significance of certain bits and pieces of information may elude your notice. For this reason, it's a wise practice to use a grease pencil to mark all "finds" on your map. And I mean everything: rubbed saplings, browsed-off branch tips, trails, tracks, scrapes, droppings, beds, even occasional sightings of the animals themselves.

In this manner, once you feel you have adequately traversed the width and breadth of the terrain, you should be able to study your map and discern specific travel patterns the deer are using as they move about their bailiwicks and engage in various activities. Even the lone, apparently isolated bed or scrape found somewhere and initially considered random or happenstance may suddenly seem to fit into a much broader pattern, like finding a key piece in a big picture puzzle. Only after this is accomplished should you begin refining your search for specific places to intercept a buck.

One important step is to distinguish between night and day trails, because seldom do whitetails follow a given travel route to some intended destination and then about-face and follow the same exact trail back in the opposite direction. Instead, they virtually always travel circuitous routes throughout their home ranges. This means that given portions of any particular trail are used during broad daylight hours, others during the dim hours of dawn and dusk, and yet others almost exclusively after full dark.

A basic tenet of successful deer hunting is simply being in the right place at the right time. You can vastly improve your chances of seeing deer if you know the approximate times of day various trail segments are being used, then invest your stand hours during those particular time frames.

After many years of hunting deer on our southern Ohio farm and an adjacent 500-acre tract, I've learned that certain trails are worth watching only during the early morning hours, some are best watched at high-noon, and others reveal travel activity just before dark. But there are some not worth watching at all because deer use them only when stars are winking overhead. This means that on any given day of the hunting season I may find myself alternately sitting on as many as three or four different stands to maximize my chances of seeing deer.

One way of distinguishing between night and day trails is to purchase any of several "game clocks" now on the market (prices average $20 to $30). About the size of a pack of cigarettes, with a flip-top cover to hide the face of the clock and protect it from the weather, these little gizmos are designed to be hung on tree trunks adjacent to deer trails and to record the exact time

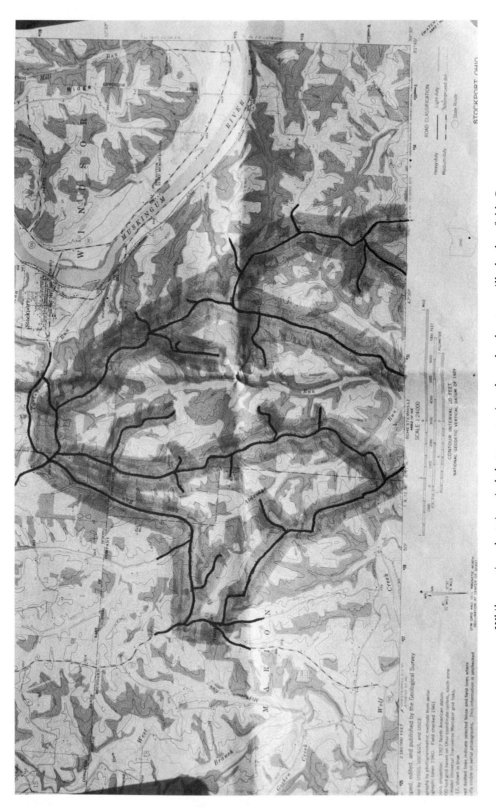

While scouting, keep in mind that on opening day other hunters will also be afield. On this topo map I've marked "hunter influence zones" found within 1,500 feet of roads and trails. I'll make a point of scouting those areas neglected by others.

To get a clear picture of deer movements and feeding behavior, mark all "finds" on your map with a grease pencil. Carry your maps afield in plastic bags to protect them from the weather. Write on the plastic rather than the map itself so that next year all marks can be quickly erased as you begin your scouting anew.

that an animal passes. By checking several clocks every day, you can peg the routines of local deer with uncanny accuracy.

A less expensive method, yet unfortunately one that's also less accurate, is to simply stretch a length of fine sewing thread across known deer trails. Make sure it is placed at least two feet above the ground so it won't be "tripped" by small animals. Then check it frequently to learn the approximate times of day deer are using those trails. Also check the direction in which hoofprints on the trail are going and jot this information on your map for still further insight as to where the animals came from and where they were going.

In coming chapters, we'll examine many other aspects of scouting that apply to specific types of hunting, such as intercepting deer during the mating period, during varied weather conditions, or in certain types of

This is a "game clock." It is used to determine the exact times each day that deer are on specific trails.

habitat such as regions where intensive agricultural practices are being carried out. But for the moment, consider one of the most advanced strategies of the decade. It's called post-season scouting.

It might seem ludicrous to engage in scouting several weeks *after* the hunting season has closed. But a large share of the country's most proficient hunters are doing this very thing. The prime times are the months of January, February, and March.

Compared to pre-season scouting, one telling advantage of post-season scouting is being able to study the activities of unmolested animals.

Think about it. During the ten-day period preceding the opening of the gun season, deer are jittery and spooky from having repeated encounters with other hunters doing their own pre-season scouting as well; not all hunters restrict their efforts to within 1,500 feet of the nearest road. Additionally, for the previous three months the animals have continually had their daily routines disturbed by the activities of small-game and bird hunters.

But when scouting is undertaken well after the season has closed, everything is back in your favor again. Now is the best possible time for observing the animals at relatively close range for virtually no one else is afield to rout the deer from their bedding sites or feeding areas until they eventually dive into cover. You can also wear full camouflage now, if you choose.

In addition to observing the deer first-hand, now also is the best time to search for and find trails and evaluate their frequency of use. With most vegetation absent, and at least occasional traces of snow on the ground, a trail that was almost indistinguishable in November becomes blatantly obvious in February. The same applies to locating bedding areas, droppings, and other sign.

However, perhaps the greatest value of post-season scouting is being able to find shed antlers. Look for them from late January until late March, when

Pre-season scouting should blend with continued in-season scouting in the hopes of piecing together as many clues as possible to the movements and location of deer. Here I examine a fresh scrape.

Shed antlers tell you of bucks that survived the hunting season, what they'll look like next year and where their general home areas are located.

they'll soon be covered by newly emerging vegetation or eaten by rodents.

When you find a shed antler, or a matched pair in the same vicinity, you can deduce several things. First, you know that a particular buck has managed to survive the hunting season and this is his home range. You know the size of his previous year's rack and can therefore make an educated guess as to what his headgear will look like the following season. And you can begin equating the presence of that shed antler with associated tracks and other sign such as old scrapes and rubs, to dope out that specific animal's behavior patterns. Likely as not, although he'll soon go into spring and then summer patterns, when next hunting season rolls around he'll be right back doing whatever allowed him to survive the previous season. What better way to learn the whereabouts and lifestyle of a whopper buck so you can begin making plans to collect him next year?

None of this is meant to suggest that post-season scouting is more important than thorough, pre-season reconnaissance missions. But, studying the animals after the season closes produces a wealth of insight that is available at no other time and can dramatically increase your chances of scoring during the next season.

7

Hunt 'Em on Their Home Turf

◆◆◆

When any veteran hunter looks back over his years of pursuing whitetails, he can probably recall at least a few incidents when he saw so many deer at one time and in one place that his eyes widened in disbelief. Likely as not, he did his necessary scouting work, then hunted long and hard without even catching a glimpse of buckskin, whereupon he then innocently pushed into a particular area and suddenly saw bobbing white flags everywhere.

I'll never forget the time I was working the Black Warrior Wildlife Management Area in Alabama's Bankhead National Forest. For several days, my enthusiasm was at a low ebb because I had meticulously studied both topo maps and aerial photos, then invested hour after arduous hour scouting the terrain by shank's mare, but other than a couple of does there seemed to be few deer in the region.

On the final day of my scheduled hunt, a crimson glow was just beginning to etch itself on the skyline, inviting dawn to center stage, and purely on impulse alone I decided to sneak-hunt instead of going back to my customary stand. Midmorning found me prowling through a cedar brake, and what happened shortly after can only be described as bittersweet. Up ahead, I spotted a sleek forkhorn nibbling on branch tips. Without hesitation, I fired and dropped him in his tracks, then instantly regretted my impulsive behavior because, at the shot, two other deer rose from their beds and bounded away, both of them handsome eight-pointers.

Another time, my hunting partner Jim Bielcheck was sitting in a tower stand in Texas where the intersection of two trails was worn trough-deep. During the first two hours of waiting, he later recalled, six different bucks wandered back and forth like traffic passing on an interstate highway. But eventually, by letting so many deer pass, he also began thinking maybe he was pressing his luck to the limit. So when one of the bigger animals reappeared, he squeezed the trigger and took possession of 185 pounds of venison and a new set of antlers for his den wall. Strangely, however, during this entire episode, I was stationed just half a mile away and saw only a couple of coyotes.

There are two logical explanations for these experiences in which hunters commonly go a long time without seeing action, and then unexpectedly find themselves attending what seems like a deer convention.

First, a stark reality of any deer hunting endeavor is that success often hinges upon luck, or, as my ever-philosophical wife would say, "having the right karma." But even luck, fate, and destiny have their limits. A hunter who consistently gets his buck every year undoubtedly can attribute a large measure of his success to knowing how to find concentrated sign, and then having the patience to wait for the deer to show.

Moreover, understanding the characteristics of the home ranges to which whitetails inextricably are tied is mandatory if their picture-puzzle lives are to be pieced together. Radio-tracking studies have shown that no matter what the state, a majority of whitetail bucks live out their entire lives within an approximate 640-acre, elliptical-shaped area that averages 1½ miles long and half a mile wide.

In one particular home-range study conducted on the Edwards Plateau in Texas, wildlife biologists live-trapped deer, outfitted them with transmitter collars, released the animals, and then monitored their travel tendencies over the next several months. Only three of the 186 study-deer ventured beyond the 1½ mile spot where they initially were captured; in fact, more than 80 percent of the deer remained within one-half mile of their catch-and-release points.

Within each buck's home range is a "core" area where the animal spends the vast majority of his time. To understand the nature of core areas, consider your own home as an analogy and you'll be able to identify the core area where you and your family members spend most of your time, too. In some houses it may be in the living room, while in others it's a large country kitchen, or perhaps a recreation room. You may periodically leave this core area to briefly visit the bathroom, laundry room, or garage, but 90 percent of the time that you're at home you can be counted upon to be in that special place where you feel most comfortable.

Whitetail bucks behave almost exactly the same. Within the perimeters of their home territories, they may occasionally travel to a nearby oak ridge to nibble upon acorns, they may briefly visit a stream bottom to drink, or they may venture off in hot pursuit of estrous does. But once their needs of the moment have been satisfied, they're right back in their core areas. Find a buck's core area and you'll find your buck. If you don't find him, rest assured he'll be back shortly. You can bet on it!

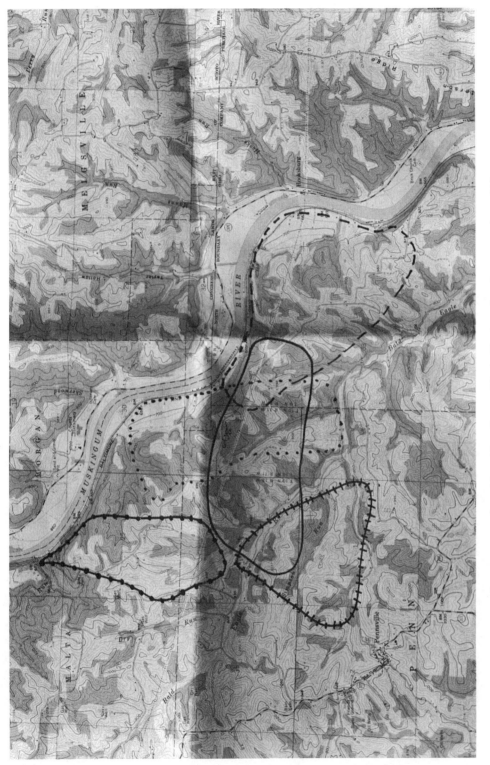

Most home ranges adopted by whitetails are elliptically shaped and average about 640 acres. Shown here are the home ranges of five study deer. Note how most of them overlap. In one study, only three of 186 deer monitored ever ventured beyond the 1½-mile spots where they were captured and released.

In most instances, a buck's core area can be identified. First, radio-tracking experiments have shown that a core area seems to average less than 40 acres in size. Second, it will offer a maximum feeling of security, which means there will be a good deal of nearly impenetrable cover to afford concealment. Third, there will be at least several different escape options available in the event the deer hears, sees, or smells the approach of something that has triggered an alarm signal. Fourth, if the terrain is rolling, hilly, or mountainous, the deer's core area will nearly always be located on higher ground as opposed to being somewhere in the adjacent lowlands, as an elevated position allows a whitetail to make the most efficient use of its senses.

With these terrain characteristics in mind, a hunter can begin scouting for core areas, and he's likely to come upon many possibilities. But the crucial part of his search depends upon locating what scientists refer to as "concentrates."

Because a buck spends most of his time in his core area, it stands to reason that signs of his presence—tracks, droppings, browse lines, beds, rubs, and scrapes—will be more prevalent in the core area than anywhere else. In addition to being profuse in number, these signs will range in age from very old to very fresh.

Let's go back to our homes and the way we live, and this point becomes even clearer. Walk through an average house and you'll see signs of the family members' presence. But notice how some rooms are immaculately clean and well-kept, indicating infrequent use. Suddenly you step into the recreation room, for example, and the place looks lived in. Slippers are sitting on the floor next to an easy chair, and on an adjacent end table there is a pipe rack and a folded edition of today's newspaper. There are schoolbooks on another table, an empty coffee cup here and there, pictures on the wall, today's mail on a nearby counter, a noticeable sag in the sofa and, at least in our case, several stains on the carpet where puppies couldn't contain their excitement over being allowed inside. In this human home range, there's no difficulty determining where the inhabitants spend most of their time.

In the world of whitetails, search for similar clues of their continual and repeated presence. Conversely, finding one set of tracks along a hillside merely indicates that a deer passed that way sometime ago. And a bed discovered in matted leaves or compressed snow only tells you a deer rested there. But such signs are merely random occurrences that may not reoccur for many days or even weeks. This brings us back to reemphasizing the importance of gearing reconnaissance missions toward a search for concentrates.

Interestingly, because the ideal composite of terrain features that commonly make up core zones are necessarily few and often widely scattered in a given region, they have a magnetic influence upon mature bucks. Numerous bucks may be drawn to each zone, which causes their home territories to overlap and, consequently, forces the deer to congregate in rather close quarters.

Therefore, it's easy to understand how a hunter can leave boot tracks across miles of acreage without seeing a deer or much sign, and then suddenly and unwittingly enter a core area and be flabbergasted to see deer and deer sign almost everywhere.

A good example of this phenomenon occurred last year when my hunting friends and I were staging drives in western Kentucky's Land-Between-the-Lakes area. We had four different tracts of terrain staked out, each of which was about 75 acres in size and could be driven in an hour's time. During the first drive a single doe was pushed to the hunters waiting on stand. Nothing was seen on the second drive, and during the third drive a spike buck popped up but was not shot at. Being a driver covering lots of ground and looking for sign as I slowly moved along, it became apparent there just

When scouting for core areas, look for sign that ranges from very old to very fresh and therefore indicates deer habitat in continual use.

weren't many deer regularly using these three areas. On the fourth drive, however, I began spotting an inordinate number of tracks and beds. Then, in the distance, shots began ringing out. As it happened, we had moved three impressive bucks to our partners up ahead, and two were taken.

But that is not the end of the story, because the following day we made drives through the same areas. Again, the first three drives proved uneventful. But on the fourth drive, through the same rolling brush country that previously gave up two bucks, two more splendid deer were taken.

Clearly, there was something very special about that particular area. Likely, it was not only the bucks' overall larger home turf, but also a hotspot where their core areas coincidentally overlapped. But exactly what it was that made the place so overwhelmingly attractive to them, compared to nearby and apparently similar areas, is not certain. That is of little consequence, however, because it is extremely difficult to pin down precisely the types of food deer may prefer in certain areas, which type of cover they may choose in accordance with the season, or any of the other nuances of their behavior. So, many times, we no longer even bother to try to second-guess them—we simply let them come out and tell us what they're doing and where, by reading the signs they've left behind.

The easiest signs to dope out are those made in conjunction with their mating activities. We'll examine these in detail later, but for the purposes of our discussion here, there is an unusual twist regarding whitetail mating behavior that most hunters don't know.

Wildlife biologists firmly believe that times are changing and that nowadays, during the rut, bucks no longer behave the same way they did when our fathers and grandfathers pursued them.

Decades ago, when deer were far less plentiful, bucks intent upon mating began expanding their home ranges, traveling widely in search of does in heat. In fact, this so-called "search and find" mating behavior is typical of most animal species when their population levels are relatively low. Some mysterious cosmic signal or genetic instinct apparently tells them to disperse over a wider-than-usual range to ensure maximum numbers of encounters and, subsequently, a higher rate of successful female impregnations.

In the case of whitetails, the effect of this natural law resulted in the toughest stand-hunting imaginable. With does being few in number and widely scattered, an amorous buck might have his line of scrapes strung out across three or four miles of countryside. And because it might take the buck two or three days to make his rounds, hunters quickly became discouraged with the prospect of parking their britches in one place.

Although it's pure speculation, I believe that this type of deer behavior caused our fathers and grandfathers to disdain "stump sitting" in favor of stillhunting and tracking deer. Even today, there still are a few pockets—usually in northern states where there are vast tracts of poor quality deer habitat—where whitetail populations are not very high and local hunters characteristically pray for opening day to reveal a new fall of tracking snow.

Fortunately, however, almost everywhere else the opposite situation exists. In a majority of states, deer numbers have soared. During the past twenty five years, Ohio's whitetail population has almost tripled, and in Pennsylvania, Texas, Alabama, and several other states, it has almost quadrupled. The result of any mushrooming animal population is that it greatly restricts the species' travel tendencies. Not only do deer begin adopting much smaller home ranges, but the competition arising between substantially increased numbers of bucks causes them to cling tenaciously to far smaller core areas and breeding territories. This state of affairs, in turn, has fostered a generation of hunters who choose to wait on stand and who, not surprisingly, are enjoying greater success than their stillhunting and tracking counterparts.

On countless occasions, my hunting partners and I have seen evidence of this increased homebody tendency of whitetails. On our farm, certain bucks are often sighted several times a day in the same vicinity. It's clear they are staying put, which is in direct contradiction to some of my colleagues who erroneously continue to tell their readers how bucks expand their home ranges during the rutting season. Only in rare situations, such as those described above, is this still true. Almost everywhere else, with bands of resident does sometimes numbering a dozen animals or more, there's simply no inclination for bucks to scour the countryside in search of mates.

In going back to scouting whitetail home ranges and narrowing the search for core areas, we noted that each individual deer's overall ranging territory generally is elliptical or oval in shape. In the final analysis, however, the actual dimensions of the range are largely determined by its natural geography. So it's wise to pay special attention to not only those areas where there exist a variety of foods and cover the animals generally prefer, but also natural barriers that might tend to inhibit their travels and thereby keep them somewhat confined.

A ready illustration that comes to mind is a swath of mixed farmland acreage, deep woods, and thick brush cover that is bordered on one side by a wide river and perhaps open prairie land on the other. Although whitetails will not hesitate to swim across a river if they feel that it's the only feasible escape route, and although they'll sometimes bolt pell-mell across wide expanses of cover-free landscape, the situation as described above is a tailor-made home range where maybe several bucks might attempt to live out their entire lives until old age takes its toll.

I once knew of a buck that lived on Blennerhasset Island directly in the middle of the Ohio River. I suppose that local hunting pressure on the mainland, or perhaps even a pack of marauding dogs, forced the deer to seek seclusion on the large island. Finding everything to his liking there, the deer decided to stay, adopting the island as his new home range rather than return to his old haunts. Although the matter of whitetails entirely abandoning their home ranges for new living circumstances elsewhere is not common, this incident points out that once deer find everything they need in the way of food, water, and cover, surrounding natural boundaries play an important role in their travel patterns.

In looking at deer sign more specifically, it should be made clear that bucks generally don't begin to make scrapes until well after most state's bowhunting seasons and some state's gun-hunting seasons have opened, so antler rubs on trees are reliable indicators of the presence of male deer and, more importantly, their core areas. As we'll see later, antler rubs are made as early as late August, and they serve both as territorial signposts and proclamations of the deer's hierarchal ranking in the local pecking order. But for the purposes of assisting the hunter in doing a proficient job of scouting, it's worth mentioning here that studies have shown that any particular buck will make approximately 105 tree rubs from August through October (whereupon tree rubbing ceases and scraping behavior begins taking place).

The significance of knowing how many tree rubs a buck can be expected to make is that the astute hunter should make a diligent effort to disregard the occasional rubbed tree he may periodically chance upon. Instead, as mentioned earlier, he should be on the lookout for "concentrates," or places where large numbers of trees have been demolished. This is the best possible indication that you are very close to a buck's core area.

During the 1982–83 hunting season, my dad and I were looking for a place to install one of several portable tree stands on the "back sixty" of my Morgan County farm. After pushing through a thornapple thicket and finally emerging on the other side, our eyes almost popped out of our heads. There before us, on a tag alder hillside, were rubs almost everywhere. The saplings had been ravaged.

After counting thirty-two rubs in an area only ¼-acre in size, we ascertained a good ambush location and then flipped a coin to see who would occupy the stand. As it turned out, luck was on my side and by 8 A.M. on opening day there was a ten-point buck hanging in my barn. But the important thing to note about this experience is that the buck was *not* taken right where we found the many antler rubs, but more than 200 yards away.

Finding concentrations of rubs is only the first accomplishment of an enterprising hunter. A buck generally makes the rubs in clusters roughly surrounding the perimeter of the core area as a type of "marking" behavior to warn other bucks, when they perchance approach, that this is *his* turf. In essence, then, rubs only serve to delineate the deer's territorial boundaries. And while the resident buck may indeed patrol his perimeter, chances are greatly enhanced of actually seeing the buck if you mark the locations of such rub concentrates on your topo map or aerial photo and then further refine your search deep within the midst of this sign.

As an analogy, consider a military installation that is surrounded by a high fence. The fence serves only to delineate the perimeter of the restricted area, and any high-ranking government officials on hand are likely to be sequestered within the middle-most areas of the compound.

With this insight at hand, we chose not to install a tree stand close to the rubbed trees. Instead, after further scouting revealed smaller concentrations of rubs elsewhere, which we duly marked on our map as well, we penetrated deeper into the buck's supposed core area to search for recently vacated beds and both old and new tracks and droppings, indicating persistent and more specifically localized use by the buck.

Although the importance of finding a buck's core area cannot be overstated, engaging in scouting during the hours of dawn and dusk when deer are most often about is an excellent way to tip the odds in your favor. Because it has been estimated that whitetails spend up to 90 percent of their time in their core areas, visually sighting individual animals themselves is a solid clue that they are, at that time, somewhere within their core areas.

However, don't make the mistake of simply looking for bucks. If you are not regularly spotting does, chances are good that the animal population in that specific region is not high. This means bucks will also be fewer in number and those which are present will have larger home ranges.

Discover the
Transition Zones

◆◆

Morning's first light was a faint glow when my friend Nels Whitcolmb hiked to his tree stand to begin his opening-day vigil.

The setting was South Carolina's Sumter National Forest, where hunters are permitted to harvest one buck per day throughout the six-month season. There was one special buck—an outstanding eight-pointer—that Whitcolmb wanted. He knew he would be satisfied with nothing less. He had seen the deer on several occasions, and although its rack wasn't especially heavy, it was a rich ebony color with white-tipped tines longer than any he had ever taken.

Whitcolmb's wish was fulfilled less than fifteen minutes after he had plunked himself down on a dead cottonwood. There he had a panoramic view of three trails that crisscrossed through a grove of black-oak saplings near the edge of a dense cypress bog. When the deer stepped into view, Whitcolmb leveled the crosshairs on the buck's lung region and squeezed the trigger. At the gun's report, the buck jumped up in the air and came down running, but traveled only a few yards before collapsing in a heap.

But there is more to the story. Less than one week later, Nels Whitcolmb collected another buck only half a mile away from the first. It was a six-pointer. A week after that, Whitcolmb scored for the third time with another eight-pointer. Only two days later he tagged an exceptionally large forkhorn that weighed 190 pounds. He then quit hunting for the season, with enough venison in his freezer to provide for his family of six until the same time next year.

Very few hunters, given the opportunity, could succeed in out-witting four decent whitetail bucks in a time frame of less than four weeks, but there

94

is still more to tell. Each of Whitcolmb's bucks was taken after he waited on stand for less than one hour. That means all four bucks were killed in less than four hours of actual hunting time! Even more noteworthy, all but two of the forty three bucks Nels Whitcolmb has killed in the last seven years have been taken in exactly the same manner. And he credits every one of those whitetails to something he initially learned from bass fishing!

"If you stop and think about it," Whitcolmb explained, "bass fishing and deer hunting have quite a lot in common. In both sports, locating your quarry is the single most important concern. When I first took up deer hunting, about seven years ago, it was natural for me to try to find those particular places where whitetails spend most of their time. Biologists have been studying and reporting deer movements in much the same way as ichthyologists study fish, using radio transmitters and plotting travel patterns on maps."

Using these techniques, biologists have been able to learn an incredible amount about the sizes and dimensions of the home ranges of individual whitetails, the core regions within each home area where bucks customarily spend most of their time, the exact nature of their mating activities, and more. But the most recent findings may prove to be the most beneficial of all. They deal with certain types of terrain configurations whitetail bucks are most likely to select as either core zones or travel corridors, if just the right composition of cover is available. Biologists and professional foresters alike call these favored regions "transition zones," and Nels Whitcolmb was among the first hunters to recognize them as dynamite places to hunt deer.

By definition, transition zones are the areas adjoining mature forests where the tall trees give way to thick groves of successively smaller saplings and ground-story vegetation before open fields and meadows begin.

These transition zones should not be confused with edges, where a dense, high-canopy forest comes to an abrupt halt and a well-defined border separates the woodland from grassy meadows or cultivated fields. Those edges will indeed be the sites of whitetail activity early in the season, particularly during the hours of dawn and dusk. But transition zones are different; they are characterized by a buffer region with regenerative cover between the forests and open ground. Here, deer may be active throughout the entire season and virtually any time of day.

It is not difficult to identify a transition zone of the type that whitetails use most often. It will be at least as wide as a football field and twice as long. It will consist of either replanted or naturally regenerative timber in which the great majority of trees are no larger than 3 to 5 inches in diameter. The trees and associated ground-level brush will be so thick and close-standing that one could not possibly walk a perfectly straight line for more than five yards without having to alter course.

"There are many reasons why transition zones attract deer," Hoyt Williamson explained last year as we embarked upon a Wisconsin deer hunt. Williamson previously worked for the U.S. Forest Service and now is em-

ployed by a commercial timber company; in both cases his job is evaluating the girth and height of saplings, using an optical device called a Relaskop. He's also one of the state's foremost authorities on transition zones, a skill he uses to good advantage in more ways than one because his first love remains whitetail hunting.

"To begin with," Williamson said, "the young trees that make up transition zones offer deer almost perfect browsing conditions. This is important for whitetail hunters to know because just about the time the hunting season opens, deer are in the process of changing their feeding habits. During the spring and summer they are primarily grazers, and therefore like to frequent meadows and open fields to dine upon clover, alfalfa, lespedeza, trefoil, horseweed, and other grasses and legumes.

"Beginning about the first week of November, depending upon the latitude, they switch. They become browsers and their fancy turns to tender twigs, branch tips, and buds. These foods obviously are not found in open fields. And the tree branches in high-canopy, climax forests are generally so far off the ground that deer can't reach them. Bingo! Whitetails will concentrate their foraging activities in the transition zones where their favorite foods are both plentiful and easily accessible."

After chatting over a morning cup of coffee, Williamson and I hiked to our blinds, located on his brother's farm just beyond the city limits of Chippewa Falls. Hoyt had scouted the terrain prior to my arrival and found a textbook transition zone. A 50-acre tract of mature birch trees was bordered on three sides by rolling pasturelands where a herd of Guernseys grazed. A pasture on the fourth side was separated from the birches by a transition zone—a wide, winding alley of mixed cover consisting of red maple saplings, birch whips, scattered pines, and tag alders.

"Gad!" I yelped, stopping for a moment to inspect the junction of four trails that came together like spokes to a wheel hub. "There must be a whole herd of deer using. . . ."

My sentence was interrupted by a snort to our left and we caught a brief glimpse of several waving tails vanishing in the distance.

"Hurry," Hoyt whispered. "Let's get into our blinds. I have a hunch they'll make a wide circle and double back. There's also a good chance they'll put other bedded deer on the move."

Moments later we were in our hideouts, the two blinds separated by 300 yards of transition zone cover and overlooking trails that meandered through dense cedars and more maple and birch saplings. Within ten min-

This typical forest edge may see deer activity early in the season because escape is close at hand and ample sunlight exposure fosters vegetative growth around the perimeter. But by the time the hunting season opens, deer will be moving to transition zones.

utes our intrusions had become absorbed as a natural part of the surroundings and songbirds resumed playing tag among the branches. I became
entranced watching the antics of a pair of nuthatches when the faint cracking
of a dry twig jolted me back to my surroundings. Two does and a yearling
approached cautiously, then disappeared behind a screen of honeysuckle.
When I slowly turned my head back, a slight movement caught my peripheral vision.

A sleek six-point buck was mincing into view as quietly as a ghost. Right
then I learned an important thing about hunting transition zones. The cover

*Transition zones are not "edges" but constitute buffer areas of thick, regenerative
saplings that separate open ground from mature forestland.*

typically is so dense, and one's vision so restricted, that deer can come within yards of a waiting hunter before he is detected. As a result, hunters hiding in ground-level blinds must remain keenly alert and noiseless, lest they give away their presence. Stillhunting is usually futile in transition zones, because it's nearly impossible to approach deer in such close quarters without forewarning them. The best bet, unquestionably, is to use a tree stand, which gives the hunter a better view down into cover that otherwise would block his line of vision from ground level.

In this case, the young buck was so close I could hear him breathe, which made me wonder whether he in turn could hear my heart pounding. It was necessary to wait anxiously until he had traveled well past my blind and was facing away before I could risk the movement of raising my rifle. Then, when the time was just right, I placed a single shot in the back of his neck, dropping him where he stood.

I had not ejected my spent .270 case when another rifle crack punctuated the morning stillness. I knew it was Hoyt who had fired, but the result was uncertain. An instant later a jubilant whoop eliminated any doubt.

"Another reason transition zones are hotspots this time of year," Williamson said when we later met and exchanged congratulations, "has to do with the seasonal change in the cover and its effect on the whitetail's shy and secretive personality."

Until late October, again depending upon latitude, forest edges may reveal a good deal of deer activity. There are many explanations for this, but one of the most plausible is the profusion of low-growing vegetation encouraged by the long periods of sunlight exposure there. Whitetails seldom venture far from concealing cover. Consequently, as fall progresses to winter, and the leaves and other greenery along forest edges turn brown, die, and fall to the ground, these edges become less and less protective for deer. Likewise, deep, mature woodlands are not safe either. The high canopy shades out much brush and understory vegetation and, in most instances, allows surprisingly long-range visibility.

This brings us back once again to transition zones. It is true that the leaves of transition-zone trees will be disappearing as elsewhere, but they were never able to shade out ground cover in the first place. Hence, there is a good deal of brush, honeysuckle, multiflora rose, and other growth in addition to the interwoven nature of the crowded saplings themselves. The deer seem to instinctively know they're not readily detected in such places and that if they are routed out, they have numerous escape options available to them.

According to Nels Whitcolmb, finding transition zones that deer can be counted upon to use frequently within their home ranges is not difficult.

"The actual tree species comprising a transition zone is not too critical," Whitcolmb claims. "Studies have shown that deer are largely opportunists when it comes to eating, and there are approximately 614 varieties of trees

Foresters use a device called a Relaskop to evaluate the height and girth of saplings. But it's enough for hunters to remember that the majority of trees should be no larger than 5 inches in diameter and they should be so numerous that you cannot walk a straight line for more than 5 yards without having to alter course.

and plants they may nibble upon throughout the year. From my experience, however, when they are browsing they take a special liking to red maple saplings, white cedar, aspen, pin oak, yellow poplar, dogwood, and arborvitae. So if you find a transition zone where any of these species predominate, you can be sure the resident deer population visits the area regularly, if in fact they don't spend all day there! The real key is the age and density of the trees; they must be young and growing close together.

"Finding transition zones is easily accomplished by hiking the countryside," Nels continued. "But I like to save both time and boot leather by first visiting a local Forest Service office, the headquarters of the state wildlife division, or the offices of a commercial timber company, to examine the huge land-use maps they have posted on their walls. I look for tracts of mature forests where partial clear-cutting of timber was made from 10 to 15 years ago. That will have been long enough for new hardwood or conifir tree seedlings to have grown to heights of 12 to 20 feet and up to 5 inches in diameter. These young trees create ideal transition zones. But even if the clear-cut wasn't intentionally replanted, many less desirable species will have sprouted of their own accord, such as sassafras, crabapple, locust, birch, tag alder, and tulip poplar. These, too, serve as splendid transition cover where the animals can find both food and hiding."

Another type of transition zone can exist where fire ravaged a portion of a large forest from 8 to 15 years ago. Since that time, all manner of regenerative growth will have thrived.

If logging activities, forest fires, or controlled burning have not occurred in the region where you like to hunt, your best bet is to lay out a topographic map and find mature woodlands, which generally are indicated by a light green color. If you orient yourself with a compass and inspect the terrain, you'll probably find transition-zone cover along the north-facing borders of the mature forest. These are not bona fide transition zones from the standpoint of consisting of regenerative cover. But because they receive less daily exposure to sunlight, the trees become choked together and their growth is stunted, simulating transition cover.

Another tip that can go a long way in helping to narrow the search for transition zones is, again, with the use of aerial photos. Small dots indicate small trees, and if they are light-colored the trees are hardwoods. Large dots indicate mature forestland, and dark-colored dots indicate conifers. When using aerial photos, the only stumbling block you may run into is that these photos are taken and periodically updated about only once every ten years; if the photos you happen to be using are more than two or three years old, plenty of changes may have taken place. Therefore, it's always wise to make an effort to obtain maps or photos that are as current as possible, then draw in any alterations or changes found during actual scouting that have occurred since the map or photo in question was printed.

Inspect abandoned farms in your hunting area, too, if access permission can be gained. In little time, unused pastures and fallow croplands will be quickly taken over by tree saplings and other growth as the terrain begins reverting back to forestland. Crabapple, hawthorn, sassafras, dogwood, and staghorn sumac are generally among the first species to make their appearances, followed by "soft" hardwoods such as poplar, aspen, boxelder, birch, and basswood, which in turn are followed by the "hard" hardwoods such as oak, maple, hickory, ash, beech, and sycamore. If wide stands of any combination of these species adjoin a mature forest, the area is well worth further investigation.

Various species of evergreens also offer ideal transition zone cover whether they were planted for commercial purposes or for wildlife cover. We've done both on our southern Ohio farm. We've planted 5,000 white pines which, in 20 years, will be cut as sawlogs, as well as 10,000 red pine, Austrian pine, and Norway spruce specifically for wildlife cover. There also are 40,000 scotch pines and Colorado blue spruce that we diligently shape and shear for Christmas trees. It seems to us that none of the above species are really favored as deer forage, and serve only as starvation rations during

In the absence of bonafide transition-zone cover, investigate north-facing slopes where minimum daily sunlight causes most trees to be stunted and crowded close together. Here, a hunter tries to rattle in a buck for his partner in just such a location.

the dead of winter when more preferred foods are depleted (the exceptions are very young trees, which have tender branchtips). Since these species usually are machine or hand-set in six or eight-foot square intervals, only those plantations in which evergreens have grown to a height of six to 15 feet offer ideal transition zone cover. Moreover, even though deer may remain within the evergreens for the greater part of each day, they'll undoubtedly feed elsewhere.

It should be emphasized that merely finding transition zones is only the prelude to filling one's deer tag. Next, it becomes necessary to learn how the animals are using the landscape. During September and October, scout primarily for rubbed trees located in conjunction with trails. During November and December, you'll want to find scrapes in conjunction with trails. Don't concern yourself too much with places where there is evidence of the animal's feeding. With the exception of evergreens, as noted earlier, it's the very nature of transition zones to offer a plenitude of food and, conse-quently, there is little pattern to their foraging activities.

Because hunting transition zones can result in very close encounters with deer, it is vitally important to evaluate carefully the predominant wind direction when selecting the location for your stand or blind. I also highly recommend the use of some type of scent, but as we noted earlier, the use of a scent in this type of close-in situation should be to divert the deer's attention *away* from your stand. Don't place scent on your clothing or around your blind, or you may become the targeted source the deer tries to home-in upon.

If you're hunting with partners, transition zones offer beautiful oppor-tunities for carefully orchestrated drives. One step that's crucial for success is that drivers be instructed to move very slowly and quietly in order to "push" the animals toward the standers. This is no time for a loud, fast-

When hunting alone in transition-zone cover, most hunters take up a stand rather than trying to stillhunt. However, small groups of hunters can make drives with good results.

paced drive, as the deer will stampede; and when they begin bounding and zigzagging through transition cover, even the best of marksmen are sure to throw up their hands in despair.

This brings us to the proverbial pot of gold at the end of the rainbow; the one type of place I always hope to find when scouting because I know in advance it means I'm absolutely assured of seeing deer. That special place is a core area within a transition zone. Every season, all my scouting efforts are geared toward this ultimate goal.

Last year, in northern Kentucky, I located such a spot. When the season opened (I thought it never would), I was perched in an old oak tree overlooking the intersection of five different deer trails, a dozen scrapes, hundreds of antler rubs on saplings, and so many beds I lost count. The cover was so thick that visibility was reduced to 25 yards. Fifty yards in one direction spring water seeped to the surface, and 100 yards in the opposite direction there was a stand of red maple saplings (a prime winter food of whitetails) that had been chewed to shreds. Unquestionably, the area was one of those exceptionally rare places where the core areas of several bucks overlapped. And because the area also was ideal transition zone cover, I couldn't have painted a better picture in my dreams.

Within the first hour of daylight that opening morning, seventeen deer passed by my stand, including five middling-size bucks. Jokingly, I wondered why they didn't occasionally bump into each other. Finally, a stunning ten-pointer came loping along. When my slug struck his chest, he fell, got up, took two wobbly steps, then fell again for good.

Yes, "being in the right place at the right time" is indeed an essential ingredient in deer hunting success. But seldom is luck the telling factor for those who consistently fill their tags with nice bucks. Make a point of finding transition zones and core areas, and if the two happen to be one and the same, the only further looking you need to do is through your favorite cookbook for a number of succulent venison recipes.

Where
Superbucks Live

◆◆◆

When a whitetail hunter makes that pre-dawn hike to his stand on opening morning, and then sits and waits for ample shooting light, many thoughts and doubts course through his mind: Did he spend enough time studying his aerial photos and topo maps? Did he do enough scouting? Has he chosen the right deer scent, consistent with the time of year and locale he's hunting? Should he occupy his stand all day, or after a few hours should he try sneak-hunting?

But above all, he feels hope. And growing anticipation. Will he succeed in taking his buck—a big one—on that first day of the season?

Then a sliver of light touches the horizon. As the glow intensifies, shots begin ringing out in the distance, heightening the hunter's excitement and expectation.

When I experienced all this during the 1985 whitetail season, I had an added enchantment. I was hunting on a small farm near the sleepy town of Kent, Ohio, which is just down the road a couple of miles from Cuyahoga Falls, where I was born and raised.

My stand was a nondescript wooden platform 10 feet high, just inside the leading edge of a transition zone consisting of black locust and sweetgum saplings. On one side of the transition zone was a 10-acre field of timothy and tall fescue, its entire perimeter dotted with fresh scrapes. On the opposite side was a climax oak forest. I knew that a nice buck had staked out this turf as his core area and exclusive rutting territory. I hadn't actually seen the deer, yet, and it was precisely this uncertainty that added immeasurably to the hunt, which should be obvious to anyone who keeps up-to-date with current events in the world of whitetail hunting.

For those who don't keep up-to-date, it was just three miles north of my stand where the world's second largest buck was found dead, with a bullet hole through one of his antler tines. Known as the "hole in the horn buck," his massive rack scored 342-⅜ points and is truly awe-inspiring to look at. A good deal of mystery surrounds the Portage County buck—especially whether the bullet that penetrated the antler continued onward and was responsible for killing the deer. But even more intriguing, most hunters know that regions that have produced outstanding trophies in the past are likely to do so again. So when I was invited to hunt this famed region, I gladly accepted.

All of this explains why I unhesitatingly passed up a forkhorn that slipped by my stand five minutes after full light. Not twenty minutes later a second buck—probably the one whose routine I had doped out—poked his head from the locust saplings to check the open meadow. After long minutes the deer eventually decided all was right with the world and stepped fully out of the cover. He began checking one of the scrapes. He was one handsome buck. I was impressed. A moment later, when my shotgun barked, he was mine.

The deer carried a wide, perfectly symmetrical eight-point rack. He probably was close to 220 pounds on the hoof, which I found incredible for a deer that later, at a check station, was determined to be only 2½ years old.

The famous "hole in the horn" buck from Kent, Ohio, attests to the reputed monster proportions whitetails are capable of attaining in certain regions of the country.

Yet such body weights and antler dimensions are not at all unusual for whitetails hereabouts.

Realistically, of course, none of us ever stand much chance of collecting a new world record deer. Nevertheless, there is indeed a little of the trophy hunter hidden in all of us. No matter how much talk there may be about what constitutes the best-eating deer, I've never met a hunter who had a big buck in his sights but decided to pass up the shot in the hope of eventually bagging a tender forkhorn instead.

In fact, many hunters live strictly for trophy hunting, imposing such high standards on themselves they just will not settle for anything less than huge-antlered male deer. Other hunters are not quite so demanding in their expectations. They'd indeed like to take a big deer, but as the season begins winding down, they begin looking upon venison for the freezer as another important consideration.

In either case, the very largest of the millions of whitetails harvested annually come from very specific regions, which means two things: A hunter who does his homework can hope to acquire a cache of succulent deer meat with the added bonus of a large rack. Conversely, the person who hunts outside this region can hope for venison, but his chances for big antlers are greatly diminished.

The region we're referring to is the upper Midwest—the heartland of America—which includes the states of Ohio, Indiana, Illinois, Iowa, Kansas, Missouri, Michigan, Wisconsin, Minnesota, North Dakota, South Dakota, and eastern Montana.

It's not that record-book deer are never taken elsewhere, just that their numbers are so few they're paled by comparison. This is easily verified by simply studying the trophy hunter's bible, known as *Records of North American Big Game* (compiled and published every six years by the Boone & Crockett Club, 205 S. Patrick St., Alexandria, VA 22314). According to the most recent (eighth) edition, over 90 percent of the top-ranked one hundred typical whitetail heads came from the above listed states, and over 95 percent of the top-ranked non-typical heads also came from the Midwest.

Equally impressive are the whitetails killed by bowhunters and duly recorded in *Bowhunting Big Game Records of North America* (compiled and published by the Pope & Young Club, 6471 Richard Ave., Placerville, CA 95667). During the club's eleventh recording period, eight of the top ten heads came from the Midwest, as did 141 of the next 187 whitetail listings.

In the few cases in which typical and non-typical record heads have come from states other than those in the Midwest, there are two plausible explanations for their occurrences. First, when you're dealing with such staggering numbers as millions of whitetails harvested nationwide every year, now and then at least a few deer will defy the odds of probability and vastly transcend normal or "average" antler development rates characteristic of a particular species or region. It's like the one turnip in your garden that, for some

This impressive whitetail was taken only a few miles from the author's home in southern Ohio. According to the Boone & Crockett Club, over 90 percent of the top-ranked heads have come from the upper Midwest.

unexplainable reason, grows twice as large as the hundreds of others in the same row.

Secondly, of the remaining record-book deer taken outside the Midwest, most have come from Texas where unique conditions prevail. Unlike nearly all other whitetail states, 99 percent of Texas hunting land falls under private ownership. This means ranchers can, and do, greatly restrict hunter access by imposing expensive leases or very stiff trespass fees, which enables them to control both hunting pressure and harvest numbers—two types of management that greatly contribute to the production of trophy racks.

So, aside from these two exceptions to the rule, the obvious question that looms to the forefront is this: Why should such an unlikely and heavily populated and industrialized state such as Ohio or Indiana be capable of consistently producing such outlandish size deer, while another state with vast expanses of rural land, such as Alabama or Mississippi, almost never gets its name into the annals of record keeping?

One reason is a law of nature that biologists refer to as Bergmann's Rule, which has to do with an animal's body size being directly proportional to the climate in which it lives. By definition, Bergmann's Rule states that "a larger body has a smaller surface area in proportion to its mass weight than a smaller body, and this form of adaptation to the climate enables the creature to more efficiently maintain its body heat during bitter cold weather to ensure the survival of the species."

This explains why whitetails are not the same animals in all regions of the country. Over eons of time, they have evolved into thirty different subspecies that have physiologically adapted in different ways to the unique climates in which they live.

The primary whitetail species is *Odocoileus virginianus*. This is the pure-strain whitetail that was first seen by early colonists when they settled in Virginia. However, as our early ancestors pioneered other regions, they eventually found many other deer, which they presumed had evolved from the Virginia deer. That was not really true, but they do reveal physical

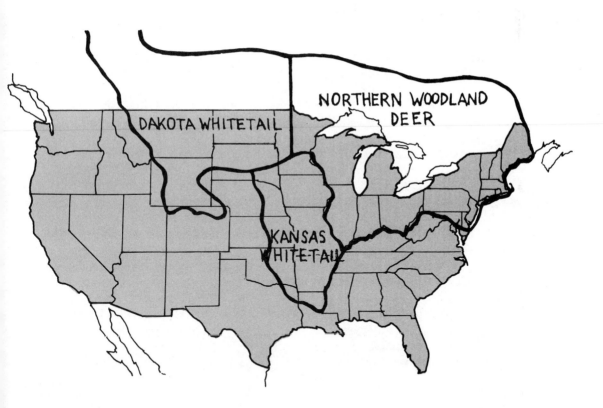

Of the 30 different whitetail subspecies, these three have the genetic capability of growing to the largest size, due to a biological theorem known as Bergmann's Rule.

characteristics that are somewhat different from *Odocoileus virginianus.* Some have a lighter or darker body coloration. Others reveal slightly different antler configurations, such as unusually thick but short tines, or long slender points, or wider main beams, or tight basket racks where the antler tines almost touch in front. But one of the most distinguishable features among the various subspecies has to do with their overall body size.

Our smallest whitetail is the Key deer, *Odocoileus virginianus clavium,* which lives in a very restricted range in hot, southernmost Florida. A fully adult Key whitetail usually weighs only about 40 pounds. When you see one bounding through the cover, you'd swear it was a greyhound and not a deer!

Also of small size, and likewise living in warm climates, are the Texas whitetail, the Coues whitetail, the Carmen Mountains whitetail, and the Arizona whitetail, all of which seldom exceed 90 pounds in weight.

At the opposite extreme is the largest whitetail subspecies, the Northern Woodland deer *(Odocoileus virginianus borealis).* This deer, exclusively found throughout the Midwest and parts of southern Canada monopolizes the record books. In the areas that these deer call home, it is not unusual for winter temperatures to occasionally dip as low as 40° below zero—and the deer have adapted well by becoming so big it often boggles the mind. The largest confirmed Northern Woodland whitetail known was a 511-pound goliath from Minnesota, followed by deer of 491 pounds and 481 pounds from Wisconsin. Then there has been a slew of others ranging from 350 to 415 pounds from Missouri, Michigan, Iowa, and Ohio. The very largest suspected whitetail ever? Well, a *600-pounder* was reportedly taken in North Dakota a decade ago, but remains unconfirmed.

Seeing these big-bodied deer close up is often enough to cause your hat to lift right off your head. Just last year, in the farm country of southern Illinois, I saw a doe I estimated at close to 400 pounds. My lower jaw hung agape as she waddled by my stand, leaving tracks almost the size of a Hereford's.

Aside from female deer, however, it stands to reason that as a male deer increases substantially in body weight, it also grows proportionately larger antlers. Every year, game wardens throughout the Midwest receive telephone calls from hunters, housewives, rural mail carriers, and others whose voices ring with excitement about the "elk" they just saw in Indiana or some other unseemly place. As it typically happens, the warden laughs at the misidentification and politely informs the caller that what he has seen is merely a very big whitetail.

All of this poses an interesting question. Why are states such as New York, New Hampshire, Vermont, Massachusetts, and Maine rarely noted in the record books? After all, they, too, are home to the Northern Woodland whitetail subspecies, and their northern latitudes also have some of the nation's coldest winter weather.

The answer to this is relatively simple. In addition to a particular subspecies having the needed genetic framework for rapid, heavy body growth and outsize antlers, the deer must also have the opportunity to realize that potential.

As an analogy, the tomato plants in your garden all may have the genetic capability of producing large, delicious fruits, but only if they are diligently watered and fertilized. Yet, if the plants do not receive the nutrients they require, they'll be thin, spindly, and never live up to their potential.

Virtually the same thing can and does happen with deer. As a result of glacial activity thousands of years ago, the upper Midwest possesses extremely fertile soil, which is used almost exclusively for intensive agricultural purposes. Whitetails, therefore, don't have to rely upon low-nutrient native foods alone but are able to grow fat and sassy upon a rich diet of soybeans, corn, alfalfa, wheat, and oats. This is a key element in their growth rates and the enormous body sizes they frequently attain, compared to their subspecies counterparts living elsewhere.

When it comes to antler growth, trace mineral substances play an equally important role. Not only is Midwest soil and water naturally endowed with high levels of phosphorus, calcium, sodium, sulphur, and dissolved nitrogen—which have been determined as most responsible for antler development—but farmers put still additional quantities of these minerals onto their land to further accelerate crop growth and yields.

But as you leave Ohio, heading eastward into unglaciated Pennsylvania, and continuing up into the northeastern states, the soil becomes progressively less and less fertile, with only small swatches here and there having important agricultural applications. In many regions, in fact, endless tracts of climax forests predominate, relegating deer to survive the best they can on spartan diets of twigs, buds, weeds, and other native vegetation of low nutritive value. In short, they just don't get enough to eat—in fact, winterkill due to starvation is common—and they don't ingest very high levels of trace mineral elements conducive to rapid antler growth.

In summary, this is the first and perhaps most important consideration a hunter should give when it comes to homing-in upon a dream buck: He should look toward one of the upper Midwest states where the Northern Woodland subspecies has not only the unique genetic potential to reach monster proportions, but also the prime habitat that allows them to do so.

The next step in narrowing the search, after a particular state has been selected for an upcoming hunt, involves a bit of easy research. If you scan through a current edition of *Records of North American Big Game,* or *Bowhunting Big Game Records of North America,* you'll quickly notice a bit of very valuable information. Next to every ranked trophy listed in the records is the actual county where the deer was taken!

It is now possible to target a specific hunting area. Let's take Ohio, for example, as the state a hunter may wish to try. Over the past several decades, seventy-eight Boone & Crockett and Pope & Young deer have been harvested in the Buckeye State. In examining every Ohio listing in the two record books, however, the astute hunter learns that of the state's eighty-eight counties, there are two or three that appear over and over again. You now know where your chances are best, and all that remains is making landowner contacts or learning where in those counties public hunting is allowed upon state or federal lands.

Curiously, few hunters ever take this approach in attempting to collect a trophy deer. Instead, they write to the state's game department, requesting county-by-county deer harvest figures. This information is often more deceptive than helpful because it only tells you where the deer population is highest (and where there subsequently are the most hunters). It does not tell you where the largest deer customarily are taken, which may be in an entirely different part of the state. Yet it is critical to learn where the monster deer are, because certain counties that have produced record-book bucks in the past are likely to continue to do so in the future, as a result of some unique combination of food and soil minerals that exist there.

Despite the cold weather that is common to the upper Midwest, deer wax fat on prime foods. This doe was so heavy she actually waddled as she walked.

To find deer with large racks, try to scout areas where there are crops that require high-nutrient, alkaline soil such as corn, soybeans, and alfalfa.

With regards to the abundance of certain trace mineral elements themselves, it's worth noting that recent research conducted at Penn State's College of Agriculture has revealed that, of all substances that contribute to antler growth, the two most influential are phosphorus and calcium. When these two minerals were added to the diets of penned deer, the animals developed much larger antlers than other test deer on restricted diets.

Said Dr. J.S. Lindzey of Penn State's Cooperative Wildlife Research Unit: "We've even had some experimental bucks produce racks with thirteen or fourteen points at only 1½ years of age!"

"With this research data," remarked Pat Karns, the top deer expert at Minnesota's Wildlife Experiment Station near Grand Rapids, "we can see a common denominator that adds up to consistently bigger bucks in certain regions than elsewhere, for lime and phosphorus are what farmers most commonly use to increase crop yields."

Detroit, Michigan deer hunter Tom Hennessey has used this insight to stack up an admirable number of trophy whitetails. In the last twenty years he has tied licenses onto thirty-one bucks sporting racks with eight points or better. "When most hunters think about pre-season scouting," Hennessey told me, "they seem preoccupied with finding deer trails, tracks, scrapes, and such signs. But my first scouting is actually done in the spring and summer. I want to find the biggest deer, and that means first locating optimum habitat where prime food and mineral-rich soil exists."

Tom Hennessey's pre-season scouting, then, generally is for a glacier-scoured agricultural region where farmers are busily planting those particular crops that require high-nutrient, alkaline soil, such as corn or legumes like soybeans or alfalfa. In unglaciated regions, he searches for evidence of

In regions where soil is infertile, look for places burned over by a forest fire in previous years. The ash deposited on the terrain neutralizes the high acid content of the soil, resulting in regenerative vegetation of higher quality. Here, son Mike and I study a scrape in a township where a fire took place five years ago.

the very same crops, knowing in advance that successfully growing them requires the landowner to artificially supplement the soil with various chemicals, minerals, and fertilizers that will simultaneously add to the antler growth rates of local deer.

"Only after my spring/summer research," Hennessey related, "do I begin thinking about refining my scouting by studying topo maps and aerial photos to learn as much as possible about the topography of the landscape, and therefore how deer are likely to be using the terrain."

Even within the natural range of the Northern Woodland deer, however, there are certain to be small pockets of unglaciated, mountainous terrain, such as Missouri's Ozarks and southeastern Ohio's Appalachians. Likewise, there are wide expanses of even glaciated, poor nutrient soil, as found in northern Minnesota and Michigan's Upper Peninsula. In any of these situations—and there are still others—determining locations where forest fires previously have occurred can be an important clue to finding big-antlered deer. Fires have the effect of depositing large quantities of ash, which neutralizes what was probably a high acid content in the soil. And this significantly improves the nutrient levels of the regenerative vegetation that subsequently takes root.

Finally, a few qualifying comments regarding the pursuit of trophy deer are justified in concluding this chapter.

While the upper Midwest—the home of the Northern Woodland subspecies—is unquestionably where the nation's largest whitetails can be found, I've known too many hunters who became so obsessed in their attempts to get their names in the record books they no longer enjoyed their deer hunting. For a time, I was a member of this fraternity as well, and passed up shots at *very* nice bucks in hopes that a veritable monster would eventually appear. Well, it never happened.

To be sure, I firmly believe there are many bucks out there, right now, that are bigger than the monster from Kent, Ohio. Game management studies have shown that any particular whitetail buck is likely to grow his best set of antlers sometime between his fifth and seventh years, but due to heavy annual harvests, less than 4 percent of all male deer ever live long enough to see even their fourth birthdays.

Consequently, because there are just not that many buster bucks skulking around, compared to the sheer numbers of hunters tramping through the puckerbrush in search of trophy racks, it's fool's play to establish unrealistic expectations for a hunt and then almost predictably come home disappointed.

In other words, there is no correlation whatever between great hunts and big bucks. Indeed, some of the most enjoyable and challenging hunts may well be concluded by the taking of average six, eight, or ten-pointers that wouldn't even begin to raise the eyebrows of those who every year find themselves severely afflicted with cases of record-book mania. Feel sorry for them, for the only venison they enjoy is that brought back to camp by others.

10

Bag a Barnyard Buck

◆◆

A biting wind raked across the soybean field before me, causing waves of rustling noises that sounded like hordes of locusts on a feeding binge. Meanwhile, a platinum-colored streak on the horizon was signaling dawn's arrival, and with it ample shooting light.

Amidst all of this, my pulse was hammering a staccato because for the last few minutes, I'd had my eyes glued to the far edge of the field where two respectable bucks and a harem of seven does stood in silhouette as they gorged themselves on beans for breakfast. The deer were still out of range of my slug-loaded shotgun, so all I could do for the moment was shiver, hunker down still deeper into my wool jacket, and wait.

I was in North Carolina. When I first entered my makeshift blind, I could see the dim glow of lights in Mel Harper's barn in the distance. Thoroughly chilled to the bone, I could envision Mel sitting in the pungent warmth of his milking stalls, entirely surrounded by patient Guernseys with their heads buried in oat bins. Add to that the heady aroma of hundreds of alfalfa hay bales stacked in an overhead mow, and the cream separator merrily humming along, and that barn positively had to be one of the most inviting and sweet-smelling places in the world.

"Ever since we began planting soybeans about five years ago," Mel had said the previous evening, "whitetails have become more plentiful around here than politicians at a liar's convention. Deer become so addicted to beans that sometimes the perimeters of our fields look like they've been run over by a lawnmower. First the deer eat the beans and pods, then the leaves and stems, and after that they paw the ground apart to get at the roots. I'd

116

feel I'd owe you a favor if you'd take one of those deer and then spread the word among your friends. Just have them stop by and ask before they hunt. If I'm not up at the house, I'll be down at the milking barn or pressing cider around back.''

Naturally, that was an offer no serious deer hunter could refuse. The following morning, after enjoying fresh eggs and home-made sausage at the insistence of Mel's wife Lora, I headed for my blind with earnest intentions of doing the required "favor" for my new-found friend. Less than one hour later, the 12-gauge Ithaca pounded my shoulder, a six-point buck slumped to the ground, and I had my main ingredient for many venison dinners. Mel apparently heard the gun's report because before I had even begun field-dressing operations, he was on his tractor and heading my way to help bring the deer to my pickup parked in his farmyard.

The significance of this particular experience is that the handsome buck I tagged was the ninth taken in similar farmland situations in recent years. But, surprisingly, the vast majority of other hunters I know seldom tap this whitetail bonanza, preferring instead to chart nonstop courses for cherished deer camps in wilderness or deeply forested regions where, unknowingly, their chances of scoring are sharply diminished.

Look at it this way. Whitetails are dominated by three driving life forces: privacy, food, and sex.

With regards to privacy, what gives deer a greater sense of security and conceals their movements better than irregular, broken terrain where a wide variety of dense understory cover offers countless mixtures of edges, openings, alleys, and travel options?

Pertaining to food, what could be more attractive to whitetails than ready access to unlimited quantities of their favorite grasses, grains, fruits, and vegetables?

And when it comes to sex, what could be more appealing to amorous bucks than the presence of numerous does that have likewise been attracted to the same vicinity due to the superb food and cover?

The answer to all three questions is not deep wilderness or climax forest-land where the bulk of the available food is high out of reach, where a distinct lack of regenerative ground-level cover makes paranoid deer feel exposed and uneasy, and where deer numbers are therefore few and widely scattered.

Instead, it's the rich agricultural lands just beyond most city limits signs that offer whitetail habitat of the highest caliber. And that's why an enterprising hunter can do no better than to begin paying more attention to hunting opportunities closer to home. He'll save gas, time, money, and yet encounter more deer than anywhere else.

Part of the reason for there being more deer per square mile in farmland country has to do with the more healthful state of the animals. In wilderness regions, many deer succumb each year to disease and winterkill as a result

Since food intake is first channeled into body growth and maintenance, and secondly to antler growth, it stands to reason deer that eat well develop the biggest racks. That's why farm-country bucks like this one invariably have larger headgear than deer living in wilderness regions.

of starvation and malnutrition. Those does that do survive are often so gaunt and haggard that they drop only one fawn in the spring. When twins are dropped, chances are high that both will be so weak they'll live but a matter of a few days.

In lush agricultural regions, however, whitetail mortality rates are not nearly so grim. The deer generally remain well-fed and healthy throughout the winter, and as a rule, does will drop twins, both of which should have high chances of survival. In many instances even triplets are conceived.

Most important of all, a farmland hunter can expect to come across deer with much larger-than-average body sizes and bucks with appreciably larger racks. Confirming this, studies have shown that whitetails exhibit a much higher conversion rate when their food intake consists largely of farm crops compared to wild foods. In other words, their gains in real body weight are far greater upon a steady diet of domesticated foods than gains achieved through an equal quantity of browse, plant life, and other native foods the animals must rely upon in non-agricultural regions. This is crucial for the trophy hunter to know, because a whitetail buck's food intake always goes first toward body growth and maintenance, and only after those requirements have been satisfied are excess nutrients channeled into antler growth and development. Admittedly, buster bucks are occasionally taken in the most unlikely places, but a check of the record books reveals that the vast majority of monster deer come from locales where agricultural activities abound.

Although farmlands, in the general sense, provide excellent habitat for whitetails, some types of farms are much better prospects for hunters. And once a hunter has secured access permission, he should also take into consideration certain strategies that are likely to prove far more successful than all others.

To begin with, forget about the huge agribusiness farms. These operations commonly sprawl over thousands of acres of terrain and are so professionally and intensively run that suitable deer habitat is virtually nonexistent. (During a certain few months there's plenty of prime food, to be sure, but rarely the needed combination of food and security cover).

Instead, concentrate your efforts upon private, family-owned farms of 500 acres or less. These are small-time operations in which landowners simply do not have the required machinery, manpower, or money to plow and plant every square inch of soil. Consequently, there are sure to be numerous brushy fencerows crisscrossing the property, small woodlots left intact, cover-filled gulleys separating the croplands, small pine plantations serving as windbreaks, and an assortment of hedges, brier patches, streamside willow groves, grassy swales, and other irregular terrain and cover features that are highly compatible with the lifestyles of whitetails.

Furthermore, you won't find $60,000 tractors with air-conditioned cabs or $120,000 combines parked in the landowner's barn, which further attests to the relative lack of efficiency with which small farms are managed. This means there is sure to be plenty of inadvertent grain spillage during harvest time, and even entire rows of crops either accidently left standing or purposely allowed to remain in order to foster wildlife populations.

Aside from the farm's size, it's imperative to go one step further and try to obtain hunting permission on those specific farms where certain crops that whitetails favor most are grown, even though neighboring farms may have similar crops. Heading the list of these favorite foods are soybeans and corn, followed by hayland crops consisting of alfalfa, timothy, red clover, orchardgrass, lespedeza, or any combination of these grass/legume species. If the farmer has some type of orchard, especially apples or peaches, all the better. Winter wheat, buckwheat, sorghum, or truck garden crops such as cabbages, navy beans, and lettuce are other favorites. One trick I've used in past years to find good numbers of deer is to make a list of what crops are being grown in the vicinity where I'd like to hunt, then attempting to gain permission on that particular farm where there is a favorite food not found on the others. In other words, let's say there are eight farms in a given township and all have devoted varying amounts of acreage to corn and alfalfa. However, on a ninth farm there is also corn, but also cabbages and a large peach orchard. Likely as not, this farm could be a real hotbed of deer activity, but the only way to find out is by scouting.

It might seem that obtaining hunting permission on private farms would be difficult indeed. That might have been true up until about 1980, and of course there will always be a small percentage of landowners who will never allow hunting under any conditions. But in many regions, just the opposite exists and farmers are now beginning to welcome hunters. An explanation for this turnabout is that in the last decade whitetail populations have exploded almost everywhere; as this is being written in 1986, current statistics tell us deer numbers have *doubled* since 1970. Because most farmers these days are operating on extremely slim profit margins—or in startling numbers of cases, according to the evening news, not making any profit at all—they don't take kindly to the prospect of deer invading their land in such numbers that they eat hundreds or sometimes thousands of dollars worth of produce, grain, or grass.

Deer hunting permission is more likely now than ever before to be greeted with a resounding "Yes!" If there is a singlemost, common obstacle to overcome it's undoubtedly the landowner's inherent (and usually justified) fear of four-wheel-drives gouging deep ruts across his hay meadows, the possibility of pastured livestock being endangered by stray shots, broken fences, or litter strewn about. If the hunter can allay all of these concerns with convincing respect and responsibility, gaining access to the land should pose no great problem.

Although farmlands generally have high whitetail populations, a hunter can't take short-cuts when it comes to scouting and other pre-season investi-

Forget about large agribusiness farms where every square inch is plowed and planted. Instead, concentrate upon small farms where in addition to plenty of food there are woodlots, briar patches, and other security cover for the animals to hide in.

gation. Because agricultural regions have such abundant supplies of food, and because the deers' cover-use and travel options are so myriad, more scouting is actually necessary than when hunting a region where cover and food are scarce and the animals are therefore more predictable.

If you haven't already studied a county plat map, a good way to begin is by laying out a topographical map and having the farmer use a felt-tipped pen to outline the perimeter of his property if it is not clearly defined with line fences. This safeguard prevents the hunter from inadvertently straying onto someone else's land and creating an embarrassing situation. Then have the farmer draw in the locations of various planted crops and other terrain features such as recently built ponds, forest slashings, or dense stands of honeysuckle. In all likelihood, the farmer will even be able to tell you where he usually sees deer around his place. All of this paints a picture that is somewhat like the pieces of a jigsaw puzzle fitted together, which allows you to make educated guesses as to where the deer are bedding, drinking, feeding, and traveling back and forth. Then it merely becomes necessary to begin leaving boot tracks to confirm those hunches.

The initial order of business should be to hike around the perimiters of planted crops in search of tracks and signs of where deer have been feeding. Those particular crops that butt up directly against security cover such as

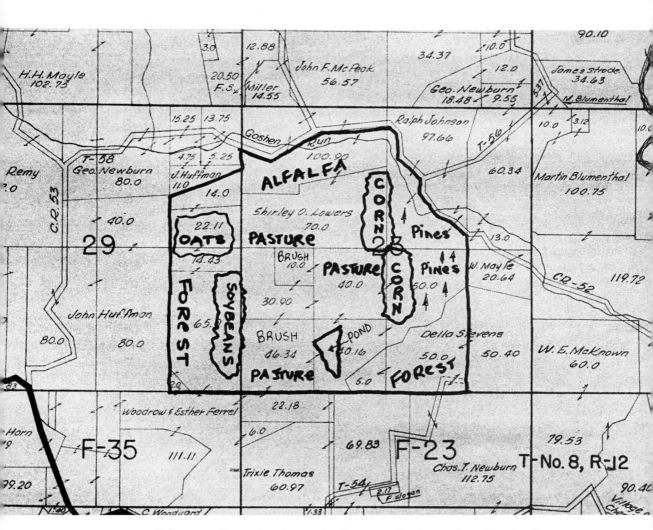

Before actually scouting the terrain, have your landowner host draw in his property boundaries on a plat map and indicate the locations of other features such as planted crops, known water sources, forestland and the like.

brush-filled gulleys, woodlot transition zones, or pine plantations are certain to reveal the greatest evidence of deer use.

While whitetails are absolutely crazy about soybeans, they also make gluttons of themselves on corn—but at first, their reaction is quite peculiar. I learned about this first-hand when we purchased our own farm in Ohio a number of years ago. I had immediately planted some acreage in corn to be used for stock feed and silage, but mainly to attract deer. None of my neighboring landowners had corn planted at that time, so I figured deer would flock to my place like ants to a picnic. Not so. Altogether, I spent dozens of hours bowhunting on various stands situated around the cornfield edges, and not a single deer ever came to sample my menu.

Totally discouraged, I called a biologist friend who specializes in whitetail behavior and pleaded for his advice. He explained that when corn is planted for the first time in a particular region, local deer simply don't know what's underneath the husks on standing cornstalks and therefore don't touch it. It sounded incredible when he next said that I'd have to *teach* the deer that corn was good to eat!

The way to do this, I learned, was by "opening up" my field. In other words, I should use a picker to harvest four or five outside rows entirely surrounding the 15-acre cornfield, ensuring a good amount of kernels, cobs, and other cut spillage was left laying exposed on the ground. Deer randomly walking the edges of the field at night could then be expected to discover the spillage, taste it, and from that time on they'd regularly come to get more corn and even use their teeth to pull off the husks of ears on still-standing stalks.

I thought the whole idea was outlandish and ridiculous. But I was at the end of my rope and took my friend's advice. Amazingly, it worked like a charm! Within only two days of opening up my field, deer were regularly visiting their new-found food source. On the third day I collected a sleek forkhorn.

It's worth mentioning that several weeks later we harvested the remainder of the corn, and several weeks after that we received an unexpected snowfall. I went to take a look at the stubble field and was shocked to find almost every square yard pockmarked with tracks. In dozens of places, there were large pawings in the snow where deer were still trying to eat spillage. Walking the perimeter of the snow-covered field, I counted 20 different trails coming from various directions and all converging upon the corn stubble.

But don't anticipate that cornfields will automatically attract deer. The corn must be a regular cash crop that is planted in the immediate vicinity every year, and the only way to learn about this is by asking the farmer how long he has been raising corn and what crops his neighbors have been planting. If the corn is a new, first-year crop in a particular region where beans, hay, wheat, or other crops have predominated in previous years, don't expect deer to begin showing up around cornfield edges until after the farmer has begun harvest operations.

After "opening up" one of my cornfields, I finally began noticing evidence of deer (above). When corn is a new, first-year crop in a region where other crops have predominated, deer may not recognize it as good to eat until after harvest operations have begun.

Partially eaten corn is not always the work of deer (left). If just the tender tip has been eaten, raccoons are the villains.

Sometimes other wildlife creatures working a cornfield can give hunters the mistaken impression the place is alive with deer. I'm reminded in particular about scouting the perimeter of a cornfield once and finding dozens upon dozens of cornstalks knocked over and the ears themselves chewed upon. I later learned the damage had been done by raccoons.

The way to tell for sure is to examine the ears themselves, although the knocked-over stalks is a dead giveaway as well. Deer don't have to knock over a cornstalk to reach the ear. But raccoons do, and when the stalk is lying on the ground, they then bite off just the tendermost 2-inch tip of each ear before moving on to the next stalk. Evaluating this sign, plus noticing a distinct absence of deer tracks, tells you the entire story.

An enigma pertaining to hunting farms planted to either corn or soybeans is the placement of stands. Many nimrods make the big mistake of electing to watch trails deep in adjacent woodlands or other dense cover, hoping to waylay deer traveling from their beds to the cropland or back again after they've fed. It's a logical tactic, but unfortunately it too often results in the hunter never catching a single glimpse of buckskin.

The reason is that farmland deer often temporarily abandon their usual dense-cover resting sites and begin bedding right in the innermost regions of the cropland itself! They simply find an irrigation ditch, or a furrow where rainwater has collected, and stay put. Even when they are standing they are completely concealed, and with plenty to eat and drink there's simply no inclination to travel any distance and risk dangerous exposure.

I learned about this aspect of whitetail behavior entirely by accident many years ago when I was sitting in a tree stand along the edge of a soybean field in Kentucky. One of the biggest bucks I've ever seen was feeding along the far side, and I desperately hoped he would eventually come to within shooting range. Then, suddenly, the deer dropped out of sight! At first I thought the old boy had detected danger and was cleverly ducking down until everything was safe again. But after a solid two-hour wait it became clear the deer had just decided to bed right there beneath the overhead canopy of bean leaves. A little later he popped up again, stretched, fed for a short while, then hit the deck again.

I never tagged that big rascal, but the education has allowed me to take two other deer in recent years by staging line-drives with several partners. We simply spread out in a straight line about 25 yards apart and begin hiking the length of the bean field, being careful to stay between the rows so as to not damage any of the plants. After making one pass, we move sideways and then come back in the opposite direction to cover new ground. Frequently, deer jump right up in front of us and begin running straight for some distant woodlot, presenting themselves briefly for clear shots at very close range.

If a farmer objects to the idea of hiking between the rows of his soybeans, it's probably not because he's worried about the walking hunters doing any damage. The damage comes when a mortally wounded deer repeatedly

Deer often bed in croplands, particularly if they are lined with irrigation ditches. By simply ducking down when danger approaches, they are as well hidden as in any woodlot.

stumbles and falls during his final 50 to 75-yard run and then hits the ground kicking, which can literally wipe out hundreds of bean plants. There are several possibilities to avoid this. One is to select a stand site somewhere along the perimeter of the field, or sneak-hunt around the perimeter, hoping to have a shot at a deer close to one of the edges. Or, stage a drive through the middle of the field, assuring the farmer in advance that no drivers will take shots, only standers along the opposite edge as the deer are leaving the field.

The sheer height of cornstalks so greatly impairs your vision that executing the same type of line-drive in a cornfield is impossible. But it is well worth any hunting party's time to stage conventional drives through cornfields in hopes of pushing deer to partners placed on stand along the opposite side of the field. Just be sure to do four things: First, obtain the farmer's permission to drive his cornfields; second, walk carefully so none of the cornstalks are damaged; third, make sure everyone wears fluorescent orange and maintains voice contact; fourth, have the drivers maintain a relatively close spacing between each other to prevent deer from slipping back between them.

The beauty of driving a cornfield in this manner is that many times you need to place only one hunter on stand! This means more than the usual number of hunters can act as drivers. The ideal situation, especially in states where center-fire rifles are legal, is to place the stand hunter halfway along the length of the biggest cornfield you can find. This will allow him to look either right or left and watch the entire edge. An accomplished shooter can thereby cover up to 350 yards of edge on either side of him for a total coverage of 700 yards. This eliminates a lot of guesswork, because you don't have to determine which particular escape trails the animals may attempt to use in leaving the cornfield. The hunter on stand simply watches the entire edge. No matter where the deer happen to step out, the stander is in perfect position to level his sights upon them.

In states where only short-range, slug-loaded shotguns are permitted for whitetail hunting, the same basic ruse can be employed. The only difference is that now, the single stand hunter is placed along one of the shorter edges he can adequately cover. The drivers thusly traverse the field lengthwise rather than through its width.

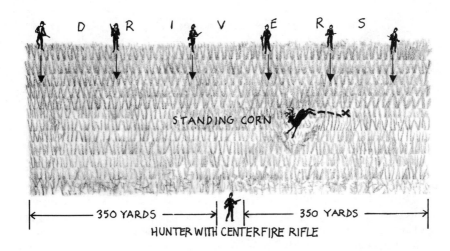

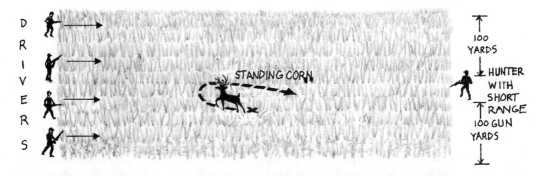

Crafty bucks love to hide in cornfields, and assembling a drive party offers the best chances for success. Only one hunter needs to be placed on stand, with all the others acting as drivers.

Whitetails especially like to bed in soybeans. Hike between the rows of beans only if you first secure the landowner's permission and you'll be rewarded with exciting action at very close range.

Hunting farms where low-growing crops are raised requires an entirely different approach because hay, small grains, and truck-garden vegetables do not give deer much in the way of daytime bedding cover. As a result, whitetails will predictably bed in nearby security cover and travel back and forth for feeding.

Alfalfa hay in particular is a drawing card for whitetails. Dawn and dusk are prime times to catch the critters in the open, especially if there is adjacent transition zone cover they can duck into at the slightest provocation. Sometimes a hunter will luck upon a single, unique vantage point from which he can watch for early or late feeding deer. But most times the best bet is having two different stands, one for morning use and another for the evening watch.

An ideal morning stand should be back inside the leading edge of adjacent security cover, to intercept deer as they are leaving the open food source and returning to bedding sites. But it is crucially important, when hiking to such a stand in pre-dawn darkness, that the hunter not walk across the open hay meadow or other cropland. Any deer feeding there will spook off and dash for the safety of cover. Instead, go the long way around and come in through a woodlot, swamp, or other dense cover from the back side, easing

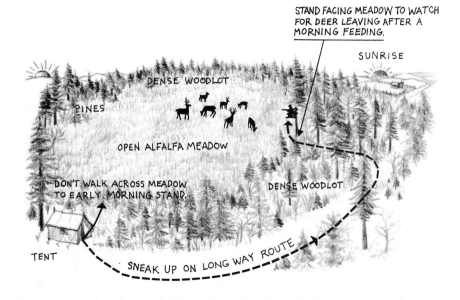

STAND FACING MEADOW TO WATCH FOR DEER LEAVING AFTER A MORNING FEEDING.

SUNRISE

DENSE WOODLOT

PINES

OPEN ALFALFA MEADOW

DON'T WALK ACROSS MEADOW TO EARLY MORNING STAND.

DENSE WOODLOT

TENT

SNEAK UP ON LONG WAY ROUTE

In hiking to an early-morning stand to watch any kind of low-growing crop, never walk directly across open ground. Sneak the long way around and come in through heavy cover on the backside or you may spook animals out of the cropland.

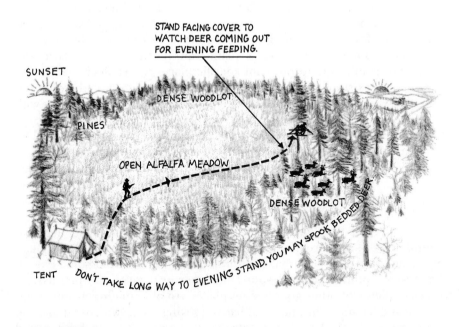

STAND FACING COVER TO WATCH DEER COMING OUT FOR EVENING FEEDING.

SUNSET

DENSE WOODLOT

PINES

OPEN ALFALFA MEADOW

DENSE WOODLOT

TENT

DON'T TAKE LONG WAY TO EVENING STAND. YOU MAY SPOOK BEDDED DEER.

If you plan to take a stand watching a low-growing crop during the evening hours, hike right across the open ground. If you take a longer route through adjacent cover, you might route deer from their beds.

up to your stand at the edge of the open meadow as quietly as possible.

When selecting an evening stand, just the opposite applies. In this situation you'll want to place your stand in such a manner that enables you to watch for deer coming from heavy cover to the open meadow or other crop. And now, it is permissible to hike across the open meadow, taking the shortest route possible to your stand. Traveling the long, roundabout route may well disturb deer bedded in the heavy cover.

The exact placement of an evening stand can often be puzzling because the degree of hunting pressure in the region predetermines the animal's behavior. If hunting pressure is light or nonexistent, the stand should be situated to watch not only the heavy-cover approach route the deer will be taking as they travel to the meadow, but also the open edges of the meadow itself. Conversely, if hunting pressure is intense, deer are not likely to step out into the open meadow to feed until after full dark. Instead, they like to mill around back inside the leading edge of the cover where cover affords concealment until darkness falls, which means you'll want your stand to likewise be farther back in.

In the above examples, we've been assuming we're whitetail hunting in a state where center-fire rifle hunters engage in both short and long-distance shooting. If the hunter is required to use a shotgun, or chooses to use primitive equipment, he'll have to be more precise in selecting his stand location. Whenever this is the case with my own hunting, I like to spend some time before the season opens using binoculars to watch likely alfalfa meadows or other low-growing croplands during the hours of dawn and dusk. This enables me to pinpoint specific places where deer seem to be entering and existing the crop area. Then I can later go directly to one of those "doorways" and select the best location for my stand, consistent with the time of day I plan to hunt.

Keep in mind that the farmland crop, whatever it happens to be, will be the focus of attention for the deer. They won't give much serious thought to acorns deep in the nearby woodlands, no matter how bountiful the mast crop is that year. And they won't show a great deal of interest in other wild foods, at least until well after nearby domesticated crops have been harvested and any residual spillage has been depleted.

One aspect of farmland hunting that is both fun and intriguing, and doesn't enter the picture when hunting other regions, has to do with selecting a stand site. You don't have to think trees only, or build some type of ground-level blind. Provided your landowner host gives you permission, there are plenty of other good hiding places. An old building is one example. I've hidden in the hay mows of barns, looking out a swinging door, and in the attics of ramshackle homesteads. I've also hidden behind rusted machinery abandoned along field edges and behind rolls of fencing.

One time my friend Al Wolter was puzzled over the best way to hunt a mammoth hay meadow. It seemed as if resident deer foiled his every effort

In farm country, it's not always necessary to think in terms of tree stands or ground-level blinds. If the farmer gives permission, you may find intriguing hiding possibilities in the hay mows of abandoned barns or the attics of old homesteads.

by never using the same trail twice in either approaching or leaving the meadow. No matter where he stationed himself, the deer always appeared somewhere else, fed toward the middle of the meadow, and then left. Finally, Al had a brainstorm. Almost spang in the middle of the meadow was a 12-foot-high stack of several thousand bales of hay that he had never paid much attention to, but now it stood out like a beacon of hope.

The next day, Al climbed on top of the hay bales and pulled up after him his rifle, a sleeping bag, a thermos bottle of tea, and a sack full of sandwiches. Next, he slightly rearranged some of the bales into a rectangular hole of sorts, unrolled his sleeping bag there, and spent the night. When his wristwatch alarm beeped softly at five o'clock the next morning, Al loaded his rifle, poured a hot drink, and began waiting.

"When it was light enough to see," Al recounted, "there were seven deer around me. One doe was actually nibbling on one of the hay bales directly below me. The eight-point buck I killed was the easiest of my career, in terms of actually making the shot, but one I spent the longest amount of time figuring out."

So when it comes to selecting a stand site on a farm, use your imagination. Many experienced bucks, I feel, have learned to look up into trees, but not many harbor suspicion over a derelict tractor, a stack of fenceposts, or even a stack of baled hay.

While whitetails everywhere depend heavily upon their senses to warn them of impending danger, something that triggers an alarm reaction in a wilderness whitetail may elicit an entirely different response from a deer living in farm country. The reason is that farmland deer have long since learned to distinguish between man's activities and categorize them as either neutral or malevolent.

When a farmer is hiking his fencelines, for example, routinely checking for places that may need mending, his stride and other behavior is entirely different than a hunter who may later choose to sneak along the same route. To the deer hiding in nearby cover, the farmer poses no threat, even though he has triggered the deer's sensory awareness. On the other hand, the deer somehow seem to know the hunter moving along is definitely cause for concern. The difference, then, between the personalities of farmland deer and wilderness deer is that a farmland whitetail will not react to the sight, smell, or sound of a human until it has made that differentiation; the wilderness whitetail will. As a result, hunters who work out of deer camps in deep forests or remote regions can expect to see practically all of their deer during the early or late hours of the day. Because deer living in such remote environments have virtually no exposure to humans during the year, they naturally believe it's safer to assume that all people are potential threats rather than to attempt any distinctions. And this causes the critters to spend the bulk of the midday periods sequestered in heavy cover.

But the same elusive behavior doesn't always apply to farmland whitetails. During the course of the year, they live in fishbowl-like environments and become so accustomed to seeing farm workers and other people in and around the area that they're not so nearly alarmed by the presence of humans or the approach of vehicles or machinery. These animals are significantly more polyphasic than deer that live elsewhere, which means they may be up and around and actively feeding and traveling almost any hour of the day without undue fear of encounters with humans.

In fact, on our own farm and on others I hunt regularly, the period between 11 A.M. and 1 P.M. is a prime time to see deer. If there is a "slow" period, which most times doesn't exist, I'd have to say it's those early-season days from 1 P.M. to 4 P.M. But I suspect this has nothing to do with avoiding humans; it's simply the hottest time of day and deer and even livestock species are inclined to find cool shade for resting. Good advice, then, for the farmland hunter is to not restrict his hunting to merely the early and late hours. He should keep at it for as long as his energy holds out, because the biggest bucks in the region may be on the move at high noon.

Finally, a side benefit of farmland hunting for whitetails is that their steady cropland diets make for incredibly good-eating animals. Over the years, some of the bucks I've taken back in the hinterland have had as much flavor as a pair of old mocassins. But whitetails raised on corn, beans, and other produce are consistently so delicious that the difference has to be tasted to be believed.

Try to bag a barnyard buck. You may never go back to the deep woods again.

11

Suburban Trophies

◆◆◆

It was a situation that seemed entirely out of keeping with what most hunters traditionally think of as big-game hunting.

Less than 300 yards from my tree stand lay a six-lane asphalt ribbon known as Interstate Highway 71. And along with "shooting light" on opening morning of Ohio's 1978 deer season came the predictable drone of bumper-to-bumper commuter traffic pulsating into the Buckeye State's capitol city of Columbus, population 950,000. Heading the opposite direction, endless streams of diesel trucks squirted out of the city limits to various destinations, burping black plumes of exhaust under the strain of heavy freight loads.

Yet not far from these congested, bustling activities, a six-point whitetail buck cautiously threaded his way through a crabapple thicket to my stand.

The deer seemed oblivious to the din of traffic punctuating the morning's lemon glow. Likely, since the time it was a spotted fawn, it had become thoroughly conditioned to these background noises continually raking through its home range. But make no mistake, the buck was just as secretive and keenly alert as any whitetail anywhere. With each step, the buck meticulously monitored the trail ahead for any sight, sound, or smell that did not belong. And that, moments later when I squeezed the trigger, made him as worthy a trophy as other bucks I've collected elsewhere in farm country and deep wilderness regions.

This hunt, as happily as it ended, actually began on a sour note. My wife and I were in a financial bind. Like most others, the spiraling inflation of the 1970s, compounded by the expense of raising kids, was eating us alive. The inevitable conclusion was that we had to begin tightening our belts, some-where. She reluctantly made her concessions. And on my side, a liberal beer allowance and the extravagant, faraway deer hunts I had been enjoying for so many years were two of the first luxuries to get the ax.

"I'm not about to give up my deer hunting altogether, even if it means going to the poorhouse," I lamented one day to my friend Tim Buciwicz at a sportman's club meeting. "But I'm getting plenty discouraged. This year at least, I'm restricted to hunting only in my own home state. And there is not an ounce of enthusiasm in my soul for going into any of the state's public hunting areas or national forest lands, because I know they'll be carpeted with wall-to-wall hunters. The competition there can only be described as fierce and a hunter who bags any kind of deer, even a spike or doe, can consider himself very lucky."

Then Buciwicz suggested an alternative that sounded even less appealing. "You know we live on a little bit of land—about 40 acres—just outside Columbus, and you're always welcome to hunt there," he offered.

"Uh, thanks for the invitation, but no thanks," I replied. "I like to hunt bigger tracts. Besides, there are probably 25,000 hunters living in Columbus and I'll bet on opening morning it will be like a stampede to the city limits signs. You'll have them pounding on your door for deer hunting permission twenty-four hours a day."

"Marge and I were worried about that possibility when we first considered buying the property," Tim explained. "But to our surprise we have had the place three years now and only two hunters have ever approached us, and that was a father and son who wanted to hunt squirrels. Our neighbor has 26 acres, and he claims virtually no one ever asks to hunt there. The two small parcels both have some deer, too," Tim said encouragingly. "Several weeks ago I saw two does and a forkhorn. And I have found some large rubs and scrapes that indicate at least one other good buck is prowling around somewhere.

"I have several hunches why we don't have much hunting pressure," Buciwicz reasoned. "The average sportsman has the misconception there couldn't possibly be good deer hunting so close to a major metropolitan region. Or, he thinks it would be a waste of time to even ask permission because he mistakenly assumes crowds of other hunters have long since beaten him to the punch and the landowner will automatically refuse hunt-ing rights to still others. Deer hunters are a peculiar breed, you know. Most of them wrongly equate whitetails, and especially trophy-sized deer, with big forests and faraway places. But it is just as likely that nice bucks, if not record-book candidates, are sneaking around right in their own backyards."

That optimistic viewpoint, along with the evidence of at least two bucks on the small acreage owned by Buciwicz and his neighbor, was all the inducement I needed. And the buck I described taking at the beginning of this chapter was the end result.

I have since learned that there are a wealth of similar, untapped deer hunting havens in every state where whitetails can be found. In many cases it is even the rule, not the exception, for deer to live to ripe old ages on these forgotten lands where a lack of disturbance allows them to grow very impressive headgear. Moreover, any innovative hunter can cash in on these little known bonanzas. He merely needs to put out of his mind the otherwise attractive looking public lands in his or other states, knowing in advance that on opening day such places will be harboring an orange-clad hunter behind every tree. It is also necessary for him to do a little research, perhaps write a few letters, and wear down a bit of boot leather.

The fact that deer can, and do, get along just fine on tracts of land that are so small as to seem totally insignificant has largely to do with the nature of the species itself. Whitetails, unlike other big game such as elk or bears, do not demand endless wilderness free from man's incessant activities. They actually thrive in close proximity to humans, as a direct result of optimum habitat and forage conditions provided by mankind.

The places where humans live, work, and play seem to eternally be carved up into what looks from above like a giant patchwork quilt, but this is certainly no disadvantage as far as whitetails are concerned. On the contrary, plenty of edges are created, which in turn afford endless travel options, both of which are high on the elusive whitetail's list of priorities. Also, it is characteristic of most areas surrounding metropolitan regions, where high canopy forests once prevailed, to have long since been transformed into extensive ground-story vegetation and regenerative second-growth woody cover, which means an abundance of readily accessible foods of the type deer dote upon most. Also, man's presence invariably means orchards, small-scale agricultural endeavors, and vegetable gardens, all of which draw deer like a magnet attracts iron filings.

It is vitally important, however, to understand that whitetails are masters of the first order when it comes to intimately knowing every geographical feature of their home ranges. And this is especially so when it comes to surviving—even flourishing—so close to civilization where the fabric of their home ranges is so disjointed. Yet while they are creatures of habit, their travel routes will vary with the seasons, and most particularly with the onset of the hunting season. When unmolested, they will regularly use familiar trails to and from their activities of feeding, drinking, mating, and bedding down. But it is their inherent nature to also have some type of "security cover" they can retreat to when pressed.

This security cover can be any type of dense brush or vegetation, a streamside thicket, or even briers and brambles large enough to hide one or more deer. But of key importance, it must be extremely difficult for a hunter to penetrate or even approach without the cover's occupants becoming well aware of the intrusion and having ample time to enact an escape via any of several exits.

This young buck has just pilfered an apple from a small orchard immediately behind a home situated on a modest 25 acres of land. He then bedded in a small copse of evergreens. Overlooked places like these often become a haven for deer when hunting pressure intensifies on nearby larger tracts of public hunting land.

I remember a situation a number of years ago that well illustrates this point. We owned a home on the outskirts of a town in southern Ohio where our modest three acres bordered on a stream. The land on the other side of the stream was a state forest where public hunting was permitted, and during the first few days of the deer season, it usually sounded like the North was attacking the South.

There was a triangular-shaped copse of thick pines near the back corner of our acreage, and deer that otherwise spent most of the year in the state forest were well aware of the dense seclusion. I say this because I regularly used the pines as a background for taking outdoor photos, and during those off-season photo sessions, never saw deer around. But I could hike back to the pines immediately after the hunting season opened and as many as six whitetails would flush out like a covey of exploding quail. I eventually doped out that here was one of their security covers. When people-pressure suddenly became intense in the state forest, the deer merely sneaked out the back door, swam the stream, hid themselves in my pines, and just plain stayed there until things cooled down or until they were routed out and had to flee to another known security cover.

This should serve as a lead for any hunter who has been working a public area with no success. If he has found ample quantities of fresh sign (trails, pellets, rubs, scrapes) to indicate at least a fair number of deer in the vicinity, but he is seeing none of them during his hunting maneuvers, he can almost always attribute his misfortune to the pressure being exerted by too many other hunters ramming around the same region. That's when he should forget about the usual haunts the deer may have been using when they were unmolested in previous weeks, and go looking for the security cover they have retreated into.

Look at it this way. If deer can be counted upon to quickly vacate the public hunting grounds to find refuge in smaller, undisturbed pockets of real estate, why not hunt those places exclusively, right from the beginning of the season?

I've already given one tip in this regard, and that has to do with checking out private holdings near much larger public hunting areas. Don't worry if the area you wish to hunt is small. Even if it is only 25 acres, an old hermit of a buck with a gnarled rack may have nevertheless staked it out as his own private little seclusion. Furthermore, it is this very type of modest size property, if it is close to any major town, that is most likely to have been discounted as a hunting possibility by the throngs of others hastening to the huge public lands.

Many of these private lands may have homes or other dwellings upon them that presently are being occupied by the landowner and his family. The only thing a hopeful hunter then needs to do is put on his friendliest smile and begin knocking on doors to inquire about trespass permission.

There are also numerous, similar tracts of property owned by absentee landowners. Generally, these are city dwellers who purchased a little land in the country with the intention of later building a home there. In some cases, asking at the nearest house down the road will reveal the name of the person who owns the land. If not, simply visit the county recorder's office. Ask to see a plat map of the township where the land is located and you'll find inscribed on the particular tract the landowner's name and the dimensions of the property; the recorder's registry of ownership will then reveal the landowner's present mailing address. Then merely write a courteous letter, or make a phone call, in hopes of securing hunting permission. If you emphasize the point that you are a local resident, an honest sportsman, and will have the highest respect for the land, it will help to get you in.

It would seem that more often than not such a strategy would result in dismal failure, and indeed there will be many rejections. But many times I have found just the opposite to be true, with an absentee landowner actually being very enthusiastic about having one or two respectable sportsmen on his place during the deer season.

When we lived in Florida, one absentee landowner responded to a phone call I made by answering, "Sure you can hunt. And by the way, every deer season I have trouble with people trespassing, dumping trash, and breaking into a shed and stealing firewood I store there. So do me a favor in return by keeping an eye on things and calling the sheriff if you spot any shenanigans." Over the years, two other landowners, one in Ohio and one in Missouri, said basically the same thing to me.

Aside from investigating the endless number of small private holdings surrounding virtually every city, there are substantial numbers of public land areas offering excellent hunting opportunities that the public itself is unaware even exists.

One example that readily comes to mind is the Wayne National Forest in my own home state of Ohio. Located in the southeastern part of the state, it comprises tens of thousands of acres. Most deer hunters from the nearby major cities are well aware of the Wayne, and hordes descend upon the main forest complex like bees to honey.

What most of the hunters do not know, however, is that the U.S. Forest Service is engaged in a continuing expansion program whereby adjacent farms and other lands are purchased whenever and wherever they become available. This gives most national forests such as the Wayne a disconnected, patchwork configuration. The primary holding draws the hunting pressure, but countless outlying segments ranging in size from 50 to 300 acres draw no attention whatever. The acquisition program is part of the Forest Service's long-term goal to absorb compatible smaller tracts that will eventually be joined together and increase the size of the whole.

Rarely are these small pieces of now-public land identified by those rustic, wooden Forest Service signs so prominently displayed at the entrances to the larger main holdings. A savvy hunter must instead visit his local USDA office to examine a wall map of all current Forest Service holdings, some of which may have been acquired only months earlier and are indicated by grease pencil marks on top of the map's plastic covering. Some of these acquisitions may be so recent that simply asking for a free copy of the printed map made available to the public is sure to *not* tell all. From the constantly updated wall-map, however, it is not at all uncommon for an astute hunter to learn of an abandoned farm or some other little chunk of deer-perfect real estate where public hunting is now allowed but there is no competition whatever from other hunters.

Reclaimed strip mine lands are another good bet. Millions of acres of this salvaged land sprawl across former coal-rich areas in the East and Midwest. These lands may often be posted, but that does not necessarily mean hunting is prohibited.

Jim Wentworth, of the Peabody Coal Company, explained the situation to me:

"We automatically post all of our lands for insurance reasons, to protect ourselves," Wentworth said. "We have hundreds of thousands of acres,

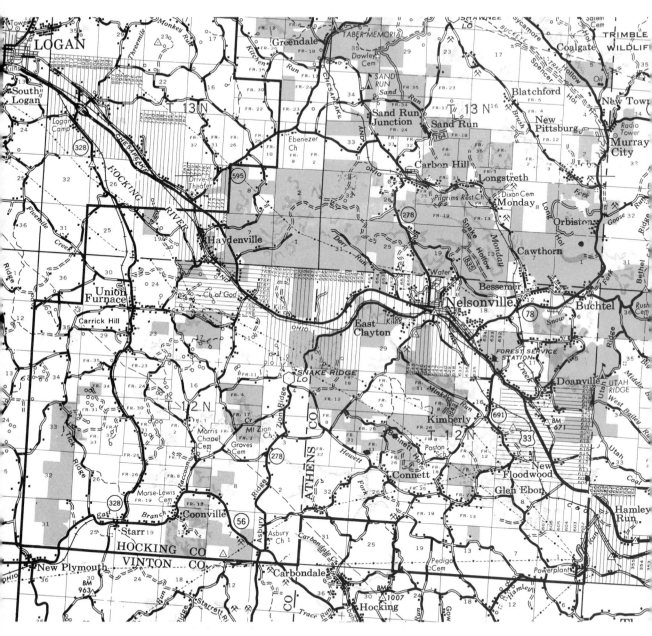

National forest lands, which are continually expanding, usually have a patchwork appearance. The larger, contiguous tracts draw all the hunting pressure while many people are not even aware that smaller parcels are also open to public hunting. It's often on one of these very tracts of land that an astute hunter can take a nice buck close to a metropolitan area.

making it impossible to patrol and supervise the property at all times. Young kids and college students know this, and during the summer, like to sneak in to swim in the strip pits where rainwater has collected, or climb the high walls and spoil banks with motorbikes. If someone drowns or falls and breaks a leg, we might find ourselves involved in an expensive lawsuit. But if the land is clearly posted with 'No Trespassing' signs, anyone who gets injured was obviously violating the law, which gets us off the hook.

"Nearly all of the coal companies I'm aware of will gladly issue free hunting permits to anyone who asks, provided they agree to remain in the extensive forests and brushlands and stay away from ongoing mining operations. But in reality, not that many hunters ever approach us. Most, apparently, in driving down roads bordering our property, see the land is posted and simply look elsewhere for a place to hunt."

Another of my favorite places to hunt—one of the first I investigate near large cities—are the various tracts of land where the city has its municipal water treatment plant, or where a utility company (electric, natural gas, or telephone) has its maintenance base. There is usually a small fenced area where equipment sheds and office buildings are located. Then there are often as many as several hundred acres of woodlands and other unused cover. I have never been able to figure out why utility companies typically have so much acreage; perhaps it is to accommodate anticipated future expansion. In any event, hunting permission can often be gained by visiting the main office and acquiring a "use permit" that enables the company to monitor the number of people on the land at any given time. In a great many cases, the only people who know this public hunting exists are deer hunters who happen to be employees of the utility company and their close friends!

Even if these parcels are characterized by many open fields and clearings, there are almost sure to be scattered fingers of brush-filled culverts, gullies choked with vegetation, wooded ridges, stream bottoms saturated with willows and tag alders, and other types of cover where whitetails bide their time.

One time in Minnesota I was hunting on the land of a water treatment facility—not far from a major city—where I saw six bucks, but only one other hunter, on opening day of the deer season.

There was some construction work going on, with pipeline ditches dug here and there, and it was amazing to watch some of those deer using the lengths of the excavation sites as efficiently as if sneaking through brush or other cover. The best buck I saw on opening day, and wanted to take, was such an artist at using the bulldozed dirt piles to hide behind as he entered and exited two adjacent hollows that I never had a clear shot at him. At least not that first day. But with his routine figured out, I changed my stand location and the second day he came loping along right on schedule. When he was close enough, I dropped him on the spot with a single shot from my .30/06. Although I will take an oath that it is true, I don't think many hunters would believe I bagged that deer not 5 miles away from towering office buildings, the incessant drone of traffic, and an enormous airport where jets continually ascended with their afterburners wide open.

Other holdings open to public hunting, often situated quite close to urban regions particularly in the southeast and south-central states, are the timber and pulp company lands. These tracts offer superb whitetail habitat because the companies practice forest management programs that involve continuous harvesting and replanting. This results in mixed stands of cover that suit deer far better than even-aged forests. Hunting is by permit, but the permits are usually free or nominally priced.

Hunters generally are just as well acquainted with these timber company lands as they are with other large tracts such as state forests and national forest lands. However, in the case of the latter, hunting pressure is unrestricted. But, for safety and other reasons (such as the presence of work crews afield), the timber companies carefully regulate how many hunters are allowed upon their lands at a given time. This has the effect of dispersing the hunters over large areas, which does not result in the same disruptive effect upon the animals' behavior as elsewhere. Consequently, each hunter stands a far better chance of success. Sometimes, a fixed number of hunters are given the opportunity to apply for seasonal-use permits. But with most such companies, it's a daily first-come, first-served affair; as soon as a predetermined number of hunters has been granted entrance to the lands, the gates are closed to all others for that day.

In going back to advice given earlier, it's worth repeating a few principles that will improve any hunter's chances of scoring, regardless of the specific nature of the property he has chosen to hunt.

First, a strong advantage is on the side of the eager sportsman who gets out early to reconnoiter hunting possibilities on various lands. The hunter who waits until opening day is almost certain to find slim pickings.

Never discount a choice looking piece of property simply because it happens to be small, is located close to a major city, has heavily traveled highways nearby, or even if it is posted. These are the very places where many bucks live in unconcerned leisure.

Finally, realize that when the guns begin booming on opening morning, deer will be quick to recognize the danger they are in and will waste no time funneling themselves in the direction of their security cover to wait out the storm. Even though there may be no other hunters parading around your own immediate turf, count upon them to be relatively close by and to eventually push deer right to you.

I won't claim that deer are so close to metropolitan centers that a hunter can take a subway to his stand. But whitetails are indeed plentiful in the inconspicuous fringe covers that are crocheted around every city in the species' natural range—places where the majority of hunters would least expect to find them.

PART III

BUCKS, DOES, AND THE RUT

12

Hunt the Domimant Buck

◆◆◆

A person who does not possess the gifts of speech or hearing can nevertheless communicate very well through the use of sign language. Likewise, whitetails often reveal their entire autobiographies by exhibiting certain body postures and mannerisms.

In both cases, as we've already noted, the key to the successful "reading" of this attempted communication is that the recipient of the assorted signals and gestures must know how to interpret them. The same thing applies to the study of physical signs the animals leave behind during their wanderings.

These thoughts flashed through my mind last year, while sitting in a tree stand, as I watched a handsome six-point buck sneaking in my direction. At least, I thought he was sneaking. As he drew closer, I sensed the deer actually was executing a sagacious retreat from some bully he had no desire to reckon with. The first tip-off was that his tail was clamped tightly against the back of his legs, and then final confirmation came when I noticed fresh scars on his flanks and shoulders. At that, I lowered my slug-loaded shotgun and allowed the timid animal to continue his escape from what, to him, obviously had not been a very pleasant experience.

My hunch paid off. An hour later, the bully himself showed up and it was patently clear why the first buck had chosen to run and hide. This deer, judging by the size of his larger rack, was at least a year older. He also was heavier in body weight, and seemed to be swaggering in an undeniably arrogant manner that proclaimed in no uncertain terms, "don't mess with me."

Here's a fine example of a dominant buck during the rut. Head high, neck swollen, antlers shining, he's truly a master of his domaine.

As I began field-dressing the buck—which wouldn't even come close to making the record book, but nonetheless stands as one of my largest deer to date—I was reminded of the complex social lives deer subscribe to and how, through the use of telling body language and spoor, they silently communicate their hierarchal rankings in the local pecking order.

Antler rubs on saplings are among the most commonly recognized signs of buck activity that hunters are likely to chance upon when scouting. Although easily identified for what they are, antler rubs are also, unquestionably, the least understood.

For generations, many hunters have maintained that antler rubs indicate places where bucks have removed their velvet and then polished and sharpened their tines. Other hunters have stalwartly claimed antler rubs are the first signs of bucks going into the annual rut, whereby they spar with tree trunks to strengthen their neck muscles in preparation for inevitable fights with other deer. Both premises are dead wrong.

When a whitetail's maximum annual antler growth has been achieved, the velvet dies, dries, and begins falling away in shreds, largely of its own accord. Upon occasion, particularly when stringy remnants of the velvet hang down and obscure the deer's vision, a buck may hasten its removal by randomly thrashing his rack against a small bush. But otherwise, this behavior is only a brief happenstance with little or no actual indication of the activity being created that a passing hunter might later detect. Once the underlying antlers are exposed, the main beams are already smooth and the tips of the tines are pointed. There is no need or instinctive desire whatever for a male deer to hone them as a gladiator readying his swords for battle.

Rather, antler rubs serve the very specific purpose of enabling each buck in the local herd to establish a breeding territory. Whitetails by nature are *not* territorial from the standpoint of ever making concerted efforts to defend their home ranges and chase away intruders. Because their ranges may well encompass several square miles and must necessarily be shared by many other individuals, defense would be virtually impossible anyway.

But despite the fact that whitetails are not territorial, they and individuals of most mammalian species must indeed acquire a space in which they feel secure before any attempt at mating can occur. Additionally, the individual must obtain a social status that would prevent restrictions being placed upon it by other members of the same species. In cases where one individual is clearly dominant, subordinates living in the same area will either leave to find their own breeding places, or, if there is no place for them within their shared home range that is not already occupied by a superior animal, not breed at all. This explains why, in most regions of the country where deer populations are at the maximum carrying capacity of the land, button bucks and spike bucks seldom impregnate does, even though they are physiologically capable of doing so.

Thus, breeding success among whitetail bucks depends chiefly upon a given individual finding a place where it feels confident and is not intimidated. It is only after these requirements of space and social status are met that a buck becomes mentally fit to reproduce. Because it takes time for this necessary social orientation to transpire, whitetail bucks usually begin attempting to establish their breeding territories as much as two months before scraping behavior and doe-chasing actually begins.

There are several ways in which whitetail bucks sort out the matter of who's who and where the niche of each is on the totem pole. There are physical signs the animals leave throughout their home ranges and espe-

Forget the myth that bucks rub their antlers on trees to remove their velvet (left), sharpen their tines, and strengthen their neck muscles for up-coming battles with other bucks. Rather, it's one of several signpost marking behaviors, each buck trying to establish a breeding territory that won't be encroached upon by other males.

cially in their core areas, which include not only antler rubs but, later, during the rut, mutilated branches hanging over scrapes. Aside from serving as visual cues, both are also anointed with saliva and forehead-gland scent to additionally reinforce each animal's attempt to delineate his territory. Should this fail and an actual encounter occurs, bucks then display various other behavioral signals such as bluffing and posturing. Finally, if these mannerisms don't resolve the issue, head-to-head combat follows (which, contrary to what romanticists would have us believe, usually entails no more than a brief pushing match).

Biologists refer to the activity of making tree rubs as signpost-marking, and there is a definite correlation between the diameters of the trees rubbed and the hierarchal rankings of the animals that made them.

Generally, thumb-size willows, tag alders, and evergreens that have been rubbed are the work of juveniles: 1½-year-old spike bucks and forkhorns.

Rubbed trees that range in diameter up to about 2½ inches are usually indicative of 2½ to 3½-year-old male deer. These are customarily six and eight-pointers possessing rather low, tight racks with slender beams and tines.

Cedars, pines, or smooth-barked saplings that are at least 3 to 4½ inches in diameter, and sometimes much larger, are favored by the oldest deer with the most worthy headgear. These bucks can be expected to be at least 3½ years old and carrying heavy eight, ten, or twelve-point racks. Of course, as the age of the deer increases, the width, height, and overall massiveness of the rack increases until the deer's health begins to decline, usually after the seventh or eighth year, which is reflected in a progressively smaller and often misshapen rack.

But none of this is carved in granite somewhere. I once watched angrily and in despair as a positively huge buck whacked to shreds a number of tiny scotch pines on my Christmas tree farm in southern Ohio. On the other hand, I once observed a forkhorn working over the 20-inch girth of an old beech. Despite occasional exceptions to the rule, though, relating the diameters of rubbed trees found during reconnaissance missions to the ages of the deer that made them is a very reliable indicator.

Although whitetails seem to have a mysterious way of visually examining a rubbed tree and equating its diameter with the social level of the deer that made it, the telling factor is recognizing and interpreting the forehead-gland scent worked into the exposed, moist cambium of the tree trunk itself. At the University of Georgia, prominent deer biologist Larry Marchington, after engaging in extensive microscopic examinations of the forehead glands of whitetail bucks, came to the conclusion there is a significant relationship between a buck's social status and its forehead-gland activity. As Marchington explains, "the position of an adult male in the hierarchy is reflected in the level of activity of his forehead glands."

Whether or not the oldest and most dominant bucks instinctively rub the largest diameter trees for the express purpose of depositing greater quantities of forehead-gland scent is not conclusively known, but is considered to indeed be the case. In any event, the glandular secretions contribute the buck's own individual scent to the rub. This, along with the visual cue of the rub, becomes a physical extension, as it were, of the deer itself.

There are numerous ways hunters can use this insight to good advantage. Foremost, since tree rubbing activity and the establishment of hierarchal ranking takes place well before the year's crop of scrapes begins dotting the countryside, the early-season hunter will want to focus his scouting upon finding the largest diameter trees that have been ravaged by bucks.

When you leave boot tracks across the terrain, trying to pin down a buck's core area, be sure to investigate pockets known to have aromatic tree species such as cedars, pines, spruces, shining sumac, cherry, or sassafras. In the absence of these, bucks will create rubs on virtually any species, but they distinctly like the ones listed above. I believe bucks have learned that the

Antler rubs serve as both visual and olfactory clues to other bucks sharing the same home range, and the diameter of the tree rubbed equates with the size of the deer that made the rub; hence, the largest rubs are made by the largest bucks. Here, I examine one of the biggest I've ever seen.

oily, resinous cambiums of these species will retain their forehead-gland scent longer; in the case of non-aromatic species, deposited scent might conceivably wash off during the next rainstorm, thereby making the rub less effective as a territorial signpost.

I make an effort to mark on a topo map or aerial photo the locations of each rub I find. If this isn't done, each find may seem totally incidental. But when you can study large numbers of rub locations on a map, your perspective broadens and often a pattern can be discerned that may indicate the travel tendencies of a dominant buck.

Although some experts like to ascertain a well-defined line of rubs extending for some distance, in the belief this indicates the regular route a buck takes in getting from Point A to Point B, I feel it's a gamble. The buck may not be using that particular trail until after full-dark; so if you want to use this technique, I suggest installing a game clock, as described previously, to find out for sure. However, I prefer to search for concentrates, or places where exceptionally large numbers of rubs seem to be intensified or consolidated in a rather small, specific area. This indicates the buck in question is spending quite a lot of time in that immediate vicinity, which increases the likelihood of seeing him.

When sitting on a stand in such an area, keep in mind there is the distinct possibility of sighting many different bucks that happen to be sharing the same home turf, and may even have overlapping core areas. This makes it necessary to solve the riddle of which one is the dominant buck and therefore, undoubtedly, the largest.

When a subordinate deer passes through the area, he'll outwardly display his inferiority. The most common subordinate posture exhibited by a low-ranking deer is a slinking-type of gait that reminds me of a retreating dog that has just been swatted on the rump with a folded newspaper for wetting on the floor. It's a "cowering" posture with the tail held tightly against the hindquarters, a somewhat sunken back and head held low. In the event that two bucks are simultaneously in sight, but are not close enough for you to evaluate their antlers, the subordinate of the two will make a concerted effort to avoid direct eye contact with the higher ranking deer, whereupon the dominant buck will allow the inferior deer to continue on his way without incident.

A dominant buck, on the other hand, is certain to reveal an entirely different personality. The best way to describe his demeanor is "proud and unafraid." With head held high, a dominant buck may actually have a somewhat prancing appearance to his gait, like a high-stepping quarterhorse. Other threatening postures include holding his tail lofted to half-mast and extended straight back, directly facing the other deer, and staring fixedly at him for long moments. If a dominant buck is fairly close, you may also note the dark hair tufts covering his tarsal glands have been erected and are rhythmically moving to dispense his own unique glandular scent. This may be followed by rub-urinating, whereby the back legs are squeezed together and the back is hunched up, to allow urine to dribble down the legs and over the glands to carry additional tarsal scent to the ground.

The difficult thing about hunting dominant bucks, as paradoxical as it sounds, is determining which is the *most* dominant animal. One time, while bowhunting in Virginia's Shenandoah Mountains, I watched two bucks from a distance as they exchanged mutual recognition of each other's hierarchal ranking. In little time the submissive deer, a six-pointer, showed respect and quickly withdrew into distant shadows. The other deer also had a six-point rack, but as he drew closer I could see the beams and tines were heavier, indicating the animal probably was a year older, and this likely attributed to his higher social status.

As I waited for this supposedly dominant buck to come within my self-imposed shooting range of 35 yards, my peripheral vision caught a slight flicker of movement far to my left. Suddenly, the six-point buck I had been watching dropped his head and turned away, and I knew what that meant. Clearly, the six-pointer was indeed of higher social ranking than the smaller six-pointer that had just beat a hasty retreat, but he was lower on the totem pole than this third deer now coming onto the scene! As slowly as possible, I turned my head to the left and there, still deep in tangled brush cover, a magnificent ten-pointer stood glaring at the deer before me. For a moment, I became unwound at this unexpected turn of events and must have spontaneously moved because somehow one of the bucks detected my presence. In a flash, both evaporated into the distance with the sound of loud snorts filling the forest.

I've always wondered if the big ten-pointer was *the* dominant buck in that region. He certainly ranked higher than both of the six-pointers, but could there have possibly been something still larger in the vicinity that he in turn would have been subordinate to? I'll never know, but such are the things wishful dreams of deer hunters are made of.

In addition to understanding how the rubbing or sign-posting behavior of whitetails enables them to establish breeding grounds and recognize their rightful places in the local pecking order, there are yet two other ruses any enterprising hunter should consider. One that might seem quite laughable, but which I am convinced works, is a technique I've been developing over the last few seasons that I call "mock-rubbing."

Most serious hunters are familiar with the advanced deer hunting strategy known as "mock-scraping," pioneered by expert Tennessee bowhunter Bob McGuire and which I then improved upon and described in the October, 1984 issue of *Outdoor Life*. Mock-rubbing is essentially born of the same philosophy because it's a viable method of fooling mother nature.

To illustrate, let's say there is a deeply gouged trail leading to a known feeding area, such as a standing cornfield, and throughout an adjacent forestland you've discovered numerous rubs of varied sizes, indicating sev-

If the disputes over dominance are not settled by rubbing trees and anointing them with scent, bucks sometimes engage in head-to-head combat, which usually is little more than a shoving contest and is rarely fatal.

eral bucks of different age classes and antler dimensions are in the immediate region. After thoroughly reconnoitering the terrain, you determine the trail leading to the corn is the best possible place to install a portable tree stand, but this gives birth to a perplexing question. What course of action do you take if a six-point buck materializes? Should you try to take him? After all, he may well be the dominant buck in that particular area. On the other hand, he may have a very low social ranking and be subordinate to several others that are far more impressive.

Mock-rubbing is the way to find out. Simply take your knife and swab the blade free of all human odor with an alcohol prep pad (these come in little, sterile, hermetically-sealed packets, available in any drugstore). Next, make phony rubs on four to six saplings that are at least 2½ inches in diameter but no larger than 3½ inches. Don't entirely girdle the saplings because this will kill the trees, and don't touch the mock-rubs with your hands or your human scent will be left behind. The trees you create rubs upon should be clearly visible from the trail, yet a comfortable shooting distance away from your stand, in accordance with the type of sporting equipment you're using.

Now, climb into your stand and carefully observe the reactions and mannerisms of any bucks that may come down the trail. When a buck spots one or more of the newly created rubs and, more specifically, the diameter of the trees that were rubbed, it will instantly display its hierarchal ranking. You can then decide whether or not the deer fulfills your expectations.

It may be premature to say I'd actually do this, but I think if a ten-pointer spotted one of my bogus rubs on a 3½-inch diameter tree and cowered, I just might let him pass, in the hopes he was using silent body language to tell me of something still larger in the region. To date, that type of opportunity hasn't yet presented itself, although I can credit the method for a six-pointer and two eight-pointers.

Another method that can be used singularly or in conjunction with mock-rubs to collect a dominant buck is the use of a revolutionary idea known as a "territorial infringement scent."

Here I'm demonstrating the mock-rubbing technique I developed as a means of determining the hierarchical ranking of whitetail bucks in the region.

Officially labeled as Dr. O's Buck Lure Safariland Hunting Corp., Box NN, McLean, VA 22101, the product is the brainchild of hunting brothers Ed, John, and Jody Boll and chemist Brian Beberwyck, who, over a six year period, developed the unique scent.

This deer scent is unlike any of those described previously in that it doesn't smell like food, mask human odor, or simulate a doe in estrus. Developed from thirteen natural ingredients, Dr. O's Buck Lure essentially duplicates the smell of a buck and, as John Boll explained to me, the best time to use the lure is well before the rut begins, when bucks are in the process of establishing their intended breeding grounds and pecking order.

Because each whitetail buck is well aware of all others inhabiting the same general area and the characteristics of their individual odors, the scent simulates, so to speak, a new kid on the block. This will ignite hierarchal investigation.

As Boll explained, "When a buck gets a whiff of the lure carried by either the wind or thermal currents, the deer becomes intent upon identifying the source so the buck that supposedly produced it may be appropriately ranked."

Equally as revolutionary as the lure is the unique application process. Using a simple golf tee with a small ball of foam sponge affixed to its top (supplied with the bottle of scent), the hunter can place the tee pad any-where he chooses within shooting range of his stand, then apply several drops of the lure to the sponge. Because the tee elevates the scent pad, the lure more readily dispenses into the air than if it were merely dribbled directly on the ground. In addition to placing the scent on the golf tee pad, squeeze a few drops onto the wet cambium of any nearby mock-rubs you've created.

Whenever a buck comes within range of the airborne scent molecules, it has an ingrained desire to investigate, and depending upon the deer's own social status, it will display either subordinate or dominant behavior. This tells the hunter whether he should try for the deer or perhaps bide his time.

"Subordinate bucks will approach the scented tee pad with a very submis-sive posture," John Boll related. "They'll be attracted to the scent and want to check it out, but they'll do so with visible caution because they know their ranking and fear the supposed buck they smell may be much bigger.

"It's an entirely another matter, however, when a dominant buck smells the lure," Boll continued. "The spectacle that follows is something few hunters have ever witnessed first-hand, and it can be an unnerving, emotion-ally-charged experience, especially if the hunter is right on the ground close to the deer. Typically, a dominant buck goes into a rage at having his breeding territory encroached upon by another deer he's not familiar with. The deer seems to literally go berserk, almost like the way in which a buck responds to the sound of rattling antlers. Its eyes bulge, the mane on his back stands up, his nostrils dilate, and he makes a beeline for the source of the scent. When it reaches the source, which in this case is the lure, the buck often becomes frustrated because he cannot make visual contact. It will often stand and paw the ground, trying to understand the source of the scent and even rub-urinating in an attempt to cover it with his own. I've seen bucks try to bury the tee pad by scuffling leaves and dirt over it with their hooves, then urinating on top of it. Others will pace around the lure, 15 to 30 yards away. I observed one buck that periodically rushed the scent in a dead run with his antlers lowered, then circled and jumped around the tee pad. Finally, it bedded down right next to the tee pad, apparently waiting for the interloping deer to return."

To be sure, there are many facets of deer behavior that must be fitted into the picture-puzzle lives of whitetails if a hunter is to fill his tag every year. But knowing a little something about the physical signs and silent body language deer use to communicate their social rankings to each other can greatly increase a hunter's chances of taking the biggest buck in the woodlot.

13

The New
Scrape Savvy

◆◆

When Pat Boone sang the hit song "Love Letters in the Sand" about the coy little beach games lovers play, the last thing he probably had in mind was whitetail deer hunting. But just like the amorous diversions guys and gals sometimes find themselves involved in, whitetails create love letters in the sand, too. They also make them in the dirt, in the grass, in the corn stubble, along the edges of grown-over fields, on old logging roads, and throughout the woodlands.

Of course, scrape hunting is not new. Hunters have been taking advantage of this chink in the armor of whitetail bucks for generations, because it is an established fact that during the rut, whitetails become less cautious and more predictable. Yet many new facets of scrape hunting have come to light in recent years, and hunters who learn to read those signs and interpret what they really mean can hope for even better success than before.

First, we should clear up one misconception about deer mating behavior. As shocking as it undoubtedly will be for even veteran deer hunters to learn, whitetail bucks do not go into rut!

Rather, bucks are much like male dogs, ready to mount females virtually anytime they will allow it. Confirmation of this was demonstrated in one study in which a buck was placed in a fenced enclosure with a doe. Most of the time he showed no interest in her from a sexual standpoint, except during the middle of November when she came into estrus. However, at random other times during the year, the doe was injected with certain hormones to artificially induce estrus, and the very instant she began discharging vaginal odors indicating her changed body chemistry (and person-

157

ality), the buck was all over her. It didn't matter whether the month was March, June, October, or any other time of year . . . he was ready for action the minute she was.

All of this must be slightly qualified, however. While a whitetail buck will try to mount a receptive doe anytime, he is capable of successfully impregnating her only when he is sporting hard, velvet-free antlers, a period during which his elevated testosterone level is resulting in a healthy, motile sperm count. Nevertheless, this means that, hypothetically, a male deer can successfully impregnate a doe seven months of the year (from September through March).

This lengthy mating period obviously does not happen in the real world of whitetails. Consequently, it's the does who actually "go into rut," or more appropriately, experience brief annual periods of sexual readiness in which they emit characteristic body odors that tell bucks they are willing to submit to their advances.

Not all does experience estrus at exactly the same time. As in the case of human females and their menstrual periods, the world of deer is an environment of individuals, each with its own unique cycle of physiological behavior that varies somewhat from others but is still within the parameters dictated by its species. When a doe does indeed naturally come into estrus, it's a receptive period that lasts only twenty-eight hours. If the doe does not conceive during this time, she loses "heat," only to experience a follow-up estrus cycle twenty-four days later. This explains why a buck may be seen chasing a doe as early as October or as late as January, but it's all within nature's scheme. First, it is the decree of all species to at least attempt to fulfill their maximum reproductive potential. And, in the case of whitetails, the length of the gestation period is such that mating must take place in the fall or early winter to ensure spring birthing followed by summer maturation, which gives fawns the highest possible chances of survival.

In any regard, it's this phenomenon of variable estrus periods among does that drives bucks crazy with wild-eyed passion, makes them do goofy things, and typically causes them to become far less cautious than otherwise. For the previous ten months, a given buck hasn't shown much interest in courting the local does in his bailiwick, simply because none has been in estrus and emitting those amorous odors that say "come hither." Suddenly, one day, the buck gets a snootful of the good stuff and the chase is on. About the time he has serviced that particular doe—or maybe even before he catches up with her—another doe comes into heat and he gets a whiff of her. Hours later, still another doe waves the welcome banner, a day later still another, and the buck literally runs himself ragged trying to cover all bases.

During this period, in areas where deer populations are high, a buck may impregnate thirty or more does over a time span of less than two weeks; moreover, each of those impregnations may require several mountings before successful conception occurs and the doe loses heat. No wonder bucks often appear so gaunt and exhausted by the time winter arrives! In fact, the mating activity is so intense and energetic that a 3½-year-old buck that weighs 225 pounds in early October may well be down to only 170 pounds by the end of December. In frigid climates, some bucks may not be able to regain their lost body weight in time to survive coming snows and the consequent scarcity of food.

But the point to be made is this. Whenever you hear other hunters say something to the effect that "the bucks are just going into the rut," you now know better. In reality, the bucks have been ready all along and it's the does who are now about to get the show rolling.

But there's something else. Contrary to what you've read and heard for decades, bucks do not purposely make scrapes in certain places for the express reason of "attracting" does! In most mammalian species, including humans, it is the role of the female to lure and attract, not the male. As a result, in the world of whitetails, it's the does who actually determine where a vast majority of scrapes are destined to be created by bucks. Does even make many of the scrapes themselves!

When a doe experiences estrus, her female hormonal secretions are transferred to the ground whenever and wherever she happens to urinate during the course of her travels. As a dog is often seen to use the claws on its back feet to tear up grass and sod in your yard after it defacates, a doe may in similar fashion use her rear hooves to scuff away leaves in the creation of a rather rudimentary scrape. This becomes an "unclaimed" or "secondary" scrape that otherwise has little mating value and simply announces to all the world there is a receptive doe in the immediate vicinity.

It should be emphasized that doe-scraping doesn't occur everytime a doe urinates. It is mostly just a happenstance. Yet its presence often misleads novice hunters into believing they've luckily found themselves in a buck's bedroom and now only need bide their time until the monster that supposedly made the scrape eventually returns. When, after several days of waiting, they've seen only does pass through the region, but no male deer, the discouraged novice throws up his hands in despair and claims scrape hunting is a waste of time.

In a majority of other instances in which bucks are indeed responsible for the creation of scrapes, it is, I repeat, the doe that often dictates their locations. As it happens, a buck chances upon a place where an estrous doe voided herself, and he instinctively proceeds to make a scrape right there, smack dab on top of the urine-dampened earth. Yet even many of these so-called "buck scrapes" as well may turn out to be "secondaries" which are destined to play little further role in the mating activities of the local whitetail population.

Although we'll go into greater detail later, the two requisites that determine whether a scrape will become a regularly visited "primary" are as follows: The scrape will be found in conjunction with others nearby and it will be located in the heart of the buck's core breeding area, as opposed to being an isolated "boundary" scrape somewhere around the perimeter of the buck's much larger home range area; and, it will predictably reveal an overhanging tree branch above it, which the male deer chews, whacks with his antlers and anoints with saliva and forehead gland scent both to proclaim his hierarchal ranking and warn other bucks away.

You've heard, I'm sure, the worn-out comment about how bucks begin traveling far and wide when they "go into the rut," in which they expand their home ranges often by several miles or more. We've already debunked the matter about bucks going into rut, and the business about them traveling widely is just as misleading.

The degree of travel any animal species engages in during the mating season is a direct function of population densities within given areas. When any particular species is relatively low in numbers, the individuals comprising that species instinctively know to disperse widely beyond their normal home ranges. This is nature's way of ensuring maximum encounters among those individuals and therefore higher-than-average levels of reproductivity. Yet as their numbers steadily increase and the range reaches maximum carrying capacity, their travels become inhibited and their home ranges shrink. Logically, if a buck has more business than he can handle right within his immediate turf, why would he be inclined to roam wide and far?

We've seen these theatrics play themselves right out on our own farm in southern Ohio where the deer population is actually too high for its own good and farmers are beginning to turn in record numbers of crop-damage claims. One evening last summer, for example, on my south meadow, which I can see clearly from my kitchen window, I counted fourteen deer in a single group. There's no telling how many others were just inside the forested edges surrounding the alfalfa that I couldn't see, nor any way of knowing how many deer were feeding at the same time on still other meadows not visible from our window. There was one buck in the group, with a seven-point rack that made him easily identifiable, and I watched him regularly as the weeks passed.

October arrived, then November and December. The deer went through their mating rituals, and I continued to see the buck in virtually the same two or three places every day of the week. Often, I saw him several times each day, proof enough he was not traveling widely. With so many lady deer beckoning for his time right there, he simply had no interest or biological inclination whatever to visit the next county.

All of this meshes very well with many scientific studies of late, and my friend Larry Marchington has been at the forefront when it comes to fitting some of these new pieces into the behavioral puzzle of whitetails. Larry is an animal research biologist at the University of Georgia and is well known for his sophisticated radio-telemetry studies of deer. With the help of other biologists, and the assistance of several state game agencies, he catches wild deer, outfits them with collar-type radio transmitters, and then monitors their movements for many months.

This has made it possible for him to plot on maps the precise home ranges and core areas of individual deer, their movement patterns, and how they interact with other deer sharing the same habitat. He knows just where they are all the time, and can even sneak up closely to watch their behavior when "does are rutting." Many of his findings have been reported in such prestigious publications as the *Journal of Wildlife Management* and the *Journal of Animal Behavior*.

"The erroneous information about deer traveling far and wide during the mating season is simply a failure of communication," Larry once told me. "Over the years I've mentioned to many outdoor writers that my studies have revealed bucks travel more during the rut, and they've misinterpreted this to mean that bucks travel greater distances. What I've since tried to clarify is that bucks travel more in the sense that they engage in far less bedding activity and are restless and more on the feet chasing after receptive does. The actual distances they travel might conceivably be far and wide in those specific regions where deer numbers are low, but since this is a rarity in most places, their travels are often confined to very small areas."

Another great fallacy pertains to the beginning of the rut. For generations, most hunters have thought that breeding activity is triggered by the first cold-weather masses sweeping down from the North. But this theory has never been able to account for the rutting phenomenon in the deep South, where even mid-winter days may be quite warm; when we lived in Florida, I used to scrape-hunt in 80° heat and frequently watched whitetails "going at it" like the end of the world was near.

In truth, it is not air temperature that triggers the so-called rut. It's a post-autumnal equinox phenomenon known as "photoperiodism." When the days begin growing noticeably shorter, a deer's behavior is changed by the decreasing amounts of daily sunlight passing through their eyes. This results in a type of reverse-stimulation effect upon the pineal gland, which is about the size of an unpopped kernel of popcorn located close to the pituitary gland. It causes its normal function of regulating body growth to cease temporarily while simultaneously spurring increases in the secretion of progesterone (the female sex hormone) to bring does to a heightened state of readiness.

Exactly when this sexual activity can be expected to peak each year, and consequently when scrape hunting is the most exciting, is unquestionably one of the most hotly contested issues in deer camps nationwide. But two scientific studies, both very similar in nature, seem to have drawn the greatest acceptance among advanced hunters and they are worth briefly recounting here.

From 1961 to 1968, New York State biologists Lawrence Jackson and William Hesselton studied the embryos of 864 dog- and road-killed does of various ages. Because the average whitetail gestation period from the time

By studying the embryos and fetuses of road-killed does, biologists have been able to pinpoint the dates each of the does was impregnated.

of conception to the time of birthing is 202 days, Jackson and Hesselton were able to determine the ages of the embryos and then, by back-dating, were able to pinpoint the times each of the 864 does were impregnated. After plugging still other variables into their rutting equation, the scientists were then able to create a graph portraying a core model of the rut for whitetail deer living anywhere in the United States.

What I've recounted here is merely a distillation of the lengthy and quite elaborate procedures that were employed. But what's especially noteworthy is that Jackson and Hesselton ascertained the date of November 15 as being the peak of the whitetail rut nationwide.

In the accompanying graph, reproduced from their research, the November 15 breeding peak is quite apparent. But notice as well that a classical bell-shaped curve encompasses the dates ranging from November 10 through November 28 before breeding activity begins to sharply taper off. Undoubtedly, this accounts for the individuality of the estrus periods of does, as described earlier, with certain does going into heat somewhat earlier or later than others comprising the same herd population under study.

In the same graph, note as well a slight resurgence of breeding activity in mid-December. This undoubtedly accounts for those does coming into estrus a second time twenty-four days later after failing, for one reason or another, to conceive during their first heat.

A second study by Robert D. McDowell (*Photoperiodism Among Breeding Eastern Whitetailed Deer,* 1970) took basically the same procedural approach but was much more elaborate in scope. McDowell recruited the help of deer biologists in nineteen states throughout the whitetail's native range to analyze the ages of embryos taken from 4,663 does. What followed was the compilation of a bar graph depicting the breeding-date peaks in conjunction with latitudinal bands segregating the country into five geographic regions.

North of the Mason-Dixon Line, McDowell's peak breeding period very closely conforms to the earlier findings of Jackson and Hesselton. But notice that the farther south one ventures, breeding activity becomes far more erratic and undefinable with regards to peaking at any specific time. To date, there are no concrete explanations for these vagaries. Several speculations have been offered, however, the most plausible of which has to do with soil fertility levels as they relate to deer habitat. Many southern states have large tracts of spartan habitat ranging from desolate swampland in the eastern-most regions to desertland as one enters Texas and continues westward. And in such areas where available forage is of low nutritional value, research has shown that deer forced to survive upon such poor diets breed significantly later than deer on high-nutrient diets elsewhere (such as the farm belt of the upper Midwest). This still doesn't explain breeding activity as early as August, but multitudes of such mysteries abound when it comes to white-tails.

In any event, we can summarize McDowell's study by saying that throughout the whitetail's northernmost range, annual breeding activity is an intense, frenetic period in which so-called scrape hunting is charged with almost explosive levels of excitement. But as one travels deeper into the southernmost ranges of whitetails, breeding seems to be a more lengthy and ongoing but also more mild-mannered activity.

In going back to the subject of scrapes and their locations being largely determined by where does randomly urinate, it's understandable that scrapes might therefore be found almost anywhere. I've discovered them in the middle of open hay meadows, in soybean fields, in the woodlands, along forested edges, and once even discovered one on the earthen dam of my farm pond only scant yards from a beached rowboat! These were simply places where does happened to randomly urinate and bucks coming across those locations, probably during the night hours, subsequently made scrapes there.

As mentioned earlier, the vast majority of these mating invitations are what biologists refer to as "secondary" scrapes and they are almost never intentionally revisited by bucks. What hunters should strive to locate are "primary" scrapes that bucks do indeed regularly visit.

There are several ways to distinguish between primary scrapes and secondary scrapes, and even methods by which an astute hunter can make an educated guess as to the size of the animals that made them.

Secondary scrapes are the ones you're most likely to find in odd places such as open fields, where you know a buck would be reluctant to expose himself during the daylight hours. Also, upon thoroughly reconnoitering the surrounding terrain and marking such scrapes on your topo map or aerial photo, they will obviously appear to be randomly placed and not bear any close relationship to trails or other scrapes. These scrapes are commonly found dotting the periphery of the buck's home range (in which case they also are sometimes called "boundary" scrapes) and if you re-check them over a period of days, you'll notice them to slowly become dried out and covered with wind-blown debris, evidence again they are not being regularly tended or "freshened."

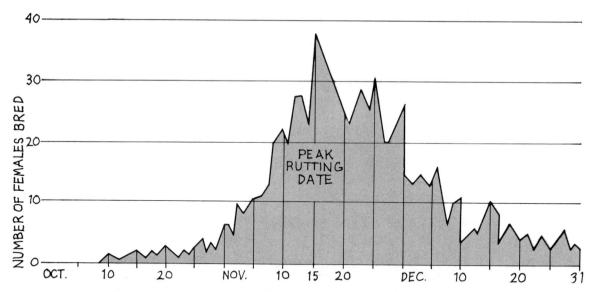

Using 864 does of various ages, biologists Jackson and Hesselton produced this graph depicting the peak breeding period for whitetails.

Opposite: *A more elaborate study by biologist Robert McDowell used embryos from 4,663 does supplied by other biologists from nineteen states to determine peak breeding periods in conjunction with latitudes. Note how the rut is more intense north of the Mason-Dixon line, spread out over a longer time period in the deep South.*

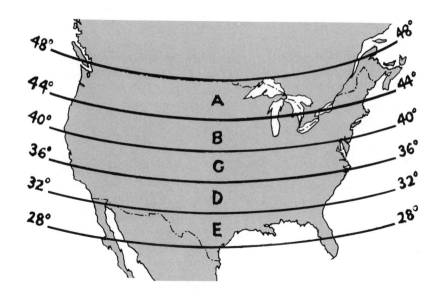

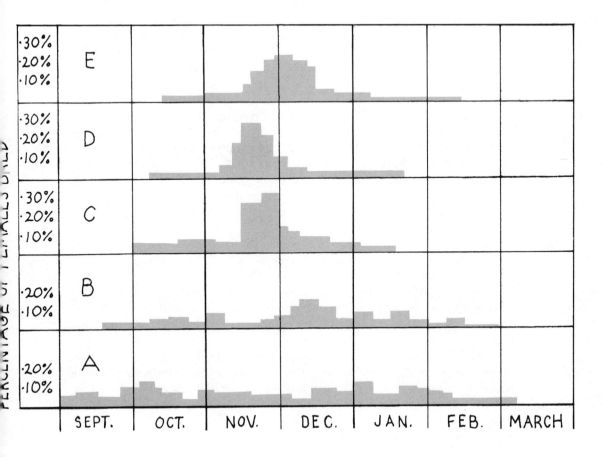

PERCENTAGE OF FEMALES BRED

Primary scrapes, on the other hand, are the love letters does and bucks like to read over and over again. In the most general sense, here's how the scenario unfolds.

It's usually the doe that determines where the scrape is eventually made by the buck in his passing discovery of a splash of estrus-flavored urine on the ground. After making the scrape, he'll want to attempt to scent-trail the doe, find her, and mate with her. Yet this trailing endeavor may not be immediately successful (in his absence, the widely circling doe may return to the scrape of her own accord), so before the buck leaves the scrape he deposits his own scent in it by rub-urinating. The procedure involves rubbing his two hind-leg tarsal glands together while simultaneously humping up his back and urinating. The urine serves as a "carrier" that runs down the legs, over the glands, and transfers the tarsal scent to the ground. If the doe drifts back into the area and detects the male tarsal scent, she instantly knows the buck is aware of her presence and lingers around in hopes he will quickly return to service her. Radio-telemetry studies have shown that, provided she is not disturbed, a doe will remain within 200 yards of a scrape she has found to be recently scent-marked by a buck.

Bucks, of course, regularly revisit those particular scrapes they themselves have scent-marked. But how frequently? Scientists say it depends upon two factors: first, the population density of deer in the vicinity, and therefore how far individual animals customarily travel; and second, how much of a buck's time is preoccupied with does he encounters as a result of this saturation level. If the local deer population is relatively small, and the animals are fairly well dispersed over a larger-than-average range, a buck may have his mating invitations strung out quite a distance. It may take him as long as two or three days to make his rounds, with many of those visitations occuring during the night hours. Conversely, in an area of highly concentrated deer, with their movements subsequently restricted, a buck may inspect each of his scrapes as often as three times a day.

These primary scrapes are the hottest places any hunter can hope to find for waylaying a love-struck buck. And since radio-telemetry studies have shown that a sexually mature male deer will make as many as twenty-seven to thirty-five primaries during the breeding period, any hunter who accepts the value of thoroughly scouting his favorite hunting grounds should have little difficulty finding a majority of them. Moreover, compared to secondary and boundary scrapes, primaries describe exactly what they are by their almost perpetual muddied state from being regularly pawed, cleaned, and anointed with fresh urine-tarsal scent.

Primary scrapes are usually found in woodland regions where the deer can go about their business without telling all the world of their intentions, and they're commonly located in conjunction with trails the animals use to and from feeding and bedding sites. Pay particular attention to the crests of ridges, saddles connecting ridgelines, old fire trails and logging roads, areas around the perimeters of small forest openings where clearcutting has taken place in the past, on terraced hill-side benches, on the slightly elevated flats adjacent to stream bottoms, and around the edges of mature woodlands.

Unlike isolated and weathered secondary scrapes, primary scrapes are commonly found near other primaries, and the hunter should especially be on the lookout for such concentrations of vigorous mating activity. Although a given buck's entourage of twenty-seven to thirty-five scrapes may appear to be strung out in a vaguely linear pattern often resembling a "star" or "cross" (that is, forming a North/South axis bisected roughly in the middle by an East/West axis, for reasons no one can explain), look closer and you'll undoubtedly ascertain a pattern within a pattern: The most frequently revisited scrapes seem to be those that are grouped or clustered. Find a place, for example, where four or five primary scrapes are located within 100 yards of each other, and you're well on your way to tagging a buck.

An illustration of this can be found in the accompanying sketch of a radio-tracking map produced by biologist Larry Marchington, which shows the locations of all the scrapes created by a buck during the breeding season. Although the so-called "star" or "cross" configuration is only barely discernible in this example, the buck's clustering of his scrapes is quite apparent. It's also easy to see how this particular buck began restricting rather than expanding his movements to a core area within his home range at the onset of the breeding season. And it's evident that there are several random, or secondary, scrapes so isolated from the others that the hunter would undoubtedly discount them as unimportant.

In the above example, I've indicated potential locations where I would seriously consider installing tree stands. Note that I have *not* elected to place stands in the midst of the clustered-scrape areas. There is evidence that when a buck's core breeding region is so intensively clustered with scrapes in specific places, that even minimal human disturbance or intrusion may cause the animal to altogether abandon that particular group of scrapes and shift his interests elsewhere. Therefore, at least in this situation, it's better to try ambushing the buck on trails connecting the scrape-clustered areas. In other instances, however, in which perhaps only a few primaries are in relatively close proximity to each other, the hunter can often situate himself within scant yards of the most frequently revisited scrape, especially if he can quickly and quietly slip into such areas. (Of course, all of this hinges upon the type of sporting equipment being used—rifle hunters have the greatest flexibility and bowhunters the least.)

Considering the wind direction is unquestionably of greatest importance because you positively do not want human scent blowing in the very direction you intend to watch for deer. Furthermore, avoiding being seen is the

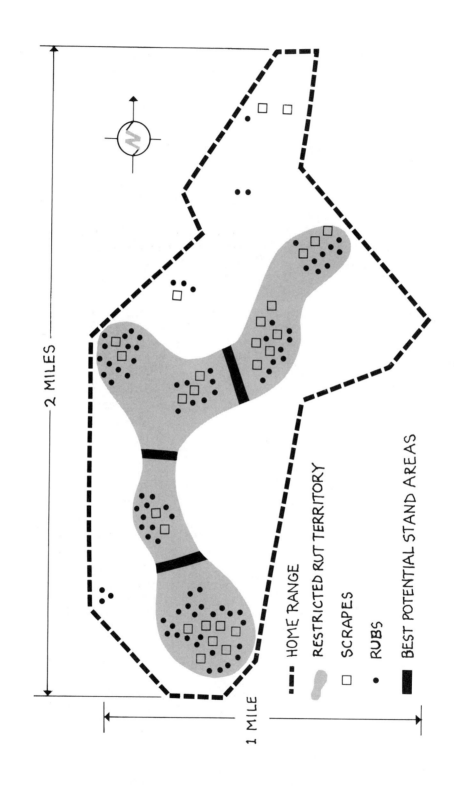

2 MILES

1 MILE

HOME RANGE

RESTRICTED RUT TERRITORY

□ SCRAPES

● RUBS

BEST POTENTIAL STAND AREAS

This sketch is a reproduction of a radio-tracking map of a buck's scraping behavior. The buck used only a small portion of his home range and his scrapes are clustered.

next concern, and this is most easily facilitated if the stand placement is such that an approaching animal is not coming straight toward you but quartering up.

Can you actually second-guess the travel direction the deer is most likely adhering to? Absolutely!

If a well-defineable trail meanders through the region, search for tracks and note the predominant direction they are facing. Bucks rarely travel the length of a trail and then about-face and go back in the opposite direction; instead, they inherently follow a circuitous route, so the imprints you find should all be headed in the same direction. Next, carefully examine the nearby scrapes you plan to watch and you'll probably be able to ascertain the direction in which dirt, weeds, duff, and other debris were thrown by the animal's hooves as he pawed the ground. You can tell which way the buck was facing when he began creating the scrape and, therefore, the likely direction he'll approach from when he periodically returns.

In addition to being able to tell the difference between secondary and primary scrapes, the actual sizes of primaries give good clues as to the ages of the male deer that made them. Small scrapes that average 6 to 8 inches in diameter are invariably half-hearted affairs on the part of immature spike bucks and forkhorns who are just beginning to learn about the opposite sex.

Scrapes averaging 12 to 18 inches in diameter are generally the work of slightly older deer, usually 2½-year-olds carrying rather smallish six and eight-point racks. This is their second mating season and they're just beginning to put their small amount of prior experience into good use. Yet they're still inferior subordinates with regards to their hierarchal rankings in the local deer populations. This places them in a rather precarious situation. On the one hand, detecting doe-in-estrus scent really turns them on, yet they must constantly be on the alert for higher ranking, more dominant males in the region.

This brings us to dominant bucks who rule the turf and make scrapes 20 inches and sometimes much larger in diameter. I once found a scrape that was about 4 feet across at its widest place! I never encountered the deer that made it, but about a week before the hunting season opened, a monster buck was struck and killed by a furniture truck on a nearby highway. That deer was estimated to be 5½ years old, it had a massive 22-point non-typical rack, and it weighed an incredible 285 pounds. I'd bet every dime in my piggy bank that this particular buck was responsible for the huge scrape I'd found.

There is yet another intriguing way of examining a scrape and calculating the size of the rack of the deer that created it. This is done by inspecting the antler tine marks characteristically found in a scrape, where the buck has dragged his rack through the dirt. Tom Townsend, a biologist with Ohio State University's School of Natural Resources, believes such sign serves as some type of marking behavior bucks use to communicate their hierarchal

When scouting, remember that the sizes of the scrapes you find indicate the ages of the animals that made them. Small scrapes such as this one have generally been made by juvenile males.

I always make a diligent search for the largest scrapes I can find. Those that are at least 20 inches in diameter, but sometimes much larger, indicate the presence of very large bucks.

rankings, but no one is really sure. In any event, carefully examine these antler marks and note the distance between the individual tine drags as well as the width of each drag furrow itself. If 5 inches or more separate the tine drags, with each furrow ¾-inch or more in width, you can be sure there is a very large deer in the area.

Aside from these many aspects of whitetail scraping behavior, many other considerations may enter the picture from time to time, often perplexing hunters to no end.

For example, regarding the huge 4-foot scrape I previously described, I sat on stand near the scrape for several days without seeing a thing, hoping desperately some deer other than the road-killed buck was responsible for making it. Although I'm a firm believer in the virtues of patience, sometimes common sense should be called to the forefront.

After several days of diligently maintaining one's vigil without reward, a hunter should not overlook the distinct possibility the buck he's waiting for already is hanging in the garage of some other lucky hunter, or met his untimely end some other way. This makes a good case in favor of doing plenty of scouting and having at least two alternate stand sites in other regions where you can quickly shift your efforts if the first location proves to be a bummer.

In addition to the size of the scrape indicating the size of the deer that made it, the antler-tine drag marks are a clue to the size and configuration of the buck's rack.

One trick I devised several years ago, however, can save the season for you. Each time you conclude an unsuccessful waiting period on stand overlooking a primary scrape, and are about to head back home with gnawing doubts circulating in your mind, take a stick and cover the scrape lightly with leaves; the stick prevents your inadvertently transferring human scent to the ground. In this manner, if the scrape is still being actively tended, next time you return for another wait on stand you'll find that in your absence the leaves will have been cleared away to bare ground.

Bucks commonly engage in this cleaning or "re-opening" behavior just the same as if the wind had covered the scrape with leaves and other debris. In any event, now you know for sure your buck is still alive and well and from this point on, patience is the key to eventually taking him. If the scrape is not re-opened within two days, you can surmise your buck is someone else's venison and immediately take up another stand some distance away to begin working another buck.

Another interesting fact about scrapes has to do with the low-hanging tree branches that are typically found in conjunction with them. The scrape itself is the mode of communication between a buck and doe. The overhead branch, however, is believed to be the mode of communication between the buck that made the scrape and other bucks sharing the same territory.

Bucks like to hook at these branches with their antlers, chew them, and deposit both saliva and secretions from their forehead glands upon them. This marking behavior, in a manner similar to their rubbing of saplings as described in the previous chapter, proclaims the buck's hierarchal ranking in the local pecking order and serves as a visible and olfactory extension of his being.

Should a subordinate buck drift through the area and detect the broken, scented branch, it will immediately assume a meek, submissive personality and slink away. Yet should a second buck of the same age and nearly equal ranking inspect the branch, likely as not he'll hang around, ready to engage in posturing, bluffing, or even battle to determine one or the other's supremacy. And, if a clearly dominant buck happens on the scene, he will often "take over" the scrape in an attempt to steal away the pleasures of the particular receptive doe in the immediate area, and he lets the original buck know by anointing the overhead branch with his own scent.

So at times it's possible, if only briefly, to witness a communal scrape situation in which it's entirely possible to sit on a given stand and witness two or more different bucks make their appearances. This is why it's a good practice for members of a hunting party to mark on a map the locations of all the primary scrapes they've found and then regularly re-check them. If a buck is killed near a particular scrape, yet in succeeding days see the scrape kept open and fresh, get somebody else in the group who hasn't filled his tag right back on that same stand—there's another, possibly larger buck still in the immediate area!

Finally, the breeding period is an excellent time of year for a hunter to tilt the odds in his favor by making use of some type of scent. I heartily recommend Tink's #69 Doe-in-Rut Lure. Although such scents can be used throughout the duration of the breeding season in your locale, my experience is that they are at their effective best during the pre-breeding and post-breeding weeks of the rut.

At the onset of the breeding season, only a small percentage of does are just beginning to enter estrus. Since the woodlands are not yet filled with the wafting odors of many ready females, bucks are therefore more likely to be attracted to the bogus scent-posts created by hunters. Conversely, during the peak period, such a large percentage of does are in heat that bucks become so preoccupied with "the real thing" it is difficult to manipulate them with a sex lure. Later, after the peak breeding period has ended and most of the does in a given region have conceived, the hunter finds himself once again back in a situation in which a scent tells a buck, "There is still another doe lingering around who hasn't yet been bred."

The best way to use such scents during the pre-breeding period is by dribbling them on trails frequented by bucks, simulating a place where a doe who recently entered estrus happened to urinate, and thereby enticing a buck to make a scrape there. Or, create a semi-circular, upwind array of scent bombs as described earlier to hold the attention of a buck drifting through the region.

During the post-breeding period, sprinkle doe-in-heat scent directly into old, weathered primary scrapes and there is an excellent chance bucks will "re-open" them and again begin tending them on a regular basis.

14

Mock-Scraping

◆◆◆

Ordinarily, I don't consider myself a practical joker, especially when it comes to playing dirty tricks on other deer hunters. But there was one particular time when it was necessary to concoct a downright underhanded scheme in the hopes of actually helping a member of our camp get his buck.

The dastardly deed took place four years ago on my farm in southern Ohio, and it involved an inexperienced hunter who was rapidly losing confidence in the stand I'd put him on. There were no readily visible trails, scrapes, or rubs in the immediate vicinity, so I couldn't seem to convince him that he'd eventually score if he'd just stay put. Knowing he was about to abandon what I considered the hottest stand in the entire township, the mental wheels of chicanery began turning.

When everyone was in camp for a lunch break, I lied about having an errand to run and then hurried to the young hunter's tree stand and, right beneath it, scratched out a huge scrape in the soft earth. I even squirted some deer scent in the bogus mating invitation to make it smell authentic, then broke the tips off an overhead branch.

Later, when the discouraged hunter returned to his stand and discovered the fresh scrape made during his brief absence, his adrenaline almost surged out of control. He didn't see anything during the remaining hours of that day nor on the following morning. But with his enthusiasm bolstered, he was now willing to stick it out as long as necessary. The next evening, the young hunter collected a sleek six-pointer at that very location.

I wasn't really surprised that the stand had eventually paid off. It was in a prime location, having given up many deer in previous years. The stand

174

was situated in a natural bottleneck connecting two brush-choked hollows. I *was* positively shocked, however, when the hunter later began describing his adventure and how he had taken his shot while the buck was pawing the scrape!

My predictable initial reaction was to assume that the hunter had merely fabricated a nice little story to go along with his deer kill, and I wasn't about to ruin his fun by spilling the beans. Besides, I didn't want to make him look foolish in front of the others in camp. But, as it sometimes happens, a practical joke has a way of backfiring upon the prankster who engineers it. The irony of this particular experience is that, in retrospect, I now believe that the young hunter was truthful in his account, and that the buck he killed had indeed been tricked into using the phony scrape!

All of this comes on the heels of new scientific findings about deer mating behavior. But, more importantly, a small coterie of expert hunters around the country are using these startling breakthroughs, along with some equally bizarre tactics, to fool Mother Nature and take more deer than ever.

I'm reminded of what happened several years ago in Ohio's Wayne National Forest. My pal, Al Wolter, then the Forest Service supervisor of Wayne, was hunting on one stand and I was on another. On opening morning, I took a splendid eight-pointer from my stand, proof enough that the scrape I was watching was a primary. But Al was willing to gamble that it was a community scrape—one being used by two or more bucks—and so he promptly abandoned his own stand and climbed into mine. Incredibly, only one hour later, he killed a nice buck that fell not more than a dozen yards from the still-steaming pile of entrails where I had field-dressed my deer. But that is not the end of the story. Four days later, when the gun season closed and the bowhunting season reopened, a friend used the same stand, overlooking the same scrape, to shoot still a third buck!

Recurring experiences such as this one blow holes in previously held theories about whitetail bucks becoming territorial during the rut and staking out mating grounds to be defended against all interlopers.

But the real blockbuster I'm about to lay on you is this: Because finding a so-called community scrape may require an extensive amount of scouting across miles of countryside, and maybe even a good deal of luck, what if you could eliminate about 90 percent of that hard work and uncertainty? What if you could simply go out into your favorite deer woods, pick a convenient location for a stand, create an *artificial* scrape right there, and then enjoy the very same results of having perhaps several bucks visit the scrape as if it were one of their own making? Or, equally shocking, what if I told you that upon indeed discovering a primary or community scrape in an unfavorable location, that you could literally pick it up and move it to another area where a more advantageous stand site was present?

These are mind-boggling propositions, to be sure, but an elite fraternity of some of the country's most advanced hunters is proving they work. The

A buck uses his front hoofs to paw out a scrape, sometimes drags his rack through it in the very place where an estrous doe previously urinated. Many scrapes are used by more than one buck.

techniques to be described very shortly fall into the broad category known as "mock-scraping," so named by Johnson City, Tennessee deer hunter Bob McGuire who is believed to be one of the originators of the method. Since then, other avid students of whitetail behavior, including Tink Nathan, Pat Ryan, and myself, have improved upon several of McGuire's early approaches and even added several new twists. In any regard, I'm convinced mock-scraping will prove to be one of the most revolutionary and widely practiced deer hunting techniques of the next two decades.

We already know that when a doe comes into estrus, in response to a chemical change in her endocrine system, she begins emitting characteristic body odors and hormonal secretions that tell male deer that she is receptive to being bred. These sexual pheromones are transferred to the ground whenever the doe urinates. Upon finding one of these urine-soaked places during his travels, a buck makes a scrape right then and there, often directly on top of the dampened, scented earth.

This explains why scrapes are frequently found along woodlot edges bordering open fields, on deer trails, on old logging roads, and sometimes deep within heavy cover. These are simply places where does commonly urinate while they are feeding or traveling to and from bedding locations.

We also know that a majority of these scrapes are destined to become boundary scrapes, or secondary scrapes, and that the enterprising hunter should refine his search for primary scrapes. These can be identified by the following characteristics: First, they are found clustered or in close conjunction with other scrapes; second, they are kept in a perpetually muddied or freshened state due to revisitation and the regular depositing of scented urine; and third, they always reveal the presence of an overhanging tree branch the male deer scent-marks with saliva and forehead gland secretions.

This brief background brings us to the subject of mock-scraping, which any hunter can easily enact in several different ways to greatly increase his chances of success.

The first method involves scouting a tract of land very quickly, just to familiarize yourself with the terrain and to get a general idea of the travel routes the animals are using. Then, without regard for any other existing deer sign such as droppings or antler rubs on saplings, pick out a convenient location for a stand. It should be situated so that you can slip in and out as quietly as possible, the prevailing wind direction should be in your favor,

You can actually make an artificial scrape and induce bucks to visit it. This is Bob McGuire, one of the pioneers in the art of mock-scraping.

and sufficient surrounding and background cover should break up your outline and mute the very slightest movements required to raise your gun or bow.

The next order of business is to use a commercially distributed doe-in-heat scent in a urine base to mark the ground where you'd like to see a buck make a primary scrape. Of critical importance is making sure that the scent is deposited beneath a tree branch hanging low enough for the deer to reach in order to engage in his own unique marking behavior. Otherwise, in keeping with a buck's typical response to random estrus-scented urine, you'll only encourage a buck to make a secondary scrape that he's not likely to intentionally revisit.

Although some expert hunters are successful just by splashing their doe scent directly on the ground, in the belief that this more closely simulates a doe having actually urinated there, most advanced hunters prefer one of several other approaches. One of Bob McGuire's early approaches was to take an entire bottle of doe scent, drill a tiny hole through the cap, insert a pipe cleaner, then use tape or wire to hang the bottle upside-down from a tree branch higher than the branch immediately over the scrape-to-be.

After using this method for an entire season, I became frustrated with it

Some of the early scent-dispensing systems I developed for mock-scraping. The largest (on the left) comes into play when a saline-diluted "maintenance" solution is desired.

because the drip-rate could not be precisely controlled; sometimes only one drop of scent would fall every five minutes, which wasn't nearly enough, and other times a steady drizzle would empty my entire scent bottle in no time, which can be extremely costly.

In an attempt to improve upon this basically sound idea, I designed a half-pint scent dispensing bottle from a jelly jar, wrapped with black tape to make it inconspicuous. With a hole drilled through the lid, I inserted a short length of ⅛-inch inside-diameter plastic tubing. I found that if I experimented by coiling the tubing, I could obtain a drip-rate of one drop per minute, whereupon I then securely taped the coils in that position.

The reason for the half-pint jar, which is far larger than most scent bottles, has to do with another ongoing experiment. I've been diluting my doe scent with 0.05 sterile normal saline solution. You can purchase saline tablets at any pharmacy, and instructions are on the package for making the solution. At first, my intention was to use a 4-to-1 saline/doe scent solution as a means of conserving the expensive doe scent, but since then I've had mixed results. On the one hand, deer seem to like the taste of the salty solution on the ground and have even been observed to lick the scrape and rub their noses in it. But when using a diluted scent, my success percentage has dropped off with regards to getting bucks to initiate mating invitations in specific locations in the first place.

So, although my work has not yet been completed, here is what I recommend. If you are a bowhunter who will be hunting during a rather lengthy season, begin by using concentrated doe scent to get your various primary scrapes well-established and regularly tended. Then switch to a saline-diluted doe scent as merely a maintenance effort to ensure the scrape remains open and regularly revisited. But if you're strictly a rifle hunter or shotgunner pursuing a one or two-week deer season, use a concentrated, urine-based, doe-in-heat scent exclusively. To this end, I then devised still another type of scent dispenser. It consists of a short piece of discarded oxygen catheter tubing (size 10 French) obtained from my family doctor, which can be inserted into a hole drilled in the cap of your bottle of scent, or fits perfectly into the flip-top spouts on the lids of most commercial scents. The heart of the system, however, is an ordinary paper clip which pinches the tubing and can be easily adjusted to obtain the exact drip-rate you desire.

Following these early and admittedly rudimentary scent-dispensing systems (don't discount them if you're on a rather tight budget, they work quite satisfactorily), Tink Nathan of Safariland Hunting Corporation invented his revolutionary Sky Skrape scent dispenser for use by mock-scraping enthusiasts.

The Sky Skrape looks almost identical to a typical I.V. infusion set as used in the medical profession. Consisting of a glass vial, which is plastic-coated to resist breakage, and a soft plastic dispensing tube with an in-line drip

Tink Nathan, head of Safari-land Hunting Corporation, has long been at the forefront in the deer-scent industry and has aided mock-scrapers with many innovative ideas.

regulator, the Sky Skrape is the state-of-the-art equipment currently used by mock-scrape hunters. The hunter unscrews the Sky Skrape's cap and fills the vial with his favorite doe-in-heat lure and then hangs the dispenser from an appropriate tree branch where he wants a buck to initiate a scrape. Using his watch, he then calibrates the drip regulator. The slowest recommended drip-rate is one microdrop per minute, which translates into one cc per hour. Since there are 30cc per liquid ounce, it's easy to calculate how long the Sky Skrape will continue to dispense scent before the glass vial needs to be refilled; in this particular case, a one-ounce bottle of doe-in-heat lure will last approximately thirty hours. But at the outset, when I'm attempting to entice a buck into initiating a scrape, I use a higher drip rate, which means refilling the glass vial with more scent every day. If you consider that many experts use several Sky Skrapes simultaneously in various locations, and that some of the premium doe-in-heat scents on the market currently cost more than $5 per fluid ounce, mock-scraping can become an expensive endeavor. So to keep these expenses moderately in line, I use undiluted, full-strength doe lures at first to get the show rolling, then switch to a saline-diluted "maintenance" solution.

The value of using some variation of scent-dispensing system is that renewed, fresh scent is continually applied to the ground one drop at a time;

otherwise, even mildly inclement weather would quickly obliterate a scent station created by a one-time application.

Whichever of the previously described approaches suit you best, check back often. Usually within one to three days, to your complete amazement, you'll find a fresh scrape exactly where the scent has been deposited on the ground. Furthermore, you'll be able to instantly confirm whether or not the established scrape is a primary merely by examining the overhanging branch to see if it has been chewed and broken. If it has, switch now to a maintenance solution of diluted scent. If the branch has not been chewed and broken, continue with a full-strength scent for at least two more days in the hope the buck that made the scrape will eventually return and add it to his list of primaries. If even this does not transpire, remove your scent dispensing system, thoroughly clean it with hot water, then re-install it in another location. There's a good chance that in your initial attempt you contaminated either the scent-dispensing system, the overhanging branch, or the nearby ground area with human scent. Go slowly, be careful, and be persistent and you will eventually succeed!

One of Nathan's latest brainstorms is this scent-dispensing system known as the Sky Skrape. Through the use of a calibrated drip regulator, a hunter can adjust the flow of scent as precisely as one microdrop per minute.

After a buck has initiated a scrape beneath your scent-dispensing system, the scrape may or may not become a primary. If it is, you'll note the overhanging tree branch has been chewed and broken as the deer marked it with saliva and forehead gland scent. This is teenage deer-hunting expert Mike Weiss, an ardent student of mock-scraping techniques.

This brings us to a second and even more intriguing aspect of mock-scraping. Let's say that during the course of your scouting you coincidentally discover an existing primary scrape that is of such awesome dimensions and reveals such large tracks and antler drag marks that your heart begins pounding like a triphammer. It's patently clear that your conscience simply will not allow you to be anywhere else on opening morning! Trouble is, there really isn't a suitable tree in the immediate vicinity for your portable stand. You desperately wish you could somehow just pick that scrape right up and relocate it a short distance away where there is indeed an ideal stand site that would offer a much better shooting advantage.

Well, in a sense, you *can* move that scrape! What I mean is that you can obliterate the original scrape and create a mock-scrape up to 100 yards away at the more favorable stand site. And you can expect the buck that's using that immediate area and that made the original scrape to instantly transfer his thoughts and energies to the new location.

To successfully destroy the original scrape, don't try to simply scuff leaves and other debris over it, because a buck will defeat your every effort by tirelessly and repeatedly reopening it. The only way to positively stop a deer from using a primary scrape is to use a small hand saw or pruning shears to cut off the scent-marked overhanging tree branch.

The importance of being careful not to contaminate the area in which you're working with human scent can't be emphasized enough. Most serious mock-scrape hunters wear some type of rubberized raincoat or parka and rubber boots and gloves; leather boots and gloves are extremely porous and become repositories for all manner of odors. In fact, I never allow my mock-scraping clothes inside the house, except to frequently wash them, upon which they go right back outside where they are stored in a large plastic bag in an open-air shed. It's also wise to periodically wash any tools or other equipment used in your mock-scraping; in addition to the hand saw or pruning shears mentioned above, from time to time you may require a small trowel, plastic pail, and 6-inch lengths of heavy bailing wire, all of which can be "de-scented" by submerging in boiling water. Remove the tools from the water with tongs, place on paper toweling to dry, then transfer to a heavy duty plastic garbage bag for carrying to your mock-scrape working area. From that point on, handle the tools only when wearing your rubber gloves.

So now you're ready to obliterate a primary scrape and create another in a new location. Keep in mind that if it is to serve as the buck's new primary scrape in that particular area, it absolutely must be situated beneath another overhanging tree branch. Beyond this, the scrape itself can be created by cutting a forked stick on location and then simply clearing away grass, sod, weeds and other matter down to bare mineral soil. Make the scrape about 18 to 20 inches in diameter, then sprinkle a liberal dose of doe-in-heat scent directly into the scrape.

Next is the icing on the cake to enhance the effectiveness of your scrape relocation. First, take the scent-marked overhanging branch you sawed off at the previous scrape location and wire it in place above the mock-scrape you've created. Tie it right to the existing overhanging branch. Second, go back still again to the old scrape location, and using your small hand trowel, shovel the top 1-inch layer of muddied soil into your pail and mix this into the soil of the mock-scrape you've created at the new location. The reason for both of these procedures is to ensure that the buck will instantly recognize the familiar scent deposits, which will lend greater authenticity to the substitute scrape and therefore promote a rapid transferal of the buck's attention to the new location.

Let's say, however, that at the location you've selected for the perfect stand site and mock-scrape there is no low-hanging tree branch for the buck to lick and chew, and therefore no apparent way to wire in place the licking branch removed from the previous scrape location. Bob McGuire suggests the following alternative.

In the immediate location, find a tall, limber sapling about an inch in diameter. Reach up as high as you can, grab the trunk, and bend the sapling over on itself so that it forms an inverted U. Next, use a length of stout nylon

MAKING A MOCK SCRAPE

1. Do not contaminate a mock-scraping site with human scent. Mike Weiss (left) displays the typical mock-scraping garb used by most hunters. Especially note the rubberized footwear and rubber gloves, which do not become repositories for human odors as do leather boots and gloves.

2. After you've created your phony scrape in a desirable location, sprinkle a liberal dose of doe-in-heat scent directly into the scrape.

3. Next, go back to the original scrape (top) and cut off an overhanging tree branch.

4. Wire the branch in place (center) directly over the top of the mock scrape.

5. Then, again return to the original scrape (right), collect the scented surface soil, and sprinkle it on the mock scrape. Although this last step is not absolutely necessary, I believe it lends authenticity to the mock scrape because the buck will recognize the familiar scent.

If your intended mock-scraping site lacks an overhanging tree branch nearby, you can create one by doubling over the crown of a sapling and tying it in place with rope.

cord (ordinary cotton rope or hemp will rot) to tie the top of the tree down, by running your rope from just beneath the crown back to the trunk. With the top of the little tree and its many limbs and branches now pointing down, make whatever adjustments in your rope that are necessary; ensure the branches are easily within reach of the buck, which means no higher than 6 feet off the ground. Then proceed as previously described, by wiring the old licking branch in place and creating the mock-scrape directly beneath.

The tremendous value of mock-scraping is that it allows a hunter to greatly extend the otherwise brief rutting period by simulating the presence of estrous does when in fact the real does living in a given region may not actually be going into heat for many weeks. But it's necessary to mention that, as effective as mock scraping is, no hunter should expect it to prove successful 100 percent of the time. Nature is riddled with too many vagaries and other unknowns to allow whitetail behavior to be completely predictable. In addition, a hunter will sometimes inadvertently and unknowingly contaminate a mock scrape area with human odor, causing whitetails, which are already paranoid to begin with, to at least temporarily avoid that specific place.

Consequently, many hunters using doe scent in an attempt to induce bucks into making scrapes like to hang their dripping bottles in as many as five or six different locations. This stacks in their favor the odds that at least one or two of the scent stations will ultimately result in a primary scrape. Scrape relocation also carries a probability factor in which, a certain percentage of the time, you simply will not be able to successfully induce a buck to transfer his interests to a new location. Checking the relocated scrape on a daily basis to see if it is being tended and periodically freshened is imperative.

This brings us to the subject of community scrapes, which offer the most exciting deer hunting imaginable because of the many different bucks that you are likely to see. Again, biologists are not positive as to why whitetails frequently share scrapes; they only know that the phenomenon does indeed occur on a regular basis.

The only real way to ascertain whether a primary or mock-scrape has become a community scrape is actually to sit on a nearby stand during the deer season and observe the behavior of the animals themselves.

If an approaching buck immediately comes in close and focuses his attention upon the scrape with his nose tight to the ground, you should take him—he's undoubtedly the dominant male in the immediate region and the very animal that has scent-marked the overhanging tree branch.

On the other hand, if an approaching deer seems reluctant to immediately come into the scrape or exhibits other timid or nervous behavior—and when he does come in, he shows more interest in the scent-marked tree branch and then quickly tucks his tail down between his legs—it's a sure sign that the deer is one of perhaps several subordinate males in the region. This submissive posture is typical of subordinate deer when they are confronted with estrus doe scent in combination with the scent of another male of greater hierarchal ranking. In this situation you've got two choices. You can take the subordinate buck, if it fulfills your expectations for the hunt (even an eight or ten-pointer may conceivably be a subordinate in the domain of a buck that's still larger). Or, you can allow the buck to pass, hoping an even larger and more dominant male will eventually show.

My friend Tom Thompson, hunting near Lexington, Kentucky last year, succeeded in making a mock scrape that eventually turned into a community scrape which he saw visited by four different bucks on various occasions. By their behavior, he made an educated guess that all of them were subordinates and so he allowed them to go about their business (if the truth be known, Tom would have been happy to take two of the deer, but they never came within his self-imposed bowhunting range of 35 yards). Finally, a fifth buck, the largest he had ever taken, stepped into view and Tompson's excellent lung shot brought the animal down after a quick 50-yard run.

A buck, especially a subordinate that has previously visited the scrape in the past and ascertained his ranking after examining the licking branch, may

Here is an example of a community scrape: two bucks sharing a breeding territory. Sometimes as many as six bucks may visit the same scrape.

If a buck shows an immediate interest in a mock scrape, he's undoubtedly the dominant male in the region, and you might as well take him. But if the deer registers more interest in the overhanging branch, as this one is doing, he is a subordinate checking another male's scent deposit to determine his own ranking in the hierarchy.

not come right up close to inspect the scrape in the future. It's my belief it doesn't want to risk a confrontation with the dominant male that is periodically tending the scrape, but he will try to mount a doe if he thinks there is little chance of getting caught in the act. From a safe distance, the subordinate subsequently takes a peek at the scrape area to see if perchance a doe is hanging around, then beats a hasty exit.

From time to time, even a dominant buck may "hang back" in heavy cover and not come in close to one of his primary scrapes. This is especially the case during the midday hours, or after several days of intense hunting pressure in a region. So when you're sitting on a stand overlooking a primary scrape or a mock-scrape, continually use your peripheral vision to scan the surrounding cover.

This aspect of whitetail behavior may even have a telling influence upon where you decide to create a mock-scrape or a stand to watch it. There is no problem, of course, if you're hunting in a state where center-fire rifles are legal, for they give you far more range of coverage. But if your state allows only shotgun hunting for whitetails and, particularly if you're bowhunting, knowing that bucks do not always have to come right in close to a scrape to "check it" may play a crucial role in the placement of your stand.

Mock-scraping is deer hunting's brand-new frontier and one of the most exciting methods to come down the pike in decades. So if you see another hunter in the woods who appears to be using a forked stick to scratch out something that looks like a buck scrape, don't be too quick to brand him a lunatic. He just might be one of the most knowledgeable and successful hunters in the county.

15

Does Are the Decision-Makers

◆◆

Most hunters maintain heady visions of bucks as monarchs of their domain, brandishing their ivory-tipped antlers in protectionist fashion as irrefutable symbols of male domination in their bailiwicks. It's quite an enchanting, almost romantic image, so often reinforced on calendars and picture post-cards.

But the truth of the matter is that whitetail bucks play rather mild-man-nered, subservient roles in the lives of deer. As shocking and disturbing as it may be to some hunters the does rule the kingdoms of deer. It's the lady deer that determine the whats, wheres, and hows of everyday life. All the while, bucks sharing the same habitat bear no responsibility whatever for their acts of procreation, and given the opportunity in almost any circum-stance would rather run and hide.

Admittedly, it is indeed a compelling experience to be sitting in a tree stand as an impressive buck approaches, stopping so often along his in-tended route to whack his antlers against saplings. But when it comes to pitting one's hunting skills against the innate chicanery of whitetails, noth-ing is more difficult to collect than an old doe with eyes, ears, and a sniffer second to none.

There's one such doe, living on the back-sixty of my farm, that I've been trying to get with a bow for more than five years. She's easily recognizable because of a knot on her left front knee—my guess is that earlier in life she broke that leg when jumping a fence—and the challenge of taking her has almost become an obsession. More than a dozen times we've had close encounters but she has always outsmarted me. If I ever do succeed, I'll undoubtedly feel a bit of remorse that our chess-like engagements are over and, fittingly, I'll rank her higher on my "trophy" list than many of the bucks I've taken.

Not all does are so cunning, of course, but most are, simply because of their longer lifespans and, consequently, the steady and repeated use of their senses to extricate themselves from sticky situations. A vast majority of bucks harvested each year are less than 2½ years old, and according to biologists at Penn State University, less than 4 percent of all whitetail bucks ever live long enough to see their fifth birthdays. But it is relatively common for does to live to the ripe old age of nine to fourteen years, an incredible period of longevity for any game species. As I said, when it comes to matching wits with whitetails, six-point and eight-point bucks are invariably wimps compared to the supreme challenge of taking a woods-wise doe that has seen the coming and passing of numerous deer seasons and knows what life is really all about during the months of October, November, and December.

Even bucks themselves owe much more to their mothers than most hunters, and even some biologists, seem willing to accept. Part of this reluctance to give credit where credit is due can be attributed to the popular talk nowadays that seems always to center around the breeding potential of trophy bucks, how we should do this or that in our game management programs to see these unique gene pools perpetuated while simultaneously reducing the number of inferior breeding animals (spikes and forkhorns), and how certain regions of the country will continue to produce larger-than-average bucks due to the unusually high number of breeding trophy males inhabiting those regions.

All of this may be true, to some extent. But we must keep in mind that newborn male fawns acquire only one-half of their body-size/antler-growth potential from their fathers. The other one-half of their beings are products of their mothers, which points out the valid need for game management programs (and hunter acceptance of those programs) geared not only to antlered deer but emphasizing total herd management policies directly affecting does as well.

Once newborn fawns are on their feet, their mother assumes complete responsibility for teaching them how to survive in the wilds. And the way young deer learn to use their visual, olfactory, and auditory senses is fascinating.

Newborn fawns are just like inquisitive children in their never-ending curiosity about their environments. For several months, they are constantly searching and smelling, tasting, getting into mischief, even romping and playing. While hiding in blinds during summer photo missions, I have had innocent fawns walk right up to me as I softly whistled or snapped my fingers. They registered no fear, simply because they had not yet been taught to.

But notice the marked difference in the behavior of a slightly older fawn, especially when it is in the close company of its mother, as it will almost continually watch and imitate her. When the doe's head jerks up, so does the fawn's as it begins exhibiting its first attempt of using the body language known as the head-bob. The doe gazes off into the distance for long moments, and so does her young one. Then the fawn stares intently at its mother to see if what she's looking at has alarmed her. She cups her ears forward and stamps her left front hoof, and the fawn does the same. Finally, convinced all is right with the world, she lowers her head again to feed, and so does the fawn. From nearby I purposely snap a twig and, immediately, up pops a big head, and so too a little one. Then I stand up from behind my blind and wave my arms.

Now the doe definitely realizes what I am. Instantly, she bolts, snorting loudly many times as she runs with her white flag waving (which says to the little one, "Follow me away from here for this place is dangerous"). The fawn, barely successful in its attempts, makes little sneezing noises as it runs off into the forest. From that time on, the fawn is imprinted with a distrust of man and in the future knows how to react in a similar situation.

In our human world, there has long been controversy as to whether a genetic/hereditary background or environmental conditioning plays the greater role in the success of one's future endeavors. Likely as not, genetics provide the potential and the environment provides (or does not provide) the opportunity to realize that potential.

But in the world of whitetails, there can be no doubt that learning is far more important than the gene pool of any particular animal. Studies have shown, in fact, that during their first and second attempts at birthing and fawning, young does are simply not very good mothers. They still lack a good deal of woods-savvy themselves, and although one or both fawns may indeed survive, the offspring don't seem to be the beneficiaries of that little "something extra" in the sly and evasive department.

Conversely, a doe that has passed her fifth birthday—which means having four years of trial-and-error fawning experience under her belt, and all the while maturing in her own right—is a professor emeritus when it comes to passing on woods wisdom to her young. Her male offspring are likely to achieve trophy-buck status, not necessarily because of a unique genetic background but mainly through their ability to survive, rather than to fall to bullets during their earlier years of life when they haven't yet had the opportunity to grow their largest racks.

Even when it comes to animal-population dynamics—the grouping of deer, their mannerisms, travel tendencies, and the hierarchal rankings they display through various types of body language—it's always an old, experienced, bossy doe who takes charge. This is in stark contrast to scenes commonly depicted on Christmas cards in which a handsome buck is shown standing boldly in some moon-drenched clearing, with any nearby does always in the background and displaying subordinate postures.

But the truth of the matter is that the artists who paint such male-domi-
nated scenes for the greeting card industry, and even for the covers of the
leading sportsmen's magazines, are, through their great lack of knowledge,
perpetuating a massive hoax upon an equally naive public. More accurately,
they should be presenting portraits of arthritic old she-deer standing front
and center, with "regal" bucks holding their tails tucked between their legs
as they cower in nearby shadows.

One of the biggest bucks I've ever seen, in fact, was so hen-pecked he
could have qualified as the Walter Mitty of whitetails. This was in western
Kentucky, during a squirrel hunting foray. I was sitting on an oak ridge
where the forest floor was carpeted with acorns and from my vantage point
I could look down upon a lush alfalfa meadow.

Suddenly, from one corner of the meadow, eight deer single-filed out of
an adjacent woodlot and began walking along the edge of the field, staying
barely inside a fringe of tall grass to remain inconspicuous. Out in front was
an absolutely huge doe that I estimate weighed at least 200 pounds. She was
followed by two much younger does, a spike buck, three yearlings, and
finally a splendid ten-pointer bringing up the rear.

Apparently, the old doe didn't want her troupe to feed in the open
meadow while it was still light. She seemed intent upon quickly leading them
along the field edge. I guessed that she wanted them to bide their time
feeding on acorns in the protection of the nearby forest and not begin
field-feeding until after full dark. Well, the big buck had the succulent alfalfa
foremost in his mind and began slowly drifting out into the meadow to
graze. Upon seeing this, the lead doe galloped to the rear of her entourage,
bit the buck on the side of the neck, then flailed at him with her hooves until
he was back in line.

As the deer neared the end of the meadow and were about to enter the
oak forest, the buck once again could not resist the temptation of the tender
grass and took several steps in the direction of the middle of the field. Up
front, the dowager doe this time merely looked back over her shoulder at
the buck. That was all it took and with his head held low he meekly slinked
back to his position at the rear of the herd.

This matriarchal society in which deer live often plays a telling role in
which particular strategies a hunter should or should not elect to use.

I do everything possible to avoid close encounters with does, particularly
overly large ones. I'd much rather go up against any-sized buck because past
experience has shown that when a buck is in the company of several does,
you can bet that an old she-deer will blow the whistle on you every time.

In some instances, there may even be two old does in the group, and this
amounts to double trouble. One of the two will rank higher in their self-
established pecking order and that individual will therefore be in charge of
all decision-making, yet the two will cooperate when it comes to monitoring
the surrounding area for danger.

One of the most common examples of this is when a group of deer is

Although it may come as a surprise to macho sportsmen, does rule the deer kingdom. They determine activity in the community of whitetails.

Newborn fawns owe half of their heredity to their mothers; unfortunately, game management programs generally focus only upon improving the gene pools of males.

Young fawns are just like inquisitive children that have a need to romp and play and get into mischief.

feeding. For the safety of the group, the two old does will take turns as "sentries," using body language to communicate with each other. While all the other deer have their heads down, and their senses occupied, one of the old does will remain with head up, keenly alert. After several minutes, the other old doe will cease feeding and raise her head to assume the sentry post and then, and only then, will the first doe lower her head to feed. It stands to reason that if you are nearby, waiting for just the right opportunity to level your sights upon a buck in the group, you may never get your chance because your slightest movement is likely to trigger an explosion of bobbing white flags.

By the same token, if you're patiently maintaining a vigil on stand and a big doe comes poking along, freeze! She may have a buck trailing somewhere behind. In cases like this, a big misconception among hunters is that the buck is smarter, allowing the doe to take the lead to forewarn him of danger up ahead. Unfortunately, this myth continues to be perpetuated by the country's deer hunting writers, but it gives bucks too much undeserved credit. What's really happening is the old doe is the self-appointed Travel Director and her suitor is merely going along with whatever she thinks best.

Interestingly enough, another reason does typically seem to exhibit better use of their senses and higher levels of cautionary behavior than bucks of the same age goes back to their early experiences as fawns. Most whitetail fawns are born in May and weaned in July. From this point on, young bucks

Here is a classical example of whitetails posting "sentries" while others feed.

Most hunters believe that bucks trail does so they'll be forewarned of danger lurking ahead, but this gives bucks undeserved credit. Actually, the doe is the Travel Director; her suitor is merely going along with whatever she decides.

begin gradually drifting away from their mother's constant care, and by October or November, they may be entirely on their own. Young does, on the other hand, commonly stay with their mothers throughout the entire winter and into the late spring, until such time as the mother is about to give birth to her next generation of offspring. As a result, doe fawns have the benefit of an additional six months of guarded supervision and teaching that their brothers do not enjoy.

Other insights into the matriarchal world of whitetails can be equally beneficial to hunters. In any given state, for example, we all know that some townships within counties seem consistently to record much higher buck harvests than nearby areas. This phenomenon can be directly attributed to the birthing characteristics of does inhabiting the other townships.

Ordinarily, given adequate habitat conditions, a doe gives birth to a single fawn her first year, twins every year thereafter, and even triplets in the cases of ideal habitat. However, when the habitat is poor and food is sparse or of poor nutritional quality, impregnated does form only one fetus of the two or more fertilized eggs they may be carrying. In nature's mysterious way, that single fawn is almost always a male, the reason being that bucks are far more prone to travel than home-body does and this increases the likelihood the new generation of offspring will leave the "starvation zone" for more suitable habitat located some distance away. Therefore, certain townships that are endowed with prime habitat actually seem to have a magnetic influence upon surrounding townships of lower quality habitat, which in time is translated into higher annual buck harvests.

But agricultural and other land-use patterns see gradual changes over time. This is why deer hunters should periodically obtain state harvest figures from their game department. Simply ascertaining which particular counties are recording the highest buck kills each year, however, is only the first step in doping out a game plan because counties in some states may encompass 100 square miles or more. What an enterprising hunter needs to learn is which specific townships within certain counties are yielding the most bucks. By penciling these figures on a county map, it's then relatively easy to figure out which regions are the so-called starvation zones and which ones bucks are constantly filtering into and adopting as their new home ranges.

16

How to Call Deer

◆◆

Long after the venison is gone, memories of the hunt that produced the succulent deer meat continue to linger. And over the years, the cumulative influence of these memories and experiences shape the deer hunter's personality. In effect, the hunter actually becomes a product of his past adventures, and this ties the knot of his marriage to deer hunting even tighter. No longer is deer hunting simply a week-long indulgence that takes place every autumn. It is a year-long affair that constitutes an integral part of his very fiber.

In my own particular case, I became a deer hunter in the fall of 1974. I had hunted whitetails for many years before that, but it was in 1974 when something happened that forever altered, or rather elevated, my level of dedication to the sport.

Sitting in a tree stand, I had decided this was the day I was going to attempt to rattle in a buck by clashing antlers together in a mock simulation of two male deer dueling with each other.

What had gotten me all fired up was a magazine article by the venerable Byron Dalrymple in which he described using the technique with good success on his ranch in Texas. In a later telephone conversation with Byron, he said rattling had become the rage in his part of the world, but due to the emotionally charged explosiveness one could expect, he did not recommend it for those with weak hearts.

As I clashed the two antlers together, I thought maybe Byron had slightly exaggerated the excitement he claimed rattling generated. But moments later, loud crashing noises in the brushy ravine below sent my blood pres-

198

sure instantly surging upward another 60 points. At first, it sounded like a hunter had gotten tangled up in a maze of vines and briers and ultimately had no choice but to bull his way out of the cover. But the calamity continued and seconds later I saw an eight-point buck charging in my direction!

By now, I had hung my rattling antlers from a nearby branch and picked up my 55-pound recurve bow, confident the buck eventually would be mine. However, the deer came only to within 50 yards of my stand when it slammed to a halt as abruptly as if it had run into an invisible wall. Then it began craning its head to one side and then the other, searching. The buck was sure he had heard two other males fighting near one of his scrapes, and now he seemed angry that he couldn't see them.

During the course of the next several minutes, the deer traveled in a 180° circle around my stand area, intensively looking for the intruders, occasionally stamping his feet, flaring his nostrils and erecting the dark tufts of hair surrounding his tarsal glands. It was incredible that the big deer couldn't hear the pounding of my heart, because it seemed like buttons would begin popping off my shirt any instant.

Apparently satisfied the two other males had heard his approach and run away, the buck then began feeding and slowly walking away. Now it was me who was becoming frustrated. Here was the first buck I'd ever even attempted to rattle in—a real dandy—and yet he was now gradually fading away back into the brushy ravine.

When the buck was almost entirely out of sight, I figured what the hell, I might as well gamble. It was a slim chance, but I picked up the antlers anyway and barely clicked the tines together just once. Instantly, the buck turned and stampeded right back up the hill like a mad dog, his rack held low to the ground as he charged ahead. Everything happened so fast that I didn't have a chance to reach for my bow. There I stood holding the rattling antlers, the buck only scant yards before me, fearing that if I even thought about moving, the deer would detect me for sure.

As it happened, I never did get a shot at that deer. Some mysterious sixth sense must have told him the whole set-up reeked of danger, and moments later he threw his tail aloft and evaporated like a puff of woodsmoke.

It was after the deer was completely out of sight that I finally looked down and noticed my hands were trembling. Then I started feeling so weak in the knees I had to sit down, sure that I'd otherwise lose my balance and fall from my elevated platform. Byron Dalrymple couldn't have been more right if he'd been a prophet.

There is an important postscript to this anecdote. The experience just recounted did not take place in Texas, where rattling was born and has long been heralded, but rather in Potter County, Pennsylvania. This points out the fallacy held by many that rattling is effective only in the brush country of the desert southwest. On the contrary, rattling will work anywhere!

It is indeed true that one's greatest success can be expected in regions

Although rattling-in deer was born in Texas, the technique has spread beyond the desert Southwest. This is Murry Burnham with one of the largest rattled-in bucks I've seen.

where high deer populations exist and where individual animals must live in close proximity to one another. This state of affairs brings numerous bucks close together, forcing them to share overlapping home ranges where they can be expected to establish and maintain very well-defined hierarchal rankings.

Also, if you haven't already assumed so, rattling works best during the rut. With the peak of the estrus period being November 15, but with many individuals coming into heat as much as two weeks earlier or later than others, this makes the entire month of November the perfect time to attempt to rattle in a buck. Yet even this bears exception, because as noted earlier, the mating season south of the Mason-Dixon line is less intense and extends in mild-mannered fashion over many months, making it plausible to attempt rattling in bucks as early as September and often as late as January.

Virtually any antlers taken from a previously killed buck can be used for rattling, but some are better than others. I personally favor a moderately heavy rack with four widely spaced and rather lengthy tines on each antler. I've also learned that rattling antlers should be replaced about once every four years because by this time they have lost so much of their moisture content that their tonal qualities begin deteriorating. Many hunters have attempted to remedy this by periodically soaking their rattling antlers in a wash tub of water, but it's a temporary measure at best; better is just to obtain a new set.

If you don't perform a bit of surgery on your antlers before using them, you'll thoroughly mutilate your hands. Using a hacksaw, first remove the sharp points on the tips of the tines. This safeguard reduces the inevitable cuts and abrasions you'll otherwise incur when clashing the antlers together. It also eliminates the potential hazard of seriously puncturing your anatomy should you slip and fall while hiking to your stand. It's wise to then saw off or sand down any rough protrusions at the bases of the antlers around the burls, or your hands will quickly become tender and sore. Finally, drill holes through the bases of the antlers and run a 2-foot length of cord or thong through to connect them. In this manner, carrying the antlers is easy by simply slinging them over your shoulder, leaving your hands free.

I prefer to rattle during the early morning hours after a moonless night, then again later in the day toward dusk. It seems that when there is bright moonlight illuminating the countryside, deer remain quite active throughout the night hours and therefore are less likely to respond to daytime rattling. I also prefer just a bit of wind, but no stronger than what you'd describe as a gentle breeze. This puts leaves, weeds, and other vegetation into motion and somewhat obscures my own necessary movements.

• Keep in mind that when a buck comes to the sound of rattling antlers, he is responding to a specific sensory cue and then making a diligent attempt to visually pinpoint the source of that noise. In effect, then, *you* become the hunted! It should therefore go without saying that in the case of bowhunters, full camouflage is essential. And in the case of rifle, shotgun, or muzzleloading hunters, attention to detail must be given in the selection of an adequately concealed blind or tree stand.

Ideally, a location either uphill or west of heavy bedding cover is best, along with the liberal use of a doe-in-estrus scent, for reasons we'll explain in greater detail later.

In many instances, the best bet of all is for two hunters to use a teamwork approach when it comes to rattling. My son Mike and I do this quite often during both bowhunting and gun-hunting seasons, for the specific purpose of diverting an approaching buck's attention.

Because a buck will attempt to home in upon the exact location of the rattling sound, he is far less likely to detect a second hunter secreted 30 yards away behind screening brush or high above in a tree stand. Two hunters working close together also increase their safety margin, for there are twice as many eyes and ears to detect the inquisitive approach of other hunters, a stark possibility on public land where the sounds of meshing antlers in the woodlands may easily draw the notice of anyone within earshot.

Finally, and especially if you're bowhunting and therefore need a relatively close shot at an animal that preferably is standing still, using a territo-

To protect your hands when rattling, saw off the tips of the tines and sand down the rough protrusions around the burrs.

When rattling-in bucks, you become the hunted. For this reason, a teamwork approach is best. As the deer tries to home-in on the rattling noise, he is unlikely to detect the second hunter nearby.

rial infringement scent can help set up that very opportunity. This type of scent was described earlier and I feel it lends authenticity to the theatrics you're attempting to stage when rattling. Moreover, the source of the scent, once detected, also helps to occupy the buck's attention, again aiding in the diversion of his senses away from the hunter's stand area and to a specific location where you hope to have your shot at a stationary animal.

It might seem as if there would be a specific procedure for rattling antlers, but I think many other deer hunting writers have unnecessarily complicated the matter with precise instructions regarding hand-holding positions, duration of rattling, loudness, and many other supposed stipulations. I believe the entire procedure is relatively easy to master if you simply try to visualize the action you are simulating and don't worry about sounding perfect.

I once talked with noted Wyoming elk guide Gabby Barris and expressed my dubious concern over my ability to produce a bugle that would sound authentic enough to dupe an old bull.

"Don't worry about how genuine the bugle will sound to *you*," Gabby consoled. "Every elk is an individual. No two ever sound exactly alike, so just produce the best representation you're capable of and in most cases it will be good enough."

Consequently, I think much the same thing applies to rattling in whitetails. At various wildlife experiment stations around the country where study-deer are confined within large, fenced enclosures, I've watched bucks bang their racks together many times and have never noticed any strikingly common denominators. Sometimes they charge and deliver awesome blows, like bighorn sheep, then twist and grind their antlers together, with legs spread for balance and splayed hooves dug into the earth for thrusting power. Other times, the deer engage each other with far less ferocity, then quickly separate to perhaps individually spar with nearby bushes or saplings before having another go at it with each other.

However, timing is indeed important, at least from the standpoint of giving any buck in the region ample opportunity to first hear the rattling and then respond to it by traveling to your location.

I like to begin a rattling sequence by first grasping the antlers at the bases with the main beams turned outward, and then whack the beams together rather loudly, to simulate two bucks first making contact with each other. Then I turn the antlers around so they are mirror images of each other—in other words, so they are positioned exactly the way they grew on the buck's head—and with tines intermeshed I simply, well, rattle them. This simulates the engaged bucks now twisting their heads and jockeying for position, so the sound should not be as loud as the initial contact sound. I do this for about forty-five seconds and periodically couple other sounds with the rattling noise, such as breaking dry twigs, stamping my feet on the earth, raking the antlers against tree bark, scuffing dry leaves or gravel with my boots, and so on.

RATTLING TECHNIQUE

There are many acceptable ways to simulate two bucks fighting. I prefer to begin a rattling sequence by hitting the backs of the antlers together as if two bucks have made initial contact.

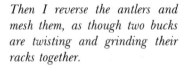

Then I reverse the antlers and mesh them, as though two bucks are twisting and grinding their racks together.

Next, I stamp the ground, drag the antlers through the leaf litter, and rake them across brush and saplings to add realism to the performance.

Next—and this is critically important—set the antlers down, pick up your bow or gun, and patiently wait as motionless as possible for at least thirty minutes. Then go through the rattling sequence again, as described above, and wait another full thirty minutes.

The great shortcoming of many hunters is enacting an acceptable rattling routine but then abandoning their posts if a buck doesn't show up almost instantaneously. Sometimes a buck will indeed charge to your location like a racehorse after you've enacted only five seconds of your first rattling sequence. But in a majority of cases it's a solid twenty minutes before they appear, and just as frequently it's not until after you've finished your second sequence do they seem to show any interest. I think that they hear the rattling but are wary of rushing headlong into any potentially suspicious or dangerous situation—especially subordinate bucks, which are well aware of more dominant animals in the area—and therefore merely take their time, perhaps circling widely at first to be able to make their approach from downwind. Then too, particularly on a very quiet day, the sound of rattling antlers can carry a very long distance and it may simply take the animal quite a long time to travel to your location. This is why an antler-rattling location should ideally be upwind of where you expect a buck is bedding. Otherwise, if the deer has to circle widely to make his approach into the wind, his arrival may be delayed or altogether discouraged. In being upwind of a suspected deer-bedding area, you should obviously be concerned about the breeze carrying your scent and alerting nearby deer. But if you place a semi-circle of scent bombs with doe-in-estrus scent, as described earlier, the problem is licked.

Most advanced hunters who are well versed in the art of rattling don't allow themselves to be glued to one specific location for more than an hour. If nothing has shown itself within thirty minutes following your second rattling sequence, move to another pre-selected site at least ¼-mile away and try again.

Whitetails will also use common vocalizations in various circumstances to communicate with each other. The hunter can simulate many of these sounds to better his chances of collecting a deer. And some sounds are even tailor-made to be used in conjunction with antler rattling to enhance the realism of one's performance.

For more than two centuries, hunters have been using assorted types of mouth calls to lure antlered big game into shooting range. The earliest of these attempts were for elk and moose, in which Indians used hollowed-out gourds, conch shells, and even blades of grass pursed tightly between the lips. Pioneers and explorers later used cone-like horns fashioned from birch bark and, still later, discarded powder horns with reeds fitted into their tip ends. Strangely, however, historical accounts reveal little or no attention ever given to calling smaller members of the deer family such as whitetails or muleys. Yet in recent years all of that has been changing and growing numbers of hunters are finding not just impressive but sometimes startling success, particularly with whitetails. Stories now abound of deer actually charging wild-eyed and ready for battle to a caller's location.

As was the case with antler-rattling, using mouth-blown calls originated in the brush country of south Texas. Curiously, however, deer were not the intended target species but rather an unexpected surprise when varmint hunters were using predator calls for coyotes, foxes, and bobcats.

Why a whitetail would eagerly respond to a call that sounds like a small mammal in distress, such as an injured rabbit, is unknown. But the fact that they do engage in such bizarre behavior is precisely why many hunters now integrate a wide variety of predator calls into their various deer hunting strategies.

My friend Bill Hoyt, of Houston, is a classic example, because he never goes deer hunting without his mouse squeaker on a lanyard around his neck and his "screaming rabbit" call in his pocket.

Interestingly, various types of predator calls that mimic small mammals in distress frequently draw the interest of deer as well.

"At first," Bill explained, "I used the rabbit call only toward the end of each vigil on stand, just before I was ready to give up for the day and go home, as sort of a last-resort measure. But after several years of noticing how it aroused the curiosity of deer, many of which I took during those final moments of waiting on stand, I began using it more frequently. The exciting thing is you never know what's going to show up. Sometimes it's a coyote, and other times a doe or small buck. In fact, it seems like young bucks are the most likely to show an interest in a predator call. To date, my largest that has been fooled by my screaming rabbit call was only a six-pointer, and I think the reason is that larger and older deer simply won't allow their curiosity to take precedence over their ingrained wariness.

"I've used my mouse squeaker with good success on big bucks," Hoyt continued. "When a buck is slowly feeding along in waist-high brush or vegetation and you can only see the ridge of his back, the squeaking noise will make him raise his head every time, to provide an easy neck shot. And one time I was sneak-hunting on a logging trail through a climax forest when up ahead I glimpsed the rump of a deer just as it was stepping off the trail into the timber. I couldn't tell whether it was a buck or doe, so I stopped immediately, raised my rifle to my shoulder, squeaked two or three times, and the deer came right back into the open to investigate. I credit that eight-pointer to my call because otherwise he would have been long gone."

It was in the late 1970s that biologists began intensively studying the vocalizations of deer. Among the most notable of these projects were those conducted by Dr. Thomas Atkeson and Dr. Larry Marchington at the University of Georgia, and Dr. Harry Jacobson of Mississippi State University, in which tape recordings of penned whitetails were scrutinized carefully and associated with specific types of behavior.

Although the biologists identified approximately fifteen distinctly different types of sounds emitted by whitetails under varying circumstances, the ones of greatest importance to hunters are: agonistic (sometimes called combative or aggressive) calls, mating grunts, alarm snorts, maternal bleats, and contact calls. If the hunter learns to identify, or interpret, these sounds he may be able to anticipate deer behavior. And if he learns to mimic several of the sounds, he can actually attract deer to his position.

Of all deer vocalizations, the *alarm snort* is undoubtedly the most recognized by hunters. A spooked deer produces this noise by violently expelling air through the nostrils with the mouth closed and in most, but not all, circumstances it is a reaction to something alien the deer has smelled but not yet actually seen or heard. Because a whitetail blatantly declares its own specific location when it makes such a sound, it is believed the snort is a means of announcing impending danger and thereby attempting to warn other nearby deer that may not be able to catch the foreign odor themselves.

Upon hearing such snorts, usually in sequence several seconds apart as the deer is enacting his speedy departure from the area, the hunter should intuitively know that he is the source of the odor. In some instances, this might mean the hunter's stand location was ill-chosen with regards to the prevailing wind direction, and without the use of a cover scent or other precautions (such as proper bathing) it was his recognizable human scent that gave him away. But it may also be that his chosen deer scent was the culprit. Perhaps the deer snorted as an adverse reaction to skunk scent or a scent used out of context. It could even have been the use of a territorial infringement lure that intimidated a small buck on the approach and caused him, in displaying his subordinate ranking, to beat a hasty retreat.

Byron Dalrymple claims he has seen hunters mimic the alarm snort to good advantage. "When deer are (bedded) in cover during the middle of the day, one hunter gets into position to watch a likely escape route. Then his partner 'blows' like a disturbed deer. After several repeats, often hidden deer will either sneak out to an edge to take a look or will go bounding from the cover, exposing themselves to shots."

In my opinion, however, although the ruse certainly has the potential of producing shots at whitetails, I feel it's a risky proposition most hunters shouldn't experiment with. For one, shots taken at hastily fleeing deer are shots too likely to only wound or cripple. But moreover, when deer panic in such a manner, it has been my experience that it may take days or even weeks for them to return to their normal behavior routines in that specific place, because they associate fear with it. If the season is only a week long, and you've only had time to scout a few key areas, you've therefore effectively reduced your chances of filling your freezer with venison. My friend Gene Wensel, the noted trophy bowhunter from Montana, even goes so far as to claim that merely missing a big buck with an arrow from a specific stand is just cause to relocate the stand, because there is little chance of getting a second shot in exactly the same place at that particular animal. And I firmly agree with him.

Agonistic calls generally consist of two types of grunts. The "low grunt" is emitted by both bucks and does on a year-around basis. It is a close-contact method of communication and represents the lowest level of aggressive interaction when one deer, invariably a subordinate, encroaches just a bit too closely upon the specific spot where a higher ranking animal is feeding or drinking. When an inferior deer takes this liberty, the higher ranking animal makes a deep, low-pitch gutteral blat. This usually wards the intruder away but if not, the dominant animal may then lay his ears back, dash forward, and administer a sharp kick with a foreleg hoof. The subordinate deer then knows to keep his distance.

The "grunt snort" is far more of a combative nature and although both males and females produce the sound, it is more common among posturing males when they are attempting to establish their hierarchal pecking order or when they are squaring off against each other during the mating season. Usually, the sound consists of two to six snorts in rapid succession, just as the deer are lunging at each other, to aid in the attempted intimidation of the other. Whenever I witness this vocal behavior, I'm reminded of the similar type of intimidation karate experts use when they shout loudly just prior to delivering kicks with the feet or blows with the hands.

Hunters can use the "grunt snort" to good advantage when rattling antlers. In fact, because it precedes the clash of antlers, using it any other time without accompanying antler sounds would be out of context.

To produce a "grunt snort" you need a call, or more appropriately a grunt tube. These are commonly sold throughout the Rocky Mountain states for use by elk hunters, but if you cannot find one locally you can always make one from an 18-inch length of plastic PVC water pipe. With your lips pursed tightly at the sides but slightly open in the very middle, as if you were about to blow through a straw, grunt into the tube by drawing small volumes of air deep from within your chest and expelling them rapidly so that it sounds like you are straining yourself to lift something very heavy. Do this four to six times between each clash of your antlers. As a precautionary note, remember the sound is supposed to be a grunt; if it sounds more like a wheeze, nearby deer may take it for an alarm snort.

In many instances, a nearby buck will be alerted to the goings-on and rush to the scene, fully expecting to find two other male deer dueling over his mating territory. The "grunt snort" also is an effective way of turning a departing deer that has been lured to rattling antlers but has not come close

To produce a "grunt snort," a grunt tube is necessary. These can be purchased in some regions, or you can make your own.

enough for a shot and now is beginning to drift out of range. In this case, however, a quick two or three grunt-snort sequence is plenty and need not be accompanied by additional antler rattling.

Maternal bleats are the soft, almost soprano-like mewings produced by fawns and yearlings when they want the attention of their mothers. In many cases, the attention they desire is to suckle and be groomed by licking, but generally this is whitetail behavior more typical of the spring and early summer months. Later in the year, during the fall and winter hunting seasons, maternal bleats usually are produced by that year's slightly older offspring that have become separated from their mothers and are uneasy about being alone. It is this maternal bleat that many commercial producers of deer calls attempt to simulate. Check mail-order hunting catalogs and sporting goods stores and you'll find such calls made by Burnham Brothers, P.S. Olt, Lohman, and others.

Interestingly, where whitetail populations are at least moderately high, adult females other than the mothers of attending fawns and yearlings commonly respond to maternal bleats. This is fine if you're willing to take a doe for freezer venison. But many hunters shy away from using a maternal bleat call, wanting to focus their energies exclusively upon bucks, and this can be a big mistake because there are two ways in which the maternal bleat call can result in antlers on the wall.

First, when an adult female is about to experience estrus but does not have a nearby, attending buck waiting for her "go ahead" signal, the doe will frequently make a similar bleat. It sounds just like the mewing of a fawn or yearling but is much louder. If you mimic this sound while sitting in a stand near a primary scrape, there's an excellent chance a buck in the vicinity will hear the supposed doe's calling to be serviced and respond to it.

Second, a doe who is just beginning to enter estrus may respond to a maternal bleat. In this instance, she hasn't peaked yet and isn't quite ready to be bred. The instinct to give attention to one of her offspring, or that of another adult female, at least for the moment supercedes her growing sexual readiness. If there is a buck in her company that is waiting for her to permit mounting, and she ambles away in response to a maternal call, the buck is positively certain to follow on her heels!

Mating grunts are extremely important for hunters to learn to recognize. Sometimes also known as "tending grunts," they are the vocalizations made by sexually excited males in two types of circumstances. A buck returning to a primary scrape and discovering fresh estrous urine will put his nose tight to the ground like a bird-dog making scent and will walk in a rapid, stiff-legged gait as he tries to catch up with the recently departed doe. Or, when the buck is actually in the company of a doe who is not yet quite ready to be serviced, he will follow closely behind, frequently closing the distance and licking her hindquarters and genital areas. Until she is ready to allow mounting, she'll ward the male away and he will drop back a short distance

"Tending grunts" are made by bucks hotly pursuing estrous deer. The sound is much like a pig rooting around in a feed bin or your stomach growling.

You can imitate a tending grunt by drawing the edge of a matchbook cover across the teeth of a rattailed comb.

and continue to grunt and follow, waiting for an indeterminate length of time before he approaches still again for another attempt.

Many years ago, when I described this tending grunt in *Outdoor Life* magazine, I said it reminded me of a euphoric hog rooting around in a feed bin. Since then, I've come to realize many urban hunters simply have never heard the sounds pigs make. Luckily, I've recently come upon an even more accurate description of the tending grunt, which anyone can recognize. It sounds precisely like your stomach growling when you're hungry!

It stands to reason that being able to identify the tending grunt is important, particularly if a doe has recently passed by your stand, because it signals the eventual appearance of a buck and the need to swiftly prepare yourself for an upcoming opportunity to shoot if the animal meets with your expectations. I positively love this type of situation because the buck is so preoccupied with catching up with the estrous doe that he seems totally oblivious to everything else going on in the immediate vicinity. He is the proverbial "sitting duck."

Although I know a few hunters who have mastered the tending grunt by using their grunt tubes, a good deal of practice is required. You have to pinch your nostrils closed with one hand, then with your mouth also closed bring short, low-pitched breaths of air up from your lungs and into your mouth. Easier, I feel, is duplicating the sound by trying to simulate someone snoring with his mouth closed; that is, by inhaling through the nostrils brief, intermittent volumes of air with your tongue pressed tightly against the roof of your mouth, to produce a distinct nasal resonance.

Still easier is buying a rat-tailed comb, holding the tail in one hand, and then drawing the double-edged side of a matchbook cover over the teeth in short, erratic stop-and-go fashion. Don't expect the sound to be very loud—a genuine tending grunt is a close-contact call—but on a quiet day it will nevertheless carry up to 75 yards.

There are two ideal times to use a tending grunt. One is when you want to try to "call back" a buck that is walking out of range after not coming close enough during an antler-rattling sequence. The other is done entirely in the absence of antler-rattling, while watching a primary scrape and imitating a buck trailing an estrous doe. If a higher ranking, dominant male is in the region, he'll be duped into thinking an estrous doe was visiting his scrape area and now is being escorted away by a subordinate, and he is not about to allow that to happen!

The *contact call* is simply a reflection of the gregarious, socially-oriented dispositions exhibited by whitetails. In short, they like to keep company with others of their own kind. Obviously, though, while drifting through a region during periods of feeding, they will occasionally fall out of sight of each other. The contact call, therefore, allows them to maintain a constant awareness of each other's locations in the absence of being able to keep visual tabs on one another.

The contact call sounds almost exactly like the low grunt described earlier but it is of longer duration and given only once. It is of special value when waiting on a stand in cover so thick that visibility is sharply limited. Should you suddenly hear a soft rustling in the leaves but nothing eventually steps into view, you might otherwise attribute the noise to a squirrel. At this time, mimicking the contact call can alleviate all doubts. If no mutual recognition response is forthcoming, you can indeed chalk up the sound as having been made by some creature other than a deer. However, if a deer is present, chances are excellent it will exchange mutual awareness by making its own contact call and perhaps slowly drifting in your direction to reorient its travel pattern with another deer it supposes is near.

Well worth mentioning at this point is something I've been experimenting with during the last two deer seasons. It comes about because of this question: "What is one of the most frustrating things that can happen to a hunter waiting quietly on stand?" In my own case, the answer is having an uncontrollable need to cough or clear my throat, yet knowing that to do so disrupts the silence and tells all the world that a human is present.

After engaging in a lot of practice, I've discovered I can effectively clear my throat and satisfy my need to cough by muffling my mouth over my jacket sleeve and simulating a contact call. It certainly is not the same valiant effort that's achieved when intentionally producing the low grunt described earlier, but it's undeniably better than hacking away in the usual manner and alerting every creature within hundreds of yards.

Finally, I'd like to emphasize that any hunter who is intent upon mastering

Records and tapes are available that allow you to hear the vocal noises of deer. Practice with your assorted calls until you can imitate the sounds—it may help you score.

the art of calling deer can take no better advice than to learn directly from the pros. Every year, numerous state wildlife departments and hunting and shooting clubs conduct deer hunting seminars where invited speakers demonstrate antler rattling techniques and various other calling methods.

And just as there have long been cassette tapes available for duck and goose hunters, there are now several that have been produced exclusively for deer hunters. What better way to learn to effectively call deer than to actually be able to listen to the sounds real deer make and then practice diligently until you can duplicate them?

In my estimation, the most recognizable and undisputed authority when it comes to calling all manner of wild critters is Murry Burnham. I suggest writing for his catalog (Burnham Brothers, Box 669, Marble Falls, TX 78654) that offers numerous types of deer calls, predator calls, cassette tapes, and instructional records.

Two other authoritative tapes I recommend are "Advanced Deer Calling and Rattling Techniques," produced jointly by Bob McGuire and deer biologists Dr. Tom Atkeson and Dr. Larry Marchington (available from B.H.P. Books, Box 3213, Johnson City, TN 37602), and "Rattling Antlers" by Tom Fleming and Dr. David Samuel (available from Locked Horns, Inc., Box 143, Davidsonville, MD 21035).

PART
IV

WHITETAILS
AND
WEATHER

17

How to Hunt Polyphasic Deer

◆◆

One of the biggest bucks of my life was taken on a day when everything started out so badly I was almost ready to throw in the towel.

This was in West Virginia's Monongahela National Forest, where I'd previously spent several days scouting transition-zone cover adjacent to a large stand of towering beech trees. I had picked out a prime location for my portable Baker ladder stand overlooking a trail intersection that was etched deeply with an uncountable number of tracks. But there was one set of widely splayed hoofprints that sent a surge of excitement through me that I'd never felt before, or since. I was certain I'd have my winter's deer meat within moments after shooting light creased the opening-day horizon, and I was equally confident the venison would be clinging to the carcass of an exceptional buck.

The following morning, bright sunlight glinting through my motel-room window brought me to an abrupt sitting position. It was 9 A.M.! My alarm clock didn't go off at 4:30 A.M. as it should have, and I had overslept.

Anyone who hasn't had the same thing happen at least once in his deer hunting career is either very lucky, or a damn liar.

I knew it would take still another hour to dress, grab my gear and hit the road, a half-hour to reach my parking place at the forest entrance, then another half-hour to hike to my stand. Skipping breakfast, I literally flew out the door, only to be greeted by a flat tire. Changing a 16-inch, 80-pound, extra-wide knobby tire on a four-wheel-drive is an adventure in itself, and I knew it would take only one additional setback for me to forget the entire day and head for a local tavern to drown my sorrows and curse my bad luck.

As it happened, I somehow made it to my stand without further incident. But after settling into my high perch, I glanced at my watch and shuddered when I learned it was almost noon. I didn't expect to see a thing, rationalizing that maybe I'd get a shot in several hours when late afternoon began blending into early evening.

Only 30 minutes later, however, I heard a scuffling in the leaves and very slowly turned around in my seat. Not more than 50 yards away, an awesome ten-point buck was methodically pawing through the ground litter in search of beechnuts. When the stock of my .243 Winchester pounded my shoulder, the warhoop that rang through the woodlands must have sounded like a berserk Apache on the warpath.

As happy as I was with how the day had made an unexpected turn-around, that experience caused me to begin seriously questioning a lot of my previous deer-hunting beliefs. Aren't whitetails, especially crafty bucks, supposed to be bedded during midday?

The answer to that question is an unequivocal "sometimes."

Recent scientific evidence is beginning to disprove the old notion about the early bird getting the worm, at least as far as deer hunters are concerned. Despite the widespread supposition that morning's first light is a prime time for deer, state-by-state statistics compiled from hunter survey cards tell a different story. According to these cards, the vast majority of whitetails taken every season are harvested between the hours of 9 and 10 in the morning.

This brings us to an inescapable conclusion: Contrary to popular belief, whitetails simply are not very active at the crack of dawn. Otherwise, a much larger percentage of deer would be taken around 7 A.M. (the legal shooting hour in most states).

Biologists classify deer as "polyphasic" creatures, which places them in the same category as animals such as rabbits and even fish such as largemouth bass. *Poly* means "many" and *phasic* means "recurring over and over again." *Polyphasic* therefore means the animal in question is well adapted to both day and night activity and consequently does whatever it wants, whenever it wants to do it.

True, whitetails commonly bed down to rest during the middle of the day. But depending upon weather conditions, mating urges, the availability of food consistent with the season, and a host of other variables, they may just as commonly feed and engage in other activities during the middle of the day and spend the night hours bedded.

The point to be made is this: In the particular county you have decided to hunt, not all the animals will be doing exactly the same thing at precisely the same time. Instead, like humans, they'll adhere to their own individual schedules and routines. This knowledge diminishes the idea that hunting success hinges upon being out early or late in the day. Actually, hunters can and should expect to encounter deer engaging in travel, feeding, and other normal activities virtually anytime.

While all of this makes a good case in favor of plunking yourself down on a stand at first light in the morning and staying put until it's too dark to see your boots that evening, there are nevertheless certain "prime times" in which you can tilt the odds in your behalf of encountering maximum numbers of animals.

Scientists have uncovered most of these so-called activity periods through radio-telemetry experiments known collectively as diel-period tracking studies. Deer are captured and outfitted with radio-transmitter collars that emit beeping signals of various frequencies to identify individual animals. Then the deer are released, and after being allowed a 48-hour recuperative period to recover from the stress of being handled, their hour-by-hour movements are plotted on topographical maps 24 hours a day, often for months at a time.

One recent study on the Fred T. Stimpson Wildlife Sanctuary in Alabama, conducted by biologists from Auburn University, shattered many long-held tenets by revealing that the vast majority of whitetail rutting activity does not in fact take place after full dark, as most hunters believed. Actually, there are two different time periods of mating intensity each day, the first being a relatively minor show of sexual behavior from 10 A.M. to 11 A.M., during which about 20 percent of the animals were attempting copulation. Later, from 2 P.M. to 3 P.M., the figure skyrockets to 50 percent!

During the breeding season, studies have shown that the most intense mating activity takes place between two and three o'clock in the afternoon. In such bright light, stands must be placed higher than usual to avoid detection.

What about the remaining 30 percent of deer that don't fall into either of those two time frames? Well, again, whitetail behavior is variable, with individual animals frequently doing their own thing whenever they are so inclined. Also, because does don't experience estrus at exactly the same time, only those animals at the peak of their cycles are likely to be the most active.

As a result, if all signs indicate the rut is in full progress in your region, sleep late if you must in the morning, quit early if you must as evening approaches, but plan to be on stand overlooking scrapes during the midafternoon hours.

But again, remember that during the previous 11 months, the animals have pretty much been left alone. Suddenly, opening day arrives and the woodlands are filled with an inordinate number of people dressed in neon colors, shooting rifles and chasing the animals hither and yon. Most of that activity, as you might suspect, begins about 9 or 10 A.M. when hunters, restless from sitting on stand for several hours, abandon their posts. It may be that they've decided to skulk around in hopes of seeing something, they yearn for a cup of coffee back at camp, or they think it's about time to hike back to the trailhead for a confab with the boys. In any event, as the hunters begin moving around, they roust deer from their beds or feeding sites and the animals predictably dodge the intruders by circling them widely. In a situation like this, it's patently clear the hunter who is able to patiently maintain his vigil is the one most likely to go undetected and eventually fill his tag.

In fact, during the last 15 years, the majority of my deer have been taken after 9 A.M. Sometimes the animals that came by my stand were placidly feeding, which told me they were following normal midday routines. Other times they were loping along with intended destinations in mind, stopping periodically to test the wind and look back over their shoulders; these deer were clearly saying they were trying to evade other hunters somewhere behind them.

Keep this in mind next time you're on stand and by mid-morning you're growing tired, cold, and bored. Other hunters stationed elsewhere are undoubtedly feeling the same way and are about to begin stirring around, and chances are good they'll soon push something in your direction. Or, in keeping with their polyphasic personalities, the deer may amble by of their own accord. Whatever the case, waiting on stand during midday probably offers double the chance of seeing deer as any other time.

If it's bitterly cold and there's no way you can sit down in a stand before morning's first light and tough it out until noon, and you know there are going to be plenty of other hunters in the vicinity, it might be best to simply avoid getting out too early. Wait until 8 or 9 A.M. before heading for your stand, with intentions of sticking it out at least until noon. I know this strategy is completely contrary to what has been written before, but it's paid off for me many times.

During cold weather, deer instinctively conserve energy. They feed and travel during the warmest times of the day (the midday hours) and rest during the coldest hours of dawn, dusk, and after dark.

There is another consideration involving midday hunting that demonstrates the way whitetails attune themselves to seasonal changes. Early in the fall, food is so plentiful that deer can quickly fill their bellies in little time. But they're now wearing their winter coats and midday temperatures can be quite warm. Consequently, the animals will want to feed early, then retire to some shaded glen or breeze-filtered ridge to sequester themselves. Toward dusk, they'll then return to feeding as soon as the air temperatures begin to drop once again.

The hunting method to use here is obvious. If you're a bowhunter and the season is sometime between August and October, the first two hours in the morning and the last two hours in the evening are likely to reveal the most animal sightings.

However, most hunters don't realize that as the season continues to progress, the deer become increasingly more midday-oriented. Food is steadily becoming less plentiful. In November and December, a deer may have to browse upon twigs and branch tips for two hours to fill its paunch with the same quantity of food it could obtain in only 15 minutes a month earlier. So if you're a rifle hunter or shotgunner, here again is still more support in favor of remaining on stand during the late-morning hours.

Finally, most states now stage special late-season hunts. In many cases, these deer hunts may be for the exclusive benefit of muzzleloader hunters or those using other primitive weapons such as crossbows. In other instances, they are special herd-reduction hunts designed to ensure the deer population does not exceed the wintering capacity of the available habitat. But whatever the exact nature of the hunt or your preference in sporting equipment, you'll want to entirely abandon the usual dawn-and-dusk patrol and instead hunt during the hours of 11 A.M. until about 3 P.M. Why? It's easy to understand if you examine a whitetail's basic biological needs.

As we've already mentioned, food supplies are at their very lowest from late December through the remaining winter months. But this is when the country also receives its coldest weather, and with food supplies being sparse, the deer instinctively know to maximize their energy resources. This prompts them to move around and feed during the warmest times each day (the midday hours) and to rest and conserve body heat during the coldest hours (dawn, dusk, and after dark).

The polyphasic nature of whitetails, however, is only a small aspect of their lifestyles. Other elements must be fitted into place for everything to come into clear focus. Take the matter of stand placement, for example.

Although whitetails may be up and around almost any time of the night or day, they have a distinct tendency toward using open areas early and late, and spending the midday hours in deep cover. But many hunters assume that when deer leave an open meadow and evaporate into thick brush or forest, they're seeking bedding sites.

Radio-telemetry studies have proven this is not the case at all, and the deer may remain on their feet for as much as several hours longer. It's just that when sunlight gets brighter and there is an associated increase in human activity, the shy critters gravitate in the direction of heavier cover to better conceal their movements.

Consequently, every serious hunter should make an effort when scouting to select several different stands that he can alternate between in accordance with the time of day and existing wind direction.

On my farm I presently have eleven permanent tree stands, plus several portable Loc-Ons and Screaming Eagles that can be installed upon a moment's notice if the need arises. By noting the wind direction, keeping in mind recent sightings of the animals themselves, and continually watching for new sign such as scrapes or increased trail use in specific areas, I'm always able to match the perfect stand to the prevailing conditions.

I may actually switch stands as many as three or four times a day. Naturally, if hunter activity is minimal in my region, an early-morning stand is likely to be somewhere along a cropland edge or overlooking a remote meadow. If hunting activity is moderate, mid-morning may see me climb out of that stand and quietly slip into another stand somewhere in second-growth transition cover. By late afternoon, I may be situated somewhere else in still deeper cover.

Of course, when hunting public lands, or as a guest on private property, it would be impractical to prepare a large number of stands for every contingency. But I always like to have at least two, and preferably three. What we're saying, then, is that the hunter who scouts minimally, installs only one stand, and then invests all his waiting hours right there regardless of the time of day or local hunting activity, is putting all of his eggs in the proverbial single basket. The disadvantages of this approach are so great it is no surprise that, statistically, only 20 percent of those who buy deer licenses each year eventually take home venison. But the hunter who remains flexible and has many options to choose from can dramatically increase his animal-per-day sightings, which in turn should increase his success percentage over the years.

So we know that during midday periods, the deer undoubtedly will have gravitated into heavier cover than where they previously were feeding during early morning twilight. But it's important to note that if the topography allows for it, the animals also will have moved in the direction of higher ground.

During midday, rising thermal currents begin sweeping toward the crests of ridges and drifting uphill into the heads of canyons, hollows, and drainages. As a result, whitetails instinctively know that higher ground is the place to be if they are to accurately test the air currents to detect anything trying to approach from below. There is also a visual advantage to being on higher ground.

The most productive stands, therefore, are located on higher ground and very close to, if not actually within, dense tangles of understory vegetation, brush cover, windblown trees, and the like. Furthermore, it's imperative that the hunter be there before the deer begin climbing for the higher elevations. If the deer beat you to the high ground, it may be impossible to hike to your stand without telling the world that you're coming.

Regardless of whether the hunter has decided to watch a trail intersection, scrapes, or known feeding areas, another matter of critical importance in placing the stand is the angle of the sun. During midday, some cover will be hidden in shadows while other spots will be bathed in light. Keep in mind that when a hunter is exposed in open places he is not only more readily visible to approaching deer, but the bright light will also tend to magnify even subtle movements he may make from time to time. Thus, a hunter will want to make sure that his stand will be well back in the shadows, away from where he expects deer to make their appearances.

For bowhunters this is easier said than done, because it is imperative they have relatively close shots, which often means placing their stands within 20 or 30 yards of trails or other sign. The cunning way to turn this seeming disadvantage into a distinct plus is to place your stand as high as state laws and practical safety considerations will allow.

My friend Jim Jorgensen has a stand from which he takes a nice buck year after year. It's on a ridge where a single pin oak carpets the ground with acorns each fall, and except for that lone tree, there simply is no other suitable cover around. Nevertheless, during midday, especially when it's very cold, the acorns are a drawing card beyond compare. To completely avoid detection, Jim's shooting platform is a measured 25 feet up in that oak tree. Once situated on his perch, he always makes use of some type of body harness or safety belt.

Jorgensen claims that deer frequently walk right beneath him during the bright midday hours, and his shots are always straight down. So effective is this shooting strategy that Jorgensen has never lost a deer in 20 years of bowhunting, and so effective is his unusually high midday stand he says he doesn't even bother to wear camouflage!

Gun hunters, of course, have a greater latitude in their stand choices. Not only can they station themselves much farther away, deep within shaded cover, but they can also use either tree stands or ground-level blinds.

Severe weather extremes may also weigh heavily upon deer behavior at certain times of day. My friend Barney Mott, a south-Texas hunter who has taken numerous trophies, seldom spends more than one hour on stand when certain conditions exist.

"Whenever we have a drought," Mott explained, "our streams and spring drainages become bone-dry washes, and in my immediate region stock tanks are far and few between. Now, water becomes more important to deer than food intake. And one of the ways they satisfy their need for water is by restricting their feeding to the late-night hours when alfalfa, clover and other grasses are heavy with dew droplets. I know it's the water they're after, not the food, because once they finish eating they continue to just lick the vegetation for long periods."

In fact, according to Mott, the animals sometimes spend the entire night in a meadow or pasture just licking for water. As soon as the early morning sun clears the horizon, the dew evaporates and the deer retreat to shaded cover to rest. So Mott's strategy is fairly well-defined. He scouts for the lushest meadow in the vicinity and situates himself before sunrise along whichever edge borders the heaviest cover, and intercepts the animals when

During very warm weather, or when there is a drought, water becomes more important to deer than food. Then they are drawn to lush meadows where they spend the night licking dew from the vegetation.

they leave at first light. Generally, he sees more deer during this single hour of the day than all other times combined.

But if a midday rainstorm suddenly begins after a long drought, Mott heads straight for one of his favorite stands.

"I don't care if it's high noon and the temperature is over 100°," Barney related. "Deer will suddenly be all over the place, drinking from puddles, water-filled tractor ruts, even ditches along roadsides."

So just chuckle next time your hunting partners begin talking about deer being "nocturnal" creatures that are most active at dawn, dusk, and during the night hours. Now you know the truth.

18

Hunting When the Freeze is On

◆◆

Without doubt, bass fishing and whitetail deer hunting are the two most popular pastimes of outdoorsmen. And as strange as it may sound, bass and deer are really very much alike, at least in the ways they respond to bitter cold weather.

Wise anglers know that bass do not experience discomfort when the water temperature plummets. They are cold-blooded creatures; their body temperatures always are the same as the water temperature. However, sudden changes in their environments do indeed precipitate changes in their behavior patterns. Generally, bass will drift away from the shallows and into deeper water as the thermometer falls because temperatures in the depths remain relatively stable on a day-to-day basis. Here, their metabolisms begin to wind down. The bass, therefore, do not require as much food. Consequently, these two alterations in their lifestyle can make them very tough to catch for all but the most experienced fishermen.

Although they are warm-blooded mammals, whitetails respond to winter's periodic onslaughts in much the same way—by abandoning their usual haunts until the weather either stabilizes or eventually reverses itself. Yet few people, aside from biologists, are aware that deer, like bass, also eat less as extremely cold weather approaches. Chemical changes take place in their bodies, causing their digestive processes to slow down. This, in turn, allows for the maintenance of various body systems at a greatly reduced rate of food intake.

Another important point about the anatomies of whitetails is that their brains are comparatively small in relation to their overall body sizes. Nature gives a creature only that equipment it needs to survive. Therefore, the integrated nervous system coursing throughout a deer's body is rudimentary at best. As a result, like most wild creatures that do not possess a sophisticated neural apparatus, a whitetail's pain threshold is quite high, making the species relatively insensitive to bitter cold. Most hunters simply are not aware of this because for generations they've been lead to believe that when the weather turns sour, deer can be expected to do this or that in order "to seek protection from the elements and be more comfortable." In reality, nothing could be further from the truth.

Body comfort actually has little to do with their changed behavior patterns. After all, the northern boundary of the whitetail's native range extends more than 150 miles beyond the United States/Canadian border to approximately 52° latitude. Anyone who has lived thereabouts, or even visited, can tell you that winter temperatures frequently *average* 20° below

Leonard Lee Rue III

Contrary to popular belief, whitetails are relatively immune to cold weather. Their rudimentary nervous systems, low pain thresholds, and superior insulation endow them with the ability to stand even below-zero temperatures without undue discomfort.

zero, and whenever there is an associated wind-chill factor it often seems as cold as 75° below zero. It just doesn't stand to reason that animal species such as whitetails would be native to such hostile climes were they not virtually immune to such weather.

We've even seen evidence of this immunity right where we live in Ohio. I don't have any explanation for it, but we often experience the most horrible winters imaginable and the 1984–85 winter was particularly severe. We had ten consecutive days in which the air temperature never climbed above 15° below zero, and on two consecutive mornings, it had dipped as low as 28° below zero. With near gale-force winds ripping across the landscape, our local radio station reported a wind-chill factor of 80° below zero and issued warnings to not go outside except in case of an emergency. Well, I stuck my head out the door just to see what it was like and within one minute I could feel the skin on my face beginning to freeze. Later that same day, through binoculars, I watched several deer feeding in corn stubble on our south meadow. I was amazed to see two nine-month-old fawns frequently stop feeding in order to romp and play as they ran in circles and chased each other through six inches of powdery snow. They obviously felt perfectly "comfortable."

In other years—also when the temperature was well below zero—I've had similar experiences with whitetails. Behind my barn there is an old tractor trail that winds its way downhill, eventually leading into a 15-acre oak forest. Many times, while hauling out firewood, I've seen deer bedded on nearby slopes. Often they have a thick dust of new-fallen snow on their backs, the hollow hairs of their coats providing such superb insulation that their body heat is unable to escape. If I approach too closely, the deer will predictably rise to their feet, shake themselves off like wet dogs and cause clouds of snowflakes to fly, then saunter off to parts unknown.

If deer are able to adapt to such gelid temperatures so easily, why is it that legions of otherwise knowledgeable and hard-working hunters so often strike out when the freeze is on?

Say, for example, that you've been hunting in balmy temperatures for several days, and you have had the opportunity to look over a number of animals but haven't seen anything of "wow" dimensions that you'd be pleased to hang in your trophy room. So you've decided to hold out a while longer, hoping the gods will smile upon you with good fortune and you'll eventually stumble onto "Mr. Big."

You wake up suddenly one morning to the sound of icy sleet pinging against your bedroom window. Bounding from the bed, you are shocked to discover that the wind is whistling and that the temperature has dropped 35° overnight.

After sitting on stand for several hours that morning without seeing a thing, you look and feel like a popsicle. So you begin moving around—sneak-hunting—but eventually conclude that the deer have vanished. By day's end, the temperature has fallen another 10°, a light skiff of hoarfrost blankets the ground, and your expectations have long since dwindled. You've forgotten entirely about taking a nice buck this season and have begun thinking that if you can somehow just manage to fill your doe tag for "freezer meat" you'll be very lucky.

The all-too-common scenario I've just recounted is the bane of all hunters living north of the Mason-Dixon Line. Because it's obvious that the deer couldn't possibly have just disappeared from the face of the earth, the best prospect for success undoubtedly lies in learning more about their behavioral reactions to severe weather.

One of the most telling clues to unraveling the mystery of their disappearance can be traced to changes in the whitetails' body chemistry—the changes that cause them to require less food. Biologists say that this is an annual occurrence, and like the rut, it is triggered by progressively shorter days and diminished periods of sunlight. Sometime around mid-November, the growth hormone thyroxin, which for the past eight months has been flooding the body, begins dissipating and will remain at a very low level until the following spring.

This shoots down another popular myth about bucks not feeding much during the rut because their thoughts are so preoccupied with sex. Actually, their reduced food intake can be attributed to a conservation measure on the part of nature. In other words, with each additional week of cold weather, food becomes less and less available, so nature accordingly reduces the animals' need for food by enacting significant changes in their body metabolisms.

Hunters should realize that as the season progresses and increasing numbers of severe arctic blasts begin descending upon their regions, deer can be expected to move around less and less in search of food. Moreover, the movements they do exhibit are no longer going to be concentrated during the traditional early and late hours of the day, but during midday when it is likely to be warmest. Again, the deer are not seeking "comfort" but rather are conserving energy more efficiently to make use of the sharply reduced food supplies.

I've seen this happen consistently. At our northern Minnesota hunting camp near Hinckley, members of our regular group begin bowhunting in October. We've learned from more than 80 years of combined experience that the odds of taking a whitetail early in the season are in our favor if we take up early morning stands, nap during midday when deer are likely to be resting in deep cover, then resume our vigils late in the afternoon.

But a full two months later, during the final days of the gun season, those in our party who still have not scored have entirely reversed their strategies. Now the order of the day is to sleep late in the morning, wait on stand during midday, then quit early. There's just not enough liklihood of seeing anything on the move—particularly at dawn's first light—to justify the oftentimes agonizing ordeal of sitting as still as a statue in weather so cold that it gnaws at your innermost fiber.

Of course, the most serious hunters—diehard veterans who are never willing to give up—may find such tactics repugnant. As far as they're concerned, they want to be in the field every available minute. That's fine and dandy, but if they want to maximize their chances for success, they should still be willing to make certain adjustments in the way they hunt.

Late in the season, and most notably when the freeze is on, they should stillhunt or sneak-hunt early and late in the day when deer are most likely to be bedded. During midday, hunters should play the waiting game on stand when deer are inclined to be traveling to and from feeding sites.

But where, exactly, do the deer go when the bottom falls out of the thermometer and ice storms or sheets of wind-driven sleet are lashing the countryside? Unquestionably, it's into thick cover on a southeast-facing slope in a low elevation area in the morning, then moving over onto a southwest-facing slope in a low elevation area in the afternoon.

Two of the most desirable types of thick cover are dense stands of head-high honeysuckle and nearly impenetrable pine plantations. The pines are

During periods of bitter cold, waiting on stand during the midday hours is the best bet. Find thick cover on a southeast- or southwest-facing slope in an area of low elevation; then locate trails to nearby feeding areas.

most often thickets of immature trees that have their whorls of branches close to the ground. In a manner of speaking, deer retreat into virtually the same types of cover as when heavy hunting pressure has them spooked.

In the face of adverse weather, whitetails retreat deep into such seclusions and wait it out. Again, trying to stay warm or achieve some other measure of comfort has little to do with their evasive behavior. Windy, stormy weather makes deer extremely restless and nervous. By their very nature, whitetails are already hypertensive and are extremely paranoid creatures. When they're no longer able to detect, classify, and catalog sounds and scents because of the competition from noisy winds and erratic air currents, they waste no time finding a place where they can maintain a low profile. Therefore, rather than allowing themselves to remain vulnerable by bedding on their customary hillside benches or ridgelines, they retreat into deep cover in the lower elevations. This not only helps to block the wind and make things quieter, but may also gives them the feeling that hiding from ready view somewhat compensates for their impaired senses.

The states where I deer hunt most frequently—Ohio, Minnesota, Wisconsin, Kentucky, West Virginia, Pennsylvania—are also the states where I pursue ruffed grouse. They, too, are very nervous, high-strung species—more so, I believe, than any other upland gamebirds—and whenever the wind is blowing they instantly vacate their usual hillside haunts. And the places where they go are precisely the same as those favored by deer under similar conditions!

Once, for a period of several days in the dead of winter, I had the opportunity to watch an eight-point whitetail buck in a fenced enclosure. This was a wild deer that had recently been captured by biologists for use in various nutrition studies. Its temporary, fenced-in home was 5 acres of relatively open hardwood forest with scattered swatches of second-growth ground cover here and there.

Whenever the weather was warm, sunny, and there was no wind, the buck had a particular place it liked to bed. The deer could see in every direction from the high hammock. Yet whenever a frontal storm system moved through the region and the wind began howling, the deer quickly vacated its usual turf. It always went downhill into a little pocket of thick multiflora rose—the only significant cover in the compound—and buried itself right in the middle.

One day as snow clouds scudded against an ominously gray sky and ice-riddled branches creaked in the wind, I watched in amazement as the buck laid on his belly for long hours, his front legs outstretched and his chin resting on the ground. But when the wind occasionally intensified with its typical freight-train drone, or an ice-laden branch suddenly crashed to the ground, the buck's head would instantly come up, swiveling in all directions. Assured that nothing was on the prowl, the buck would then quickly duck back down again. Moments later his head would be up, down, then back up again. Under these conditions, the buck's entire personality was like a violin string about to snap.

A biologist at the research station told me that during one terrible winter storm, the penned buck stayed put for four consecutive days until the weather finally abated. I'm confident that the penned buck would have preferred access to much thicker and deeper cover to increase his feeling of security. I'm also certain that unconfined deer in their native habitat behave much the same way when the freeze is on.

In addition to tangled jungles of honeysuckle and conifer forests, white-tails also like to retreat into swamps when the weather is unsettled. Swamps are always located in low-lying terrain and are somewhat sheltered from the brunt of the weather.

But no matter what type of cover deer may elect to use for hiding, hunting them when the freeze is on can be an exercise in exasperation because the animals are so alert to any signs of danger. But there are several tactics that seem to be far more productive than others.

First, of course, pay attention to weather forecasts. Deer seem to have built-in barometers that give them advance notice when hostile weather is about to assault their regions. They take advantage of this insight by stock-ing up on groceries, instinctively knowing that once the bitter weather strikes, it will preclude safe traveling to and from feeding sites for perhaps several days. Then, immediately after the frontal system has passed and calmness again prevails, the deer come out of hiding and return to their favorite food plots. Consequently, stand-hunting or sneak-hunting—just before and immediately after a storm—are two key strategies.

Low-pressure fronts are most likely to bring with them windy, blizzard-like conditions that are sure to curtail deer movements. Conversely, high pressure fronts *usually* bring moderating weather. The real fun begins when one of these high pressure systems, with above-freezing temperatures, sud-denly comes near the tag end of the deer season. The phenomenon, often referred to as the "January thaw," not only brings deer out to feed but may also reveal a resurgence of rutting activity. You just have to hope that the unpredictable arrival of the "thaw" coincides with that 28-day, post-estrus peak in which previously unbred does are coming back into heat a second or third time. If the stars are in your favor, breeding activity will be going on, and the biggest bucks will be right in the thick of it.

After the passage of a severe frontal system, cornfields can be prime places to find your venison. Particularly throughout the Midwest and the northern border states, it is becoming an increasingly popular agricultural practice to leave corn standing as long as possible. In the past, it was either combined or chopped for silage sometime in October or November. But with grain-elevator storage costs escalating like never before, and future market prices uncertain, many farmers nowadays are leaving the corn in the field until such time as they have a specific need for it or until the price increases, which it often does in February and March.

Already-picked cornfields are also good bets because a substantial amount of harvest residue may continue to draw deer months after the crop has been combined. On our own cornfields we're sometimes amazed to see a dozen deer at a time pawing through a foot of snow cover to find spillage.

I emphasize the importance of finding corn when the freeze is on because native wild foods are becoming more and more sparse with each additional week of winter weather. Other popular agricultural foods such as soybeans are rarely allowed to remain in the field beyond their peak harvest times, so corn is a deer magnet beyond compare.

Hunting during a storm can also pay off. The best opportunity occurs during the passage of a weak low-pressure system in which the temperature does not fall dramatically. This usually means that the wind velocity will not be too fierce and any precipitation is likely to be in the form of huge wet snowflakes that begin clinging to brush and tree branches like giant globs of cotton candy. Under such conditions, whitetails don't seem to become as jittery and frantic about their safety and may continue to feed during midday periods. The fluffy snow itself may also pacify them just enough during nonfeeding periods so that they will remain tied to their usual haunts rather than dive headlong into thick security cover.

Hunting during the most ravaging freeze-outs offers the least chance of success. Now, patiently waiting on stand is inherently a futile endeavor. The animals simply will not come to you, and this makes it necessary for you to go find them by skulking through swamps, honeysuckle, brush thickets, or evergreens.

Never try to approach such cover on level ground. Any deer hiding within it will merely vamoose out the other side, giving you only a fleeting glimpse of their flags. Instead, try to dope out the lay of the land—or better yet, study your topographical map—and then approach from high ground. This will allow you to look down and through the cover, and will make it far easier to spot bedded or sneaking deer.

Another tack is to team up with a partner, which is the way I really prefer to hunt under conditions that have forced deer into hiding. The key to success is in being so intimately familiar with the terrain from previous scouting missions that you know exactly where an old buck is going to lay up when the weather turns sour, *and* the precise escape trail he can be counted upon using in an attempt to sneak away from approaching danger. One hunter then establishes himself overlooking that route, while his partner enters the cover from the opposite side and disturbs the buck just enough to make him attempt to slip out the back door.

During the 1985–86 whitetail season in Ohio, my friend Al Wolter and I enacted this strategy and it worked like a charm. I enjoyed the fantastic luck of taking a nice eight-pointer only five minutes after sitting on stand on

Hunting during a storm can pay off. I like to sneak-hunt when wet snowflakes cling to cover like big gobs of cotton candy. The animals seem to be less jittery, and I can walk in the woods silently.

opening morning—and was flabbergasted to receive a trophy at the deer check station for having harvested the very first buck of the season in Morgan County—but Al had decided to hold out for something really splendid or take nothing at all.

By the time the final day of the season rolled around, however, Al changed his mind and decided his home freezer needed more venison after all. Trouble was, the previous night a storm-front had moved into the area. Blizzard-like snowflakes were flying horizontally, creating a veritable white-out that reduced visibility to 25 yards. There was only one hope for success and that meant putting Al on The Last Chance Stand (all of my stands have names, this one appropriately so because it's where I station hunters who have yet to score). The stand is located at the end of a steep hollow choked with honeysuckle and it overlooks a well-worn escape trail bucks use when routed from the vegetation. When I was sure Al was in position, I then entered the cover at the head of the drainage and simply began hiking toward him. I had scarcely progressed a dozen yards or so when Al's shotgun cracked in the distance, maybe 100 yards ahead of me. Then I heard his traditional warhoop and knew the season for both of us now was officially over.

Hunters can enact this ploy virtually anywhere there is dense security cover. All it takes is plenty of planning in the form of reconnoitering the terrain for the most likely escape route, then investing plenty of patience and unselfishness to slowly push deer to each other. But keep in mind that if the deer have been spooked by intense hunting pressure during the week, they will be reluctant to leave their hiding places or travel far. This is a tailor-made situation in which neither of the two partners have filled their tags, because chances are good it will be the moving hunter who kicks out a deer at very close range and is awarded the shot.

Another option is to round up several hunters and begin staging drives, particularly in the case of expansive pine plantations. This is the same type of situation, not unlike hunting rabbits, where the drivers themselves are likely to see just as much shooting action as the hunters placed on stands. Remember, when deer have retreated into the catacombs of thick cover they are extremely reluctant to expose themselves or to sever their close ties with that cover. As a result, a buck pushed out by a driver may *appear* to be in the process of charting a bounding and weaving escape flight that is destined to take him into the next county, but he'll probably travel less than 50 yards before he quickly ducks back down to resume hiding.

Because the drivers are likely to be engaging in shooting from time to time, those hunters placed on stand should use portable tree stands situated as high as practical so they are not in the direct line of fire of their approaching partners. Also—and this cannot be emphasized too strongly—every hunter participating in such a maneuver should be fully clad in fluorescent orange clothing and should maintain loud voice contact so everyone is well aware of each other's location.

When hunting during freezing stormy weather, wise garment selection also requires careful thought. For sneak-hunting or stillhunting, wool is always the best bet because it is nearly noiseless when the fabric grates against brambles and brush. But when toughing out long hours on stand, the relatively open weave of wool fabric allows wind to quickly make you feel like an ice cube. Then, I rely exclusively upon down-filled duds, bundling up like a snowman, with a tightly woven nylon exterior shell to thwart the wind.

I'd be the last to say that hunting deer when the freeze is on is purely enjoyable. Human beings just weren't designed for bitterly cold weather. But when such conditions prevail, any hunter can indeed fill his tag. Just keep in mind the changed behavior the animals are certain to begin exhibiting and plan your strategy accordingly.

19

Deer Hunting
When it Sizzles

◆◆

Throughout the Northeast and upper Midwest, generations of whitetail hunters have come to rely upon "good tracking snow" as the most accurate barometer of success.

However, sometimes mother nature throws them a curve in the form of sultry temperatures that seem more in keeping with August than what they've come to expect in late November. With furled brows they find themselves dismayed as to where the animals are and what tactics might prove best. And as it often happens, many simply relegate their outings to watching a waterhole somewhere, hoping to ambush something that might wander by.

For many years I was a member of that very fraternity. Then one autumn I was invited to hunt deer on an old plantation in Butler County, deep in southern Alabama. The temperature was a blistering 96°, quite atypical from their usual 80° deer hunting weather. But not only did every member of our party eventually collect a nice deer, but I also had a startling revelation.

These hunters, it suddenly dawned on me, probably never hunted deer in the snow. Some of them didn't even own insulated boots or long johns. To them, numb fingers were something you momentarily experienced when adding more ice cubes to your favorite drink at day's end. But these southern hunters consistently enjoyed just as much success as my cronies living north of the Mason-Dixon Line.

Talk about throwing still another wive's tale into a cocked hat! Clearly, as I learned, the old adage about "good tracking snow" being a requisite for success was nothing more than pure nonsense.

Now that whitetails now range over a vast expanse of the continent and have colonized an infinite variety of terrains, few concrete axioms can be laid down that will apply to each and every situation when hunters unexpectedly are faced with hot weather. But by taking a page from the southern deer hunter's notebook, then plugging local conditions into the equation, hunters everywhere can tilt the balance in their favor.

First consider a whitetail's need for water. They are required to drink periodically, which is not a trait shared by all members of the animal kingdom. Many animals, particularly small game species and members of the rodent family, seldom need to drink because they can metabolically manufacture their own water from the foods they eat. Deer, on the other hand, have a daily requirement of 1½ to 3 quarts of water per 100 pounds of body weight. This rate is variable because factors such as extent of exercise, air temperatures, evaporation rates, and the percentage of mineral salts in the animal's customary diet play a major role in the frequency with which body fluids must be replaced.

Even the specific foods whitetails may be tied to influences their water requirements. Curiously enough, warm temperatures during the fall and winter hunting seasons may see the species exhibit a higher water intake than any other time of year. With succulent vegetation rapidly disappearing and the animals making a transition to low-moisture-content woody material (browse such as twigs and branch tips), additional water intake is necessary for the digestion process. Also, after early October, deer are wrapped in their heavy coats in order to retain as much body heat as possible and to insulate themselves from temperatures which, under normal conditions for that time of year, should be ranging from cool to bitter cold.

Many hunters presume deer satisfy their need to drink by regularly visiting obvious sources such as lake shores and streams, but this may hold true only in certain parts of the country. From the arid Plains states, down through Texas, and into the desert Southwest, hiding in cover and watching a *resata* (stock pond) may indeed be the secret to collecting many venison dinners, as may watching a bubbling creek or lakefront where scouting has revealed the convergence of several deer trails. In such perpetually parched regions, whitetails are intimately aware of the locations of major, widely separated water sources and home in upon them with regularity.

However, exactly the opposite situation exists in a majority of other whitetail states where a plentitude of water is to be found in many forms. Our farm in southern Ohio comes to mind as a ready example. Here, I've seen deer drinking at the conspicuous water sources such as the small lake behind our house, from all three streams that meander through the acreage, and from the several springs pockmarking the landscape. But I've just as often seen them drink from many inconspicuous places such as roadside culverts, drainage ditches, puddles where recent rainfall has gathered, and sheet metal stock tanks in pastures. Once, I even saw a small buck drinking from

Deer satisfy their thirst primarily in lakes and rivers. In most states, however, an abundance of water is found in other forms as well.

In blistering hot weather, even an apparently dry creek bed such as this may reveal tiny spring seepages and pools.

a rainwater-filled tractor rut and another time observed a doe licking a wet rock face in a shaded gorge where a bare rivulet of water slowly seeped from a fissure in the granite.

In most regions of the country there is an abundance of surface water, and the deer there are opportunists when it comes to drinking. As a result, parking your britches on a stump overlooking any particular water source can prove to be a dismal failure. But in arid regions, or when severe droughts are associated with hot weather, a lone source of water somewhere can attract deer from afar.

At the 21st Annual Conference of the Southeastern Association of Game and Fish Commissioners, biologist E.D. Michael shed still more light on the drinking habits of deer, which should benefit serious hunters who have studied local conditions and decided that water-watching might indeed pay off.

Among his many research findings, Michael learned of three peak times of drinking activity. They are 7 A.M., 11 A.M., and from 4 P.M. to 6 P.M. If deer could talk, we could ask them to explain these rather arbitrary drinking times—perhaps their cud-chewing periods and related body metabolisms

Deer also drink from rainwater-filled puddles, stock tanks, roadside culverts, and many other less conspicuous places.

are a determining influence—but in any event the wise hunter will want to keep these times in mind, especially when hunting in arid climates.

During the remaining hours of the day, whitetails may involve themselves in any number of other activities, provided weather conditions and air temperatures are normal for that time of year. But if unseasonably warm weather begins baking the countryside, there are some very specific types of behavior they're most likely to engage in. And still again, the topography of the terrain determines where they'll be and what they'll be up to.

Throughout the southernmost reaches of the whitetail's range where a generally mild late-season climate allows farmers to extend their crop-growing operations well into the fall and early winter months, grain fields often provide unparalleled hot-weather hunting excitement.

I remember one October when my pal Jerry Bartlett and I were hunting in Sumter County, South Carolina. The temperature had pushed well into the nineties and our logical conclusion was to sneak-hunt the ridgelines where we figured slight breezes would offer deer some respite from the heat. We were dead wrong and found the sun to be pounding the ridges relentlessly, so we next plodded downhill into a winding, narrow bottomland bordered by sheer hillsides. It was shady there, but not a wisp of air could move and it was like being in a sauna with the lights turned off. No deer were there, either.

Finally we decided to hike back to our trucks for lunch. As we walked the last few yards out of the bottom and came to an adjoining 10-acre soybean field, Jerry suddenly spotted a six-point buck standing in the middle of the beans. Then the buck just as suddenly dropped down and out of sight, like he had fallen through a trapdoor.

"This is going to be the easiest deer we've ever taken," I whispered.

After a momentary confab, we crouched low and began slinking across the bean field, confident that when we got within 25 yards of the buck it would stand up and we'd have fleeting seconds to drop him at point-blank range before he was able to run away. We never really decided which one of us would take the shot, but it doesn't make any difference because we never had a chance to put our plan into action. Before we had covered half the distance to the buck's location, four does that we didn't know about rocketed out of the beans several yards in front of us. Seconds later, the buck followed on their heels, leaving us the ones that were flushed—with embarrassment.

Nevertheless, through nothing more than pure chance, we'd made an intriguing discovery. To make a long story short, we forgot about eating lunch and simply hunted every soybean field we could find where we were able to secure trespass permission. In each case, our method was first to hike slowly around the perimeters of the fields, in the hope something might be bedded along one of the edges, and then walk between the bean rows themselves, criss-crossing the middle of the fields. In all, we jumped more than a dozen does and five bucks that afternoon, and attached our tags to three of the latter.

In retrospect, it's obvious why the deer had elected to bed in the bean fields on this torrid day. The waist-high canopy of overhead cover offered concealment and shade from the sun, irrigation furrows between the rows of beans provided a ready source of drinking water, and the deer had instant access to one of their all-time favorite foods. What more could they want?

For the very same reasons, cornfields can be havens for whitetails during heat spells. Even in northern climates, where for decades it has been traditional to cut corn before the first frost, it is becoming increasingly common to leave the corn unharvested in the fields late into the winter or until such time as it is sold or needed for stock forage in order to reduce or eliminate storage expenses. Thus, if the weather is unseasonably warm, find still-standing corn and you'll undoubtedly find deer.

The difficulty of hunting deer in standing corn is one's sharply reduced range of vision. Hunting alone or with a partner just won't do, because the deer are reluctant to leave the corn and will lead you on a merry chase for hours. They'll crash out ahead of you, making all kinds of commotion as they flush wildly through the dry and brittle cornstalks, and you'll be lucky to just catch a blurred glimpse of buckskin. With distance gained, they'll then downshift into sneak-gear, and maybe even resume bedding, until such time as you once again approach just a bit to closely and experience an encore of their previous performance.

Consequently, there are only two ways to obtain shooting opportunities at deer in corn. One is to assemble a relatively large number of hunters—at least eight—and begin making drives. Yet this can be extremely dangerous if the participating members don't take special safety precautions. If hunters designated to wait on stand are positioned at ground-level vantage points, they won't be able to see the drivers moving through the corn, so it's imperative they instead make use of portable tree stands to give them a clear view from above the corn. In this manner, not only will they be able to see both the drivers and the deer moving ahead of them, but any shots taken will be at a sharp downward angle toward the ground.

The second ruse is to sneak-hunt through the corn by yourself, or with a partner moving along a parallel route not more than several rows apart so that you're occasionally able to catch glimpses of each other's orange clothing. But the secret to any success you hope to achieve in this type of hunting is that it *must* be done on a day when there is a moderate to brisk wind. This will cause the corn to rattle noisily, effectively camouflaging each instance in which you brush against dry leaves and stalks and create noise. Any shots are virtually always close-range affairs as a bedded deer is just rising to his feet. Many times, if a buck happens to be facing the opposite direction, you'll be able to take him right in his bed.

Again, the lay of the land and the types of cover native to the area undeniably have the most telling influences upon deer location and their behavior patterns during hot weather. About the only universal application is that hot weather prompts whitetails to be far more active than usual during the night hours. By the time the morning sun has lifted entirely off the horizon, you can count upon the vast majority of animals to be tucked away in their selected hiding places for the remainder of the day, and although they may rise around 11 A.M. to stretch their legs and drink, they are not likely to travel far.

As a result, the prime time to sit in a tree stand or in a ground-level blind is the first hour or two of morning light. After that, you might as well abandon your post and go searching for the animals because they are not likely to come to you—not even at dusk. During hot weather periods, it generally takes a while for the evening air to begin cooling down. Consequently, deer may not begin stirring around until two or even three hours after full dark.

As to where the animals bide their time during the midday hours, we've already seen that grain fields are premier attractions. In non-agricultural regions, think "shade." In many parts of the upper Midwest, throughout the Plains states, in scattered portions of the South, or for that matter wherever the terrain is relatively flat, mature woodlands are automatically eliminated from consideration. The hardwoods there have long since lost their leafy canopies, which allows the bright sun to almost fry the forest floor.

In every part of the country, whitetails are far more active than usual at night during hot weather than during the day.

When temperatures are far above normal, deer like to bed along the edges of forested north-facing slopes where thick brush and successively aged hardwoods are bathed in shade for the greater part of each day.

Heavily forested regions can reward the hunter with explosive action. Look for blown-down trees where deer are likely to find both shade and concealment in the tangled branches and limbs.

However, in the predominantly hilly or mountainous regions throughout the Northeast, down the Atlantic coast into the Carolinas, then sweeping westward into the Ozarks, the story is entirely different. Now, the ideal place to gingerly poke along is a forested north-facing slope where a mixture of thick, dead brush and successively-aged hardwoods are bathed in shade for the greater part of each day. The next best bet, beginning several hours after sunrise, is a very steep east-facing slope.

In any region inhabited by whitetails, whether flat or hilly, stands of evergreens and cedars remain green and "leafy" throughout the year. If they're surrounded by wide expanses of territory exposed to the sun, virtually every deer in the immediate vicinity may be secreted deep within their confines.

The trick again is to locate middle-aged conifer plantations. Acreage with tall, mature trees won't hold deer because their lower branches have long since died from lack of sunlight, which leaves the understory void of cover. Immature trees that still have dense whorls of branches close to the ground have not yet towered high enough to provide understory shade from the sun. Those which are middle-aged, however, ranging from 20 to 30 feet in height, afford the best of both worlds: shade *and* concealment.

Once again, this thick cover makes for close-range shooting opportunities. In fact, because the predictably present carpet of pine needles offers such silent footing, it's frequently possible to walk right up on bedded deer. Soft wool clothing aids the effort by not signalling your approach when pine boughs occasionally swish against you.

Once I was sitting on a bowhunting stand on a private farm near Atlanta and, after several hours of seeing nothing, decided to hike to an alternate stand. The shortest distance meant going straight through a plantation of white pine. I was intent upon getting into my alternate stand as quickly as possible and was therefore moving along at a good pace. Sneak-hunting was the farthest thing from my mind and I didn't even have an arrow nocked on my bowstring.

Then up ahead I spied a dead buck. It appeared to be a smallish six-pointer and my first guess was that it had been the attempted target of a poacher, or maybe it had been hit by a car on the nearby road, had escaped into the supposed safety of the thick pines, and eventually expired right there. I walked over to take a closer look at the animal and when I came to within 10 yards it suddenly sprang to life and dashed off. That sucker wasn't dead at all but had merely been sleeping in the heat of midday! He was in a location where he probably never expected to encounter a human being and the combination of the noiseless footing on soft pine needles and my wool clothing had allowed me to walk right up on him. Although I had absolutely no chance to take that deer, it's happenstance occurrences like this that add immeasurably to the education of a deer hunter and may well contribute to his success on another day, in another place.

On the most sultry days, when high air temperatures find themselves combined with oppressive humidity levels, whitetails also seem to gravitate toward those shaded areas closely bordered by cool, moving water. Find a stream capable of supporting trout tumbling down from higher elevations, or a smallmouth bass river rushing through a rocky gorge, and the swath of terrain bordering its northerly or easterly sides will seem almost air conditioned due to the shade and the "misting" effect of the bubbling water.

How close deer will be to the actual edge of the watercourse, where it's coolest, depends chiefly upon how much noise the water is creating. The animals don't want their sense of hearing impaired to the extent that they are vulnerable to close approach.

The water may be slapping rocks and boiling through shallow rapids, which is typical in the canyon-like land area stretching eastward from Missouri and Arkansas, through Kentucky and West Virginia, and down into North Carolina and northern Alabama. Then, look for the deer to bed singly in pockets and recesses high above the water, or in small groups of two or three in the shade of boulders, outcroppings, or small clumps of cedars or hawthornes. In this situation, approaching the deer's suspected locations from above, by skulking along the rim of the gorge and peering down into the jumbled cover formations, can be quite effective.

But if the water is only serenely gliding along, which is common in the flatlands of Michigan, up through Minnesota and into the Dakotas, deer may bed in relatively large groups right at the water's edge wherever there is shade afforded by willows or thick stands of tag alders. The density of the cover, however, offers little choice other than to drive the animals out to partners stationed at downstream or upstream vantage points. This can be a very tricky proposition, as I once learned during such a drive along the banks of Minnesota's Kettle River.

The drive ran like a well-oiled machine and every hunter on stand saw deer. Unfortunately, they were all does. The one buck that had been consorting with the lady deer, we later learned, refused to follow after them as they attempted to escape in a northerly direction. Instead, he ran directly west, dove into the river, and began swimming toward the opposite shore. We spotted him—a nice eight-pointer—just as he climbed out of the water and up the muddy bank where he stood for long moments, gawking at us. It was as if he had clairvoyantly sensed the predicament we'd have been in if one of us had dropped him with an easy 75-yard shot, because it would have taken us two days of back-breaking labor to drag him from that side of the river to the nearest access road, and that state of affairs bought his ticket to freedom.

Again, forested ridges are not always breeze-filtered or very sought-out places by deer in hot weather, due to the absence of a high canopy of leaves in fall and winter to block the assault of the bright sun. But there are several notable exceptions.

If you can find an exceptionally large tree, such as a beech, sycamore, or maple that has recently been uprooted by a tornado or was felled by lightning or high winds, it may well serve as an oasis where a sly buck has chosen to hide. For approximately two years afterward, the latticework of branches and limbs offers a dark maze of hiding places. A crafty deer may belly-crawl right into the interior and not budge unless an equally crafty hunter actually kicks the limbs with his boots. This type of deer hunting definitely is not for the weak-hearted because nothing is more unnerving than a whitetail buck crashing out of such cover a few yards away.

In subsequent years, the felled tree's location is worth many repeat visits. With sunlight now permitted to bathe the forest floor in that very area, thick ground vegetation is sure to have taken root and sprouted. The species you should most hope to find are those remaining thick and leafy throughout most of the year, such as rhododendron, laurel, multiflora rose, greenbrier, and particularly honeysuckle.

In our region of southeastern Ohio, honeysuckle commonly is head-high and so nightmarishly dense that whitetails bull their way through and under the stuff. In time, they create an endless network of passageways and tunnels beneath the greenery. Because honeysuckle grows best on south-facing slopes and may even blanket entire hillsides in almost impenetrable jungle-like fashion, such a place is ideal to escape both hunting pressure and the unrelenting heat of midday sun.

When deer are hiding in honeysuckle, the sport that follows ranks as possibly the toughest whitetail hunting anywhere, except perhaps when deer are hiding in the vast seas of thornbrush and cactus of south Texas. In both cases, even the hunter who is quick with a rifle is destined to a discouragingly low success rate if he chooses to hunt alone. About the only tactic that merits consideration is a well-planned pincer movement with large numbers of drivers spaced close together to prevent the animals from dodging the hunters and sneaking back through the drive line. Or, find the main trails deer use to enter and leave such cover and be there, in a portable tree stand or self-standing tower, at least one hour before morning's first light.

Hunting deer during unseasonably warm weather doesn't mean the balance is tipped decidedly in the animals' favor. It only means their habits will have temporarily changed in order to adapt to the prevailing conditions. If you keep the words water, shade, and cover in mind, you'll be right where the deer themselves have decided is the best place to be.

20

Be a Weather-Watcher

◆◆◆

Ask five deer hunters to name the best rifle caliber for whitetails and you're certain to receive five different answers. But ask one hundred hunters to describe the most difficult hunting conditions they've ever experienced, and you can bet this month's rent all of their answers will have something to do with severe weather extremes.

Weather influences the behavior of whitetails more than any other aspect of their environments. Although this weather may range from bitter cold to searing heat, in between these two extremes are a wide variety of other, less intense conditions that typify fall and winter deer hunting. Most are in some way associated with storms, and at times they can have a dramatic impact upon the nature of feeding and bedding activities of deer, as well as the travel routes used to and from those locations.

Of the many specific types of unsettled weather that may prevail from time to time, frontal conditions and related barometric changes seem to have the greatest effects.

Those particular cold fronts typified by falling barometric pressures and violent weather generally see a sharp change in normal deer behavior. (Not all cold fronts fall into this category, nor are all so severe). And those particular warm fronts typified by steadily rising barometric pressures and calming weather usually are just the opposite and tend to stimulate deer activities. (Again, there are exceptions).

However, in any case it is not a sudden drop in air temperature that makes deer dive into hiding, nor a gradual rise in temperature that causes a resurgence of activity. Rather, it is the unsettled weather itself, associated with the leading edge of a low pressure front, especially the increased wind velocity, which plays havoc with their abilities to use their sensory apparatus effectively. The calm that follows hours or days later, and generally is associated with a high pressure system, is the animals' pacifier and encourages them to resume their former behavior.

It's worth emphasizing again that in any situation involving the onslaught of frontal conditions, whitetails, from a strictly physiological standpoint, are virtually immune to severe weather. They do not have extensive collateral blood circulation through their extremities, nor low pain thresholds, nor sophisticated central nervous systems to relay signals of discomfort to their brains. Their core temperatures are easily maintained by special winter coats acquired in September, which are comprised of thick, hollow hairs that trap air and retain heat as efficiently and in exactly the same manner as DuPont's Holofil insulation. (DuPont's "miracle" insulation was developed by synthetically copying the winter hair of deer).

This brings us back to frontal systems—north or south, cold or warm— exerting their influence upon deer behavior by causing their senses to become virtually inoperative.

Place yourself in a whitetail's world. You live within very close proximity to man, which in itself makes you feel continually jittery. Your genetic framework has a strong aversion toward predators; long ago you had to watch out for wolves and big cats, but nowadays the danger comes from coyotes and free-roaming dogs.

Consequently, within your adopted home range, it's clear that survival depends on your being able to monitor your surroundings. When weather conditions are relatively calm, your keen senses of vision, hearing, and smell are superbly geared to the task of forewarning you of danger.

Suddenly, the weather begins to change and your bailiwick becomes a frenzied kaleidoscope of swaying tree trunks and ground cover, howling winds, clacking limbs, and erratic air currents that sweep through from one direction only to reverse themselves in some other chaotic fashion.

Your predictable reaction, of course, is to chart a non-stop course for some type of protected seclusion, hunker down, and wait for the tempest to subside. It also stands to reason that if you could somehow forecast this coming weather a day or two in advance, or even only hours in advance, you'd seize the opportunity to stock up on food to see you through the tough times of hiding and inactivity. Furthermore, the minute the weather conditions stabilized, allowing you once again to make effective use of your senses, you'd be on your feet again, heading for some favorite food source and then a watering site.

Until we can teach whitetails to talk, all of this is speculative. Other unknown factors may enter the picture, but scientists who study whitetail behavior contend this is basically the way the species operates in the face of changing weather conditions.

Where do the deer go? In any given region, deer are restricted by the landform options available to them. As a general rule, however, whenever possible they will go downhill and into the thickest cover they can find on a south-facing slope.

At the approach of stormy weather, dense pine plantations are especially favored by deer, as are cedar brakes, stands of brushwood in low elevations, and stands of honeysuckle, rhododendron, and laurel. But remember: Whitetails do not retreat into such places seeking "comfort" but rather security during a brief period in which their senses are impaired.

Now, let's place ourselves in a different realm, as deer hunters in search of our quarry. Because whitetails seem to possess internal barometers enabling them to forecast the approach of frontal systems, it's best to use the same strategy to beat them at their own game.

This means diligently keeping abreast of weather reports, and even buying a barometer that can be checked daily. (A word of precaution: Many people buy a barometer, hang it on a wall someplace, then receive totally erroneous information. Every barometer must first be calibrated to the particular elevation above sea level where you live—or plan to hunt—and instructions packed with each instrument tell you how. Then, check your barometer's readings against those given by a meteorologist during a local newscast to ensure your barometer is functioning accurately.)

If it is possible to plan your hunting days somewhat in advance, watch for a barometer reading that is beginning to fall. This indicates a rapidly approaching storm front and deer will be out in full force, even during what might otherwise be unfavorable midday periods. Now is when a hunter should enact his sneak-hunting skills around the perimeters of corn and soybean fields, alfalfa meadows, or on the crests of oak ridges carpeted with acorns. Or, he may elect to wait on stand overlooking trails leading from deep security cover to known feeding sites.

Exactly the same approach should be used the day or two after a frontal system has passed through your region and the barometer has once again begun to rise, heralding moderating conditions that allow deer to move out of their secluded hiding places.

It's even possible to go one step further in this pre-hunt planning with regards to distant hunting trips. Say, for example, your favorite deer hunting location is 100 miles west from your home. You're packed and ready to leave for several days to visit that region, but upon checking a weather report you learn the area is presently besieged by a low-pressure system and terrible weather. In this instance, following through with your intended plans would unquestionably be a big mistake. Not only would you probably take a physical beating from the weather, but the animals would be holed-up in damned-awful places and deer sightings would therefore be minimal. Because most weather systems generally travel from west to east, your home area is about to receive the same bad weather in a day or two. Check your barometer and you'll undoubtedly see the first signs of it beginning to fall. Your best move would be to cancel your plans in order to hunt closer to home during pre-front conditions, as deer are likely to be up and around almost everywhere. Or, at least delay your visit to the western part of the state by several days in order to hunt moderating, post-frontal conditions.

If your close-to-home hunting grounds are presently under assault by in-progress frontal conditions, you have three options. One is to delay your intended hunting for several days until the barometer begins to rise again, signaling the eventual arrival of a high-pressure system. The second is to pick some area of the state you like to hunt that is far to the *east* of your home, where you can ply your efforts during pre-front, deer-active conditions. And the third is to drive to the western part of the state to hunt post-front, deer-active conditions.

To be sure, many times we simply can't pick the best hunting days to be afield, nor can we travel far from home on the spur of the moment. Job and family responsibilities for many of us entail very regimented lifestyles that allow hunting only on certain prescribed days of the week, regardless of what the weather may hold in store. Or, upon occasion, we may find ourselves far from home, embarking upon that big once-a-year campaign we've looked forward to for so many months, when adverse weather may threaten the success of the outing.

In either case, there are a few time-tested ways to at least slightly swing the odds back in your favor. First, if your home is your base of operations for one or two-day local hunts, closely monitor weather conditions as we described earlier, so you'll know whether to hunt feeding areas or deep security cover.

When away from home, it's not likely you'll have a barometer in camp, but you may have a radio for tuning in local weather forecasts. If not, learn to be a sky-watcher in order to anticipate approaching weather systems, and thereby know which hunting techniques are likely to prove the most effective.

Alto-cumulus clouds gathering on the north or northwest horizon, with accompanying winds blowing from the south or southwest, are sure indications of a falling barometer and an approaching cold front. Depending upon the latitude, the temperature may be dropping rapidly, or only a few degrees at a time, but in any case now's the time to be afield from the crack of dawn until late evening. Pack a lunch, hunt pre-scouted feeding areas, and don't even think about giving up until it's so dark you can't see the tops of your boots.

The actual arrival of the front generally will be hallmarked by the presence of either alto-cumulus clouds that have grown steadily darker, or alto-stratus clouds that give the sky a solid gray overcast. The wind velocity will have increased dramatically and it will be coming from the south, southwest, or even the southeast. Beginning spits of rain or sleet are still another portent of even more turmoil in the offing.

Alto-cumulus clouds gathering on the north or northwest horizon with winds from the south or southwest indicate a falling barometer and the approach of a cold frontal system. Now is the time to hunt scouted feeding areas.

Alto-stratus clouds are accompanied by strong winds from the south, southwest, or southeast and often the beginning of rain, sleet, or driving snow. Now, waiting on stand is a futile endeavor. Still-hunting is the recommended tactic.

Expert skywatchers know the arrival of scattered cumulus clouds means the approach of a high-pressure system and moderating weather conditions. Again, this is the time to intercept deer at their customary feeding grounds.

Until the front entirely passes through the region, waiting on stand for deer to come to you is a futile endeavor. If they move at all during these weather conditions their travels will be extremely short, both in duration and distance covered.

This is a perfect opportunity for stillhunting. Because of the noisy wind, you need not worry about silent moving as the rustling ground leaves and creaking tree trunks will obliterate any noises you may periodically make. It is necessary, however, to move slowly, with long pauses in between each forward advance. Amidst the continual movement of surrounding cover, it will be difficult for deer to pick out the specific, brief movement of a hunter. Don't allow your scent to obviously travel ahead of your line of progress if the prevailing wind is clearly coursing in a particular direction; otherwise, its swirling, unpredictable direction from one moment to the next may actually be to your advantage, as deer will not be able to ascertain the exact direction the scent is coming from. This will cause them to stay put longer until their other senses can positively identify something not to their liking.

When hunting low-elevation, protected cover, try to avoid traveling across level ground. More often than not, your only reward will be fleeting glimpses of bobbing white flags. Better, whenever possible, is to remain on slightly elevated terrain, such as sidehills or terraced benches, that allow an unobstructed view down into thick cover to spot bedded deer or those attempting to sneak away.

These circumstances also are tailor-made for holding drives with partners. But, I've learned from past experience that frontal conditions that have forced deer into hiding do not require as many hunters placed on stand as might otherwise be warranted. One stand-hunter, or perhaps two, overlooking strategic locations such as escape trails, may be plenty, with all the remaining hunters in the party spread out in a long drive line that moves slowly and silently. Under such conditions, whitetails pushed from their beds are quite reluctant to travel long distances. With their senses impaired by the weather, they feel more visible and vulnerable the longer they remain on their feet.

Consequently, it's common for a deer to be rousted from its hiding place by drivers, only to travel a short way and then quickly hunker back down again, or immediately turn right or left in an attempt to circle the hunter who jumped it. This means that if you move a deer from its bed, you may have a shot at it. But more than likely, it will be the driver to your immediate right or left who sees the action; only infrequently will a stander placed farther ahead see the animal come loping toward him.

If it seems, a day or two later, that the front may be showing signs of leaving the region, again check the sky for confirmation. A clear night sky with a light breeze from the north or northwest, or very high and scattered cumulus clouds with gentle breezes from the north or northwest, both usually mean the approach of a high pressure system, moderating conditions, and eventually fair weather. Now's the time to once again have high hopes of intercepting deer at their customary feeding grounds.

But if the sky remains overcast and winds continue emanating from some southerly direction, expect continued foul weather. Particularly across the Midwest, it's not unusual for two or three succeeding cold fronts in a row to pass through the region before the arrival of another high pressure system. Ohio seems especially plagued by weather designed to torment deer hunters, and it seems that about once every three years the annual deer harvest simply doesn't measure up to the projections and expectations of the Division of Wildlife. Invariably, the reason is that a low pressure system began moving across the state shortly before opening day, followed a couple of days later by a second cold front, and then a third. Understandably, with the Buckeye State having only a six-day deer hunting season, shotgunners simply don't enjoy much shotgunning. The deer have retreated into thick security cover and just don't move or engage in otherwise normal behavior. Sometimes the weather is so terrible, even the hunters themselves are forced to sound the retreat call. And even when a high-pressure warm front does eventually arrive, its leading edge may be characterized by unsettled weather. By then it's of no consequence anyway, because the last day of the season is now history.

There's no argument from me that hunting in the face of brutal frontal conditions is difficult for both the body and the spirit. But by acquiring a fundamental knowledge of how weather systems travel across the country, and how whitetails react to pre-front, resident, and post-frontal conditions, any serious hunter can expect to return to camp with more than just memories of the day afield.

PART V

REFINING BASIC TECHNIQUES

21

Sneak-Hunt Your Buck

◆◆◆

An old proverb says, "Man learns more from his failures than from his successes." Whoever coined the adage may have had deer hunters in mind because when it comes to sneak-hunting, or stillhunting, one quickly becomes aware of more than just a few stark realities.

First, while it may be enchanting to think of ourselves as modern-day Hiawathas when we creep into our favorite deer woods, senses dulled by the softness of 20th-century living quickly take their toll and we find that trying to get close enough to a deer in order to place a telling shot is fraught with frustration and disappointment.

Let's face the facts. None of us can see as well as a deer, smell as well as a deer, or silently slip through the forest like a deer. Indeed, we don't even know our way around the forest all that well.

Deer, on the other hand, have absolutely nothing better to do with their time but try to survive, make little deer once a year, and thoroughly acquaint themselves with their habitat. They're out there, rain or shine, 365 days a year.

The point is this: Of all the many different types of deer hunting strategies, sneak-hunting is unquestionably the most difficult. Therefore, I recommend it for only the most serious hunters who are willing to invest the required time and effort to learn to do it right. Yet balancing the rather dubious success rate that even an advanced hunter might come to enjoy is a nice pay-back. With whitetails being so incredibly crafty and cunning, the bucks you do take while stillhunting will afford far more personal satisfaction than deer taken by any other method.

My own most memorable buck would make an inveterate trophy hunter blush with embarrassment because that deer's vital statistics included being only 2½ years of age, weighing only 155 pounds and wearing a modest (okay, call it puny) six-point rack. But I never worked so hard for any buck in my life. I met that buck one-on-one, playing by his rules on his home turf, and when I won I knew I'd earned my venison. Although I've taken much larger deer before and since, there's not a single one that brings back as much memorable pride.

This was the year I made a commitment that I would not allow the entire season to pass with my butt glued to a board high up in a tree. I'd sneak-hunted before without a smidgen of success, but that made the possibility of eventually scoring seem all the more challenging. Finally, I decided *this* was the season.

I saw the buck three times in three days, and each time it was only a fleeting glimpse of his south end heading north. That was when I learned the first rule of successfully sneak-hunting a buck: You have to spot your quarry before it spots you. If it's the other way around, forget it, because any whitetail knows how to get from Point A to Point B with such evasive slickery the most sagacious CIA official would turn green with envy.

One way to see more deer, obviously, is to do your homework so your later efforts will be engaged in those places where there is a noteworthy deer population. This means not only studying harvest figures from previous years, but also doing plenty of scouting. It's also important that you scout during the early and late hours of the day, because such an approach allows you to derive two benefits for the price of one: In addition to being able to find and evaluate signs of the animals' presence, you're likely to see them as well because dawn and dusk generally are prime times for them to be on their feet.

Deer tend to come into fairly open feeding areas early and late in the day, so it stands to reason that some of the finest stillhunting opportunities are to be had on lush meadows, croplands, creek and river bottomlands, and forest edges where low browse is available. But don't venture into these open, brightly illuminated places. Stay back inside the edges of the available cover and cling to the shadows. Whitetails, especially if they are hard-hunted, are usually on the lookout for a whole man, and they seem to have difficulty identifying one when they can only see a part, such as an arm. Therefore, when you are about to peer into an open meadow or along the edge of a woodlot, try to look around a tree trunk or hedgerow. The surrounding cover will break up your outline.

Sometimes it's easy to spot deer from ridges and hilltops, but never silhouette yourself against the sky. Travel just below the crest, watching ahead and below to your side. From time to time, I also like to look over the crest, particularly when I know that on the other side is a clearing, a stand of oaks that recently dropped a good acorn crop, or some other food source. When I do so, I try to peer through brush or other cover.

With a likely area picked out, the next order of business is forming a realistic attitude. My experience has always been to lower my hunt expectations. There just aren't that many Boone & Crockett deer running around out there, and when it comes to sneak-hunting, *any* buck collected is a worthy trophy. Not only that, but the thing most aspiring still-hunters need more than anything else is field-smarts, a few successful encounters, and experience. Learning to sneak-hunt with visions of record-book bucks in mind is one of the surest ways to mentally defeat yourself right from the beginning.

The second rule is something many hunters just never seem to accept when it comes to sneak-hunting: The distance you travel during a day's hunting is meaningless in terms of your anticipated success. On some sneak-hunting endeavors I've spent more than an hour negotiating only 100 yards of difficult cover, and many experts say I move too fast! So when a member of your hunting party returns to camp boasting that he must have hiked eight miles that day, he's ripped his bloomers as a skilled sneak-hunter.

In a sense, this brings us back to the first rule, which has to do with seeing your buck before it sees you. One way *not* to have that happen is by hurriedly

When sneak-hunting, always stay in cover and move slowly. In thickets like this one, taking an hour to travel a hundred yards may be moving too fast.

legging it mile after mile. Deer are highly adept at detecting movement because of a high number of rods, or daylight-adapted motion detectors, in their eyes, and it's this feature of their anatomy that usually spells a hunter's undoing. When he's statue-still, a hunter may not be noticed for what he is, even at short ranges. But the instant he begins moving his arms and legs, every deer in the neighborhood knows it and takes appropriate evasive action . . . which, coincidentally enough, is usually freezing in place.

So heed the timeless advice Ottawa chieftain Pontiac repeatedly gave his braves when leading the Indian rebellion against the English in 1763. He admonished them to "Walk a little, watch a lot." In other words, the less you walk, the more you see. This is exactly the tactic I used on that first buck I successfully sneak-hunted and described earlier. I melted into his environment and became just another tree, but one whose roots weren't permanently anchored in place.

Even the time of day a hunter chooses to skulk through deer cover can weigh heavily upon the outcome. Surprisingly, the vast majority of hunters do the opposite of what they should, by plunking down somewhere in a stand or blind early and late in the day, then sneak-hunting during midday when most deer may be bedded.

This just may be the primary reason why sneak-hunting has traditionally carried such a low success percentage in most hunting circles. When deer are bedded, they'll undoubtedly have chosen a location designed to afford the utmost security. In order to monitor their surroundings, they'll most likely be on high ground, which allows them to have a good view of everything around them as well as test the rising thermal currents of air carrying the scent of anything that may approach from below. They'll also very likely be in dense cover, which is not easy to navigate without making noise.

So the deer now have four distinct advantages working in their favor: They're lying down and difficult to spot, and because of their chosen vantage points can quite easily see, hear, or smell anything coming around that may present a threat.

Given this, how can a noisy, smelly, moving hunter get his venison? Well, in most instances he can't, which is exactly the way the deer plan it. Oh, it does happen upon occasion, but usually as a result of one hunter's misfortune turning into another hunter's luck. That noisy, smelly, moving hunter unknowingly alerts the deer and rousts them from their beds, and in making their escapes they accidently stumble into another hunter doing his thing some distance away.

Therefore, a cardinal rule of stillhunting is this: Do your sneak-hunting early and late in the day when you'd ordinarily be tempted to wait on stand. Your chances of success will skyrocket.

Early and late in the day the deer are most probably moving around, and generally not in dense cover. This means they're much easier to see. Also, they're probably feeding, at least intermittently, or drinking, or traveling to or from feeding and drinking places, or they may have courtship on their minds. In any event, the nature of whatever activity they're involved in at least partly occupies their senses with things other than their immediate security. This preoccupation is their Achilles heel.

The way I learned about this started out as bad luck, but quickly turned to good. Because of a tight work schedule one fall, I didn't have time to either scout or prepare a new stand. The only option was going to the tree stand I'd built the previous year, hoping deer were still using the trail it overlooked.

So there I was, fifteen minutes before shooting light on opening morning, horrified to discover the stand had fallen into disrepair and couldn't be used! The first alternative was to curse my bad luck and go home. The second alternative was try to repair the stand, but in so doing I would probably make so much noise no deer would stay in the vicinity. And the third alternative was to forget about sitting on stand and begin sneak-hunting.

As it happened, I saw more deer that morning than I'd ever seen while perched in a tree stand. What's more, they never saw me. By staying in shadows, just inside the leading edges of woodlots and brush cover, I skulked along at a snail's pace, checking out alfalfa meadows and clover pastures. The deer I saw would periodically jerk their heads up to survey their surroundings, but when they were convinced that nothing was amiss they'd lower their heads again to continue their breakfast. That was when I'd move forward a few more steps to a renewed vantage point.

I took a sleek forkhorn buck that morning, which may not sound like much. But considering how the morning had started out, and my gloomy attitude when looking at my broken-down stand, it was like finding gold in a mudhole.

There's a three-pronged system that works best for most accomplished sneak-hunters. First, meticulously scan the terrain ahead of your line of travel, searching diligently for deer. With nothing in sight, now search the ground immediately in front of you to plan your forthcoming two or three steps. Naturally, you'll want to tread only upon noiseless ground materials such as flat rocks, damp earth, hardpan, wet leaves, soft snow, or pine needles, as opposed to crusted snow, dry twigs, crunchy leaves, loose gravel, or brittle duff. This may necessitate traveling a zigzag route rather than straight-line; of course, you'll also want to make use of intervening cover to hide behind. With your footfalls so planned, you now quickly pan the distant landscape again, to confirm your first inspection, and if again you see no deer you now move forward in slow motion.

Then it's back to the same routine again: Pan the terrain, plan footfalls, pan the terrain again, then move.

This is a crucial aspect of sneak-hunting, but few hunters realize that you only need to move a few feet at a time to gain a new view of your surroundings. As you move only two or three steps to a new location, you'll find yourself looking through the same cover but with a different angle of vision and, consequently, spying an entirely new scene. Sooner or later, this small change in the way you see things will enable you to spot a deer, but because you're traveling so slowly, the deer will not likely see you.

The quietest way to walk is by using what is known as the rolling compression step. I learned this from Steve Carter of Springfield, Missouri, one of the most proficient stillhunters I know.

"Moving quietly is almost as important as moving slowly," Steve tells beginners in the college-level nature course he teaches. "In fact, it is such an artform that some of my biologist colleagues—the famed Valerius Geist, in particular—have actually developed the ability to sneak up and touch a deer!"

A bit skeptical about this, I once hiked with Carter to a nearby forest containing mixed hardwoods and brush for a casual test of his skill. I began stillhunting as quietly as I could, and he told me he would follow at about 5 yards behind and occasionally offer advice or corrections.

About fifteen minutes passed, and Steve hadn't said a word. I was beginning to feel smug. Finally, I turned around to ask him a question and he was gone! He was absolutely nowhere in sight and yet he had managed to disappear without making a sound. He made his point, and I realized how quietly a hunter can move if he knows how. A bit later, a voice said "Hello, John" directly behind me and I almost fell down with startled surprise. Steve had circled around and returned, again without my hearing the rustle of a single leaf.

"You have to learn a new way of walking," Steve told me. "Take very short steps because if you try to combine your regular long stride with a very slow forward movement, you'll frequently come close to losing your balance, and when you try to regain your footing your spontaneous reflexes will work more quickly than your mind, causing you to place your foot where you may not want it. And that is likely to cause noise. In using the rolling compression step, you can put your heel down first, or your toes, whichever happens to be the most comfortable to you and allows for the greatest balance. I prefer to put my toes down first because when wearing soft-soled boots I have a greater degree of sensitivity in feeling the ground cover I'm stepping upon. In any event, after your toe or heel is planted, then 'roll' down the remainder of your foot very slowly to minimize any sound. As you are rolling-down your foot, if you begin to feel a twig or some other noisemaker, simply roll your foot back in the opposite direction to release the pressure being exerted upon it and move it several inches to the right or left. Once that particular foot is firmly planted ahead, then and only then should you transfer all of your weight to that foot and begin thinking about bringing the trailing foot forward in the same manner as before."

In addition to learning a new way of walking, it's also necessary to learn a new way of "seeing."

The problem with our human vision, as it relates to deer hunting, is that when we look off into the distance we tend to pinpoint our focus upon a small area. As a result, if an animal 100 yards away is just 10 yards outside of your concentrated area of focus, you probably will not see it. You then may erroneously conclude no deer are around, begin your next forward advance, suddenly hear a loud snort, and moments later see a deer bounding away. All of this occurred because deer do not identify things by first looking at them in pinpoint focus. Instead, they view their surroundings with a wide-angle perspective that allows them to catch the slightest of movements, even when they are taking place around the outermost periphery of their visual scope. After that movement is detected, then they pinpoint their focus upon it for further classification.

Successful sneak-hunters are those who have trained themselves, when panning the terrain ahead of their line of progress, to at first not intently look at any particular feature but with eyes moving slowly from right to left, then back again, concentrating upon picking up any movement that may be taking place in the distance. Only after no movement is spotted do they take the cover and terrain apart piece by piece.

This is where learning to recognize small parts of a deer's anatomy proves invaluable because you'll seldom see the whole animal at first, especially in deep and shady cover. A curved white stick in a trellis of dead brush, for example, may actually be an antler tine; a horizontal line in a stand of vertical saplings may be a deer's back; a black shiny nose, a white throat patch, the glint of an eye, or a swatch of brown in a tangle of greenbrier may lead to the completion of the picture puzzle. The expert stillhunter often discovers that what he has been looking at is really only an odd-shaped tree branch, a rock, or some other inanimate terrain feature, but sooner or later it will turn out to be part of a deer.

Once I was stillhunting in a copse of cedars in Michigan's Upper Peninsula and came to a blowdown. With my eyes I slowly took the fallen cedar apart and detected what appeared to be the antlers of a big buck bedded in the tangled branches. The longer I looked, the more I strained to see better, and the more I became convinced that my eyes were only playing tricks on me. It was too good to be true, and I finally decided I was only seeing branches that closely resembled a buck's headpiece. I finally lowered my rifle and took a step forward. There was a loud snort and one of the biggest deer I've ever seen catapulted out of the blowdown and sped away. But there's an unusual twist to this story. Two days later I came to the same blowdown and shot a smaller deer that was bedded in exactly the same spot.

Another important element of sneak-hunting is the direction of the wind. But don't worry about the worn-out advice of always having the wind in your face. It can be a cross-wind, or one that is traveling obliquely. Just don't allow your scent to travel directly ahead of your intended route.

When whitetails are in heavy cover, you seldom see a whole animal at first. Learn to recognize parts of a deer such as the horizontal line of the back amongst vertical saplings, a black shiny nose, a white throat patch, or the curve of an antler beam.

A related weather phenomenon—thermal air currents—are more localized in nature. They travel up and down rather than horizontally, and are caused by changes in the temperature.

Under stable or consistent weather conditions, thermal air currents drift downhill beginning in the late evening and last through the early morning. "Downhill" also means down valleys, down canyons, down creek bottoms, and so on, to lower elevations. Then, beginning sometime during the late morning, the thermal air currents reverse themselves to head back in the opposite direction, uphill, to the crests of ridges and to the heads of canyons and draws.

Periods of unsettled weather are sure to affect the directional movement of thermal air currents. Rapidly clearing weather after a storm front sends the currents wafting to higher elevations, but a rapidly approaching frontal system, or one that already is in progress, causes them to cascade downhill.

When there is no rolling terrain, hill country, or mountains, and the topography is relatively flat, thermal air currents drift out of heavy cover areas such as forests to more open places during the evening hours. This continues until early morning the following day. Then about midmorning there is a reversal, with the thermal drift from the open places toward heavy cover.

Despite all of this, a critical thing to keep in mind is that a prevailing wind will cancel out any thermal air currents.

With this knowledge, it's easy for a smart hunter to better his chances of catching deer unaware. First, keep in mind that deer continually test the wind for any ravels of scent that may indicate approaching danger. When the air "seems" still, however, deer use the thermals to serve as their sentries.

You may have already noticed the effect of this, but not known exactly how or why it was happening. For example, it's one reason why crafty bucks head for higher ground to spend midday. They do it to have a good view of what's going on below, as stated earlier, and also because the typical upslope drift of the thermals during the daylight hours will warn them well in advance of anything on the prowl. Conversely, "most" deer spend "most" of the night and dawn hours at the lower elevations; that is usually where food and water are most plentiful, but the thermal air currents have now shifted and lower ground is simply the place to be if those air currents are to be used as warning signals of anything approaching. In flat country, the same principle applies. The deer move into heavy cover to spend the late morning and early afternoon hours, partly to hide and rest, but also because the thermals will be in their favor; in the evening and early morning they are able to move into more open areas to feed and drink and yet still be on the alert.

It is common to see large numbers of deer feeding in open areas during midday periods immediately after the passage of a frontal system. Again, the animals are immune to severe weather but retreat into cover more because their sensory capabilities are impaired during such periods. The apparent oddity, then, of coming upon deer feeding in open places after the weather has cleared is a result of thermal air currents. The upslope drift of the currents, or in flatlands the movement of thermals from heavy cover to open areas, both of which are generally associated with dusk-to-dawn periods, suddenly takes place during, say, the late morning or early afternoon. This allows whitetails to stock up on groceries while still being fully attuned to anything and everything that is going on around them.

I said hunters could benefit from such insight, and here's how. When sneak-hunting, plan your movements in advance to have thermal air patterns working in your favor instead of against you. In other words, deer have tied their movements and behavior to the currents, and if you tailor your movements to them as well, you'll stand a far greater chance of seeing game. In hill country, this means hunting upslope in the direction of bedding sites until no later than perhaps 10 A.M. Through the late morning, afternoon, and sometimes even into the very early evening, you must be on high ground such as ridges, hillside benches, and canyon rims. In the flatlands, stay deep in the forests and heavy-cover regions during midday, and work the downslope edges and clearings only during the evening or very early in the morning.

If time allows, you can even practice sneak-hunting during the off-season. Get out in the woods and brush country, make a guess as to where you might expect to find a deer feeding, then try to approach to within shooting range. If you want, combine the activity with squirrel hunting, as bushytails are almost as difficult to sneak-hunt as deer. One hunter I know takes a full-size paper deer target and stands it up on wooden stakes. Then he tries to sneak up to the target from five different directions. After that, he places the target somewhere else, with entirely different terrain posing a new challenge.

One ruse that whitetail scouts often employ with good success is to follow deer trails. Because trails are tramped down from continual use, deer nearly always choose the easiest routes in order to navigate variable terrain with mixed cover. A hunter can wend his way down the same trails much more easily and silently than if he tries to just bull his way through the briars and brambles. Moreover, if he notes the way such trails lead uphill and down, from heavy cover to feeding areas and such, and then studies the direction of tracks found on those trails, he should be able to learn plenty about how resident animals are using thermals to their advantage during the course of their travels.

But the question often arises: What do you do if you make a mistake and snap a dry twig or inadvertantly allow thorns to grate against your clothing? First, accept it as part of the game because it happens to the best of hunters. But also remember that there is a big difference between what a deer hears, and what a deer hears that frightens it.

Lots of noises permeate the places where deer live and they become accustomed to hearing all kinds of racket such as falling walnuts, squirrels rustling in ground leaves, birds flitting about, and dead branches clacking in the wind. Consequently, deer are continually getting an earful. However, they have the innate ability to catalogue what they hear as either normal or potentially unsafe.

If you make a noise that alerts a nearby deer, it will attune its senses and wait for further noises to allow it to classify what it heard. If you immediately come to a halt and make no further noises, the deer will eventually set its mind at ease and return to its former feeding or other activity. As a result, it's not the occasional, blundering noise a hunter sometimes makes that spells his undoing, but the rhythmic cadence of continuing noises that a deer evaluates as detrimental to his hide.

When there is snow on the ground, many sneak-hunters combine their stillhunting efforts with tracking. But it usually isn't worthwhile to follow tracks discovered late in the day. Deer customarily bed during midday, so the tracks were probably made that morning and the animal may be far away.

The easiest way to move quietly through heavy cover is to stay right on the same trails the deer themselves use.

By the same token, even if the deer is relatively close, remember how difficult it is to sneak up on a bedded deer that has all of his senses riveted upon his surroundings. All of this makes a good case in favor of following tracks only when they are discovered at dawn; the deer that made them is likely to be nearby, on his feet, and moving slowly.

One mistake made by many hunters following tracks is to follow the same exact route taken by the deer while continually looking at the imprints in the snow right next to your boots. The error here is not realizing that traveling deer constantly monitor their back trails, which invites detection of your presence if you are on the same trail.

Much wiser is to sneak-hunt along a parallel course to the tracks. Stay as far away from the tracks as you possibly can while still being able to note the direction they are going; in most instances, the distance will be about 25 or 30 yards. Also, try to stay within thin cover, plotting each forward move in such a manner that trees, brush, bushes, or other cover will help to hide your movements. Of utmost importance, spend minimum time looking at the tracks because they only tell you one thing: Where an animal once stood. Where you want to focus your attention is far ahead in the distance where the tracks are leading, in hopes of eventually spotting the deer itself.

When following tracks, remember that the animal up ahead is constantly monitoring its backtrail. To avoid detection, walk parallel to the tracks, remaining in cover.

When you finally come within sight of a deer, whether by following tracks or simply during the course of sneak-hunting, you may be able to successfully conclude the hunt then and there. But if the shooting range is too long, you'll have to stalk the animal.

If the deer is moving, try to anticipate its direction so you can intercept it at some location farther ahead of its line of travel. If you have a long way to go and there is such cover as a steep knoll, dense forest, or rocky ledge that will completely hide your movements, remove any cartridge you may have chambered and take off at a trot. Otherwise, walk slowly and carefully, keeping a low profile. Moreover, move only when the deer is looking elsewhere or when the animal has his vision momentarily blocked by a tree trunk or boulder, using the rolling compression technique of executing your footfalls.

Although few hunters who come upon large imprints in snow cover can resist the temptation to follow after them, many of the country's most highly skilled hunters are now doing precisely the opposite. Using the advanced strategy known as "backtracking," they strive instead to learn where the animal has been.

Understand the logic behind this unconventional tactic and you'll probably be intrigued with the results, too.

The premise upon which backtracking rests is that the largest and wariest bucks constantly survey their backtrails, ever alert to anything that may be following them, which makes sneaking up behind some old monarch and catching him unaware a dubious proposition at best. Yet because whitetails customarily travel throughout their home ranges in wide circles that eventually bring them back to their starting points—usually a core area where they spend most of their time—and because they are far less suspicious about what's up ahead than what's behind, backtracking can be positively lethal.

Although it's possible to be sneak-hunting along a buck's backtrack and eventually see the animal coming in your direction, a hunter more commonly finds the deer's bedding area, whereupon he then selects a hiding station in nearby cover or deep shadows and begins playing the waiting game, biding his time until the deer returns. In this manner I've bushwhacked two bucks that had absolutely no idea I was waiting for them in what they undoubtedly thought was the safest place in their entire home range.

Let's pose one final situation that frequently occurs. You're doing a commendable job of sneak-hunting, but a nearby buck nevertheless detects your presence and makes off for parts unknown. As you listen to his snorts, you feel like a real klutz, but you shouldn't allow such commonplace happenings to mentally defeat you.

Sit down and be patient for at least fifteen minutes. Deer that are not outright spooked often acquire a curiosity about what alerted them, and sometimes they make a wide circle that brings them right back to their former area of activity in the hopes they can get a look at whatever initially routed them out. This means you may yet get a shot, especially if you pay close attention *not* to the direction in which the deer departed, but actually behind you and to either side.

If, after a full fifteen minutes, no deer returns to the immediate area, you may then elect to continue sneak-hunting in the same general direction the animal departed. The deer probably didn't go far. Unlike elk or mule deer, which may go 5 miles when spooked, whitetails invariably take off like rockets until they're just out of sight and come to a screeching halt within 200 yards, dive back into heavy trailside cover, and resume their slinking behavior.

Exactly how you pursue a deer "once jumped" depends upon the nature of the terrain. As a general rule, whitetails hold to the same type of cover and elevation as when you first moved them. Consequently, if you start a deer in a stand of cedars, chances are good the deer will stay in the cedars rather than breaking for nearby hardwoods. And if you start a deer in a swamp, it will probably remain in the swamp rather than evacuate for a nearby pine plantation. Similarly, in mountainous terrain, a deer started on a sidehill will predictably follow that sidehill on approximately the same contour level. Start a deer on a ridge and he'll probably continue to cling to that high ground for as long as possible.

With knowledge of this behavioral trait in mind, you should be able to analyze the surrounding topography and not only make an educated guess as to where the animal might be farther ahead but, just as important, how to best approach it.

Admittedly, sneak-hunting is far from the easiest way of collecting horns, hides and venison. But I will guarantee that any deer you do attach your tag to will remain etched in your memory far longer than those taken in any other manner.

22

Perfect Deer Stands and Blinds

◆◆◆

To be entirely candid, when you're using a .270 rifle and can pop off a round at an unsuspecting animal up to 300 yards away, things like scent drift or how deer catalog various sounds become virtually meaningless in terms of stand placement. This presumes the gun hunter has thoroughly studied the topography of the area, is aware of all available deer sign, knows exactly what the animals are doing, and has selected a stand that gives him wide-ranging coverage of the terrain.

On the other hand, bowhunting stands and blinds differ from those that would be used by gun hunters in one significant way. You must place yourself much, much closer to your quarry, and when a deer finally comes within range, the smallest error in judgement or planning can become magnified to such proportions that it may easily cost you your prize. Actually, two types of errors may enter the picture for there are errors of omission (things we should have done, but didn't) and errors of commission (things we did, but shouldn't have). And it's usually the errors of commission that prove to be the most noticeable because when all your hopes rest upon a single arrow, the shooting distance is so close you can see vapor coming from a buck's nostrils and count the bumps on his antler burrs. At that near range, even the faint scratching noise of whisker stubble against your collar may send him crashing away through the brush.

Bowhunting stands must therefore be selected with great care. Having an almost point-blank shot is, of course, the primary consideration. But the shooting circumstances themselves must be such that not even the tiniest oversight is allowed to work to your disadvantage.

Sometimes, everything happens just right. And herein is what separates the advanced hunter from the beginner, because on future outings the expert remembers what worked well before and strives to duplicate those same shooting conditions time and again.

By "perfect" stands and blinds, I'm not necessarily referring to actual places but rather attributes of certain places that distinctly tilt the odds in the hunter's favor. Naturally, the higher the number of these desirable features that can be incorporated into a given stand location, the greater the hunter's chance of scoring.

Bowhunters register great concern over the smallest of details when it comes to selecting their stands, so it's logical that the enterprising gun hunter who does likewise—takes a page from the bowhunter's notebook, as it were—can enhance his chances of success. Moreover, there are certain to be many times when the gun hunter, despite the long-range capability of his firearm, finds himself in a region where the nature of the cover mandates a stand that is certain to afford nothing other than close-in encounters with deer. That's when a gun hunter's acquired knowledge of "perfect" stand placement becomes vital.

One aspect I consider critically important is what I call the sunlight factor, yet surprisingly few hunters ever evaluate this element when scouting for a stand.

Most hunters do their scouting during midday when the sun is almost directly overhead, completely overlooking the fact that they'll probably be doing most of their shooting early or late in the day when the sun is low on the horizon. I usually learn things through the school of hard-knocks, so this facet of my deer hunting education once cost me a dandy buck.

I was in southern Ohio, seated in what I thought was an ideal stand, watching a trail intersection in a thornapple thicket from a nearby cottonwood tree. As dusk approached and the sun began sinking to the skyline, it became increasingly more difficult to see the trail. Then, just when the sun had become almost too blinding to look at, a nice six-pointer finally appeared. But by this time my burning eyes were squinted almost closed, with stinging tears streaming down my face. I slowly raised my arm to wipe my eyes with my jacket sleeve and apparently the deer caught the movement, because the next thing I knew he was gone.

Aside from the difficulty of looking directly into the sun without discomfort, bright sunlight shining straight in your direction tends to magnify even the slightest of movements you may make.

Why not turn this situation entirely around to work exactly the same way, *against* the deer? If you're exclusively an early-morning hunter, you'll want your chosen stand to be such that the rising sun in the east is on your back and slanting in the direction where you most expect deer to approach. If you're an evening hunter, you'll want your back to the west to achieve the same end. If you hunt both mornings and evenings, you'll need two entirely different stands.

With this accomplished, any deer that approach will have great difficulty

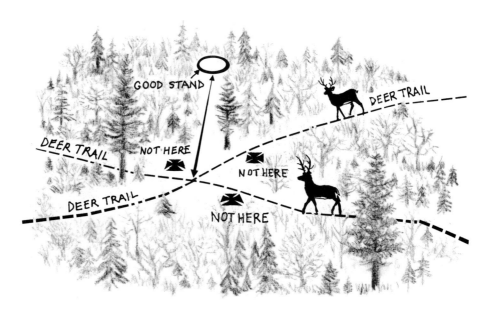

A cardinal rule of stand selection is to choose a site where you can watch the places you expect deer to emerge from cover. The actual distance from these points depends on your choice of rifle.

seeing you because to look in your direction will mean staring directly into glaring bright light.

Because crafty bucks often seem to suddenly materialize in some of the most unexpected places, remember to situate your stand within cover where long tentacles of shadows will help to break up your outline. This goes back to what was said earlier about slight movements being much more readily detectable in brightly illuminated places. Some hunters like to have a collage of heavy brush, vegetation, or tree branches directly behind them. This is infinitely better than being out in the open, but better still is being some distance back in from the leading edge of the cover, where your body outline becomes almost completely absorbed. This is especially necessary on behalf of bowhunters watching trail crossings, primary scrapes, and such. But in some instances, gun hunters will indeed want to be right at the leading edge of the cover—those in which they desire to maintain coverage down a rather lengthy corridor separating two tracts of heavy cover, such as an old logging road or perhaps a utility line right-of-way.

Regarding terrain features themselves, there also are several ideal situations to look for. My friend Jim Mirron, a Wisconsin trophy hunter, especially likes to find funnels or bottlenecks of cover the deer must pass through as they travel from one place to another.

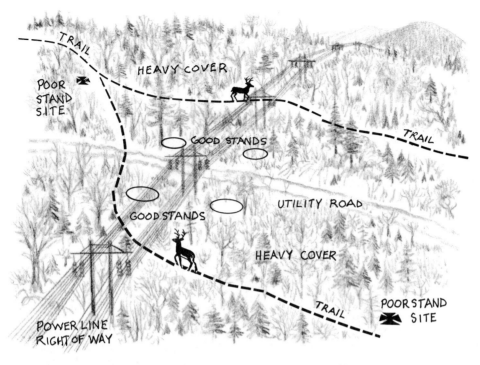

One instance in which a gun hunter can effectively take a stand right along the open, leading edge of cover is when he desires to maintain coverage down a long corridor such as a power-line right-of-way or an old logging road.

Look for bottlenecks where deer trails converge, forcing animals to squeeze themselves through narrow passages rather than going straight uphill or downhill.

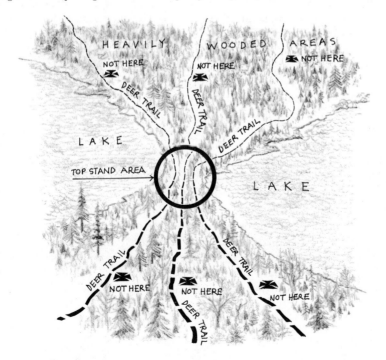

"If there are two large tracts of wooded acreage that are connected by a narrow aisle of saplings," Mirron explained during a recent hunt, "deer trading back and forth between the two forested areas are almost certain to sneak through the aisle of second-growth cover rather than risk exposing themselves in the open."

Later, he proved his point by arrowing a splendid buck in a corridor of birchwhips that was barely 30 yards wide.

Similarly, in a long bottomland or canyon, look for a necked-down area that takes on somewhat of an hourglass appearance. Rather than go straight uphill or downhill in steep terrain, deer prefer to stay on level ground and squeeze themselves through the narrow gap in order to gain access to one end of the bottomland or the other. A like situation might be where a narrow finger of land separates two adjoining lakefronts.

In mountain country, where sheer hillsides pitch off steeply, find a terraced bench or shelf that follows the natural contour of the mountain for a good distance. You can be certain it will reveal a heavily worn trail that has been used regularly by generations of deer.

Not too long ago, I was hunting near Bluefield, West Virginia where the terrain is so precipitous that the locals jokingly claim they're all born with one leg shorter than the other so they can get around the hill-country without undue difficulty. Anyway, one of the premier strategies here-abouts—and which should work anywhere there is similar topography—is simply sitting on one mountainside just as if you were mule deer hunting out West and using binoculars to glass the distant, opposite slope for travel-ing deer. Whenever you see two or more animals, they'll invariably be single-filing themselves along, staying right on benches. If you're gun hunt-ing and the distance separating the two opposite-facing slopes is not more than 300 yards or so, you might be able to pick off an animal right from where you've been doing your glassing. If you're a bowhunter, you'll want to mark on your topo map which particular benches have revealed the most traffic so you can subsequently scout those specific shelves for stand loca-tions that will afford close shooting.

Sometimes, in fact, you'll really strike it lucky and find a steep mountain-side with several terraced benches that stairstep their way from higher elevations to lower, with each bench revealing a trail. Now, the perfect set-up might be establishing a stand right on the contour edge of one bench you wish to cover and from that position being able to simultaneously view a second terrace immediately below.

I cannot emphasize too strongly the importance of situating stands in a manner that allows you to maintain coverage of more than one direction from which deer may approach. A hunter watching a single trail has only two chances of seeing deer, as they come from either the right or left. On the other hand, by simply watching a place where two trails cross, he now has the opportunity to bushwhack deer coming from any of four different direc-tions.

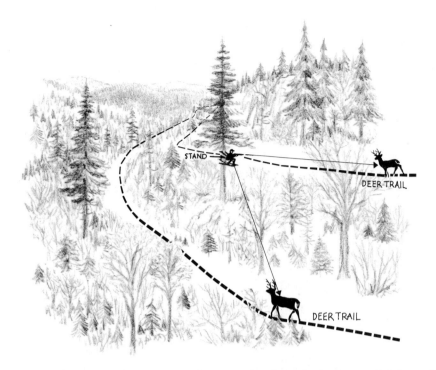

In steep, mountainous terrain a stand on a terraced bench showing a definite trail provides a good view of two possible deer approaches.

Another example of a stand that allows you to watch more than one trail—this one on a saddle connecting two ridges. Always look for these multiple trail crossings.

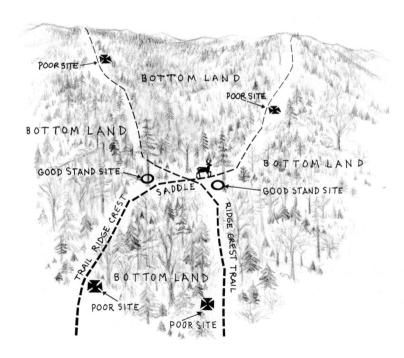

A while ago in Missouri, I chanced upon an area find where four trails intersected upon a low saddle that connected a series of finger ridges sloping down from a steep mountain. That meant deer crossing the saddle might come from any of eight different directions!

When I reported this news back in camp, the other three members of our group agreed we should all hunt that specific saddle, and the fairest way to do it would be to work in shifts. The plan was for one of us to climb into the designated stand for a three-hour period and then, like clockwork, that hunter would come down out of the tree as his replacement climbed up. We also agreed that each day we'd rotate our shifts so each hunter would have ample opportunity to hunt various time periods, but as it happened that wasn't necessary. By the end of the very first day, we had three bucks and a very big doe hanging on our game pole.

Over the years, I've tried long and hard to find multiple trail crossings but have only once succeeded in finding a place where more than four trails converged. It was in Texas, as I had described earlier, where I located five trails crossing each other that resembled spokes radiating from the hub of a wheel. But this doesn't mean such occurrences are necessarily rare finds, only that most hunters don't invest enough legwork in their scouting for high-traffic areas that will reward them with optimum numbers of deer sightings. As my friend Glenn Helgeland, an expert bowhunter from Mequon, Wisconsin, is fond of saying, "You can avoid re-inventing the wheel by learning from other people's experiences, but there must come a time when the bookin' stops and the lookin' begins."

But in expansive tracts of land saturated lessly with heavy cover, whitetails don't seem to use specific trails as religiously as they do when there are irregularly shaped mixtures of heavy cover, thin cover, and openings such as forest clearings and farm meadows. Instead, they exhibit a tendency to just randomly filter through the region with no set pattern to their movements. This can be exasperating because you expect the deer to be traveling like slot cars on tracks, yet in scouting you find droppings, hoofprints, and other sign seemingly scattered over almost every square yard of ground.

I believe there's only one way to unravel this mystery: to examine the broad, overall picture in hopes of finding "magnets" in specific places that the deer periodically home in on during the course of their travels.

For example, in a huge forest comprised mainly of maple and beech trees intermingled with rhododendron in those places where sunlight can reach the ground, a single towering oak that bears a heavy mast crop each year can be a hotspot worth its weight in venison. Or, in agricultural communities where a majority of farmers plant wheat, an isolated patch of soybeans will attract deer from afar. The same applies to an apple orchard in the heart of corn country.

So always be on the alert for an "oasis" of sorts when reconnoitering the vast deer country before you. Search for something uniquely favored by deer, but stands alone from that which predominates in the region. Conversely, when it comes to anything that is plentiful and widespread, finding specific places that reveal regular visitation is chancy at best. These particular sources of food, water, or cover should probably be scratched from your list as prospective stand sites.

In looking at the most desirable characteristics of certain stand sites themselves, a majority of hunters nowadays have long since come to appreciate the value of having some type of elevated vantage point. It's not that deer never look up—they do, indeed—but simply that they're not accustomed to looking up on a regular basis and something overhead is therefore less likely to draw their notice.

A perfect stand site will *never* be on an elevation that is lower than the plane occupied by the deer, because to do so invites ready detection. Slightly better is being on the same elevation as the deer, and best of all is to be on an elevation much higher than the deer's line of vision.

Of course, the longer the estimated shooting distance to that particular spot where you plan to take your deer, the less important stand height becomes. If you're using a centerfire rifle and guestimate you'll probably be making a 175-yard shot when your buck steps out of a distant canebrake, it may not be necessary to use a tree stand. If you are using a slug-loaded shotgun, watching several primary scrapes from 60 or 75 yards away, a tree stand may or may not be necessary. But if you're bowhunting and you know your shot will be within 25 yards, there is no question about it; a tree stand will greatly increase your chances of success. In all other cases, if there is even marginal doubt as to whether you'll see deer close, far, or at some intermediate range, best advice is to play it safe and climb a tree.

Older hunters or others who do not wish to climb trees should try to find a ground-level blind that will give them some elevated advantage. This might be on a hummock, a knoll, just below the crest of a ridge (to avoid having your silhouette looming on the skyline), or perhaps on a promontory or ledge outcropping. Then, when using camouflage cloth or brush or pine boughs to construct the blind, build it so you can take your shot around one side or the other; never attempt a shot directly over the top of the blind because you'll give away your location. Again, this concern is critical when bowhunting, but as the shooting distance increases it becomes less and less important.

The philosophy behind situating a blind on high ground is exactly the reason why western mule deer hunters have never become as fanatical about using portable tree stands as eastern whitetail hunters. They don't have to use tree stands to enjoy the same shooting advantages, because in the West it's easy to find an elevated vantage point. There are exceptions to this, of course, but I'd venture a guess that if the eastern half of the country were as steep and rugged as the Rocky Mountain states, tree stands never would have become as popular as they are.

278

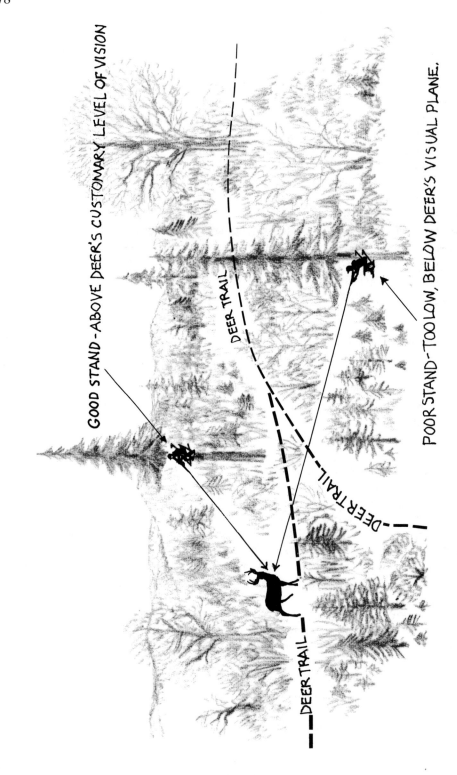

GOOD STAND - ABOVE DEER'S CUSTOMARY LEVEL OF VISION

POOR STAND - TOO LOW, BELOW DEER'S VISUAL PLANE.

DEER TRAIL

DEER TRAIL

DEER TRAIL

A good stand site will rarely, if ever, be on an elevation that is lower than the plane occupied by the deer.

Ground-level blinds can be just as effective as tree stands, but they too ought to be on higher ground than the deer trails you're watching.

When it comes to selecting a particular tree for a stand in a region you've scouted, many accomplished experts—especially bowhunters—even fine-tune their approach by studying specific species. I, for one, distinctly like pine trees that have long needles such as white pine.

Early in the season, when autumn foliage still is present to help hide your man-form, virtually any type of tree may suffice. But when bowhunting over the course of what may be a four-month-long season, or when starting the season bowhunting and then later switching to a firearm, you must be able to anticipate what a given tree will look like as the weeks wear on. In time, most species become almost entirely denuded, making you stand out clearly. Yet pine trees and certain other evergreens such as cedars retain their bushy boughs year-around, to afford excellent concealment no matter what the time of year.

My pal Barney Smith, who pursues whitetails in western Kentucky where there are few pine trees, recommends selecting an oak tree for your stand.

"Even though an oak tree's leaves will eventually turn brown and die," Smith advises, "much of the foliage remains securely affixed to the branches long into the dead of winter. The same is true of the popular species—white, yellow, and tulip."

One feature I like to see incorporated into a bow-stand site is moderately thick brush, saplings, or tall vegetation along trail edges leading to my sphere of coverage. The cover should be dense enough that I can just barely see through it to detect the moving outline of a deer. This way, If I see a buck threading his way in my direction and he is approaching from behind dense screening cover, I can adjust my stance if necessary and raise my bow. Then, when the deer has almost but not quite stepped into view, I can draw my bow. All of this is accomplished very slowly and with little chance of the deer seeing the movement through the cover. When it takes just one or two more steps beyond the screening cover and into the shooting alley I've previously cut, no additional movement is necessary on my part other than merely relaxing my fingertips to send the arrow on its way.

Early in the season when foliage is present, you can use any tree for a stand. However, eventually leaf-drop may expose you. This is why I distinctly favor pine trees; they retain their leafy boughs year-round.

Again, though, wind direction is more responsible for defeating hunters than any other factor. And in many cases, hunters have no one to blame but themselves when a buck bolts after catching a whiff of man-scent. Admittedly, in regions with steep terrain, finger-ridges extending in random directions, winding drainages, forest windbreaks and other terrain features that play havoc with the prevailing wind direction, you sometimes feel like you just want to throw your hands up in despair. But the astute hunter learns to tailor his hunting strategies to existing conditions, and this means being willing to switch tactics when necessary.

If the day is greeted with swirling, eddying wind currents, take advantage of the splendid opportunity to sneak-hunt or stage drives. You know deer aren't going to be moving much on their own and will allow hunters to approach quite closely in hopes they'll eventually pass. On the other hand, if the weather calms around midday, head directly back to your stand because now, after being holed up, the deer will be out feeding.

Thermals have an influence as well. As noted previously, in the absence of a prevailing wind deer will scent-check air currents that each day travel uphill and downhill, and from open places to heavy cover and vice-versa, as a result of changing air temperatures. Consequently, there is no better argument in favor of readying as many different stand sites as possible for a given deer hunt.

During the course of hunting one specific buck over a period of several days, I've changed stand sites as many as five or six different times as conditions changed. For example, if I'm watching a trail intersection from a stand situated 30 yards to the southwest and a storm front suddenly begins approaching from that direction, I'll probably climb down and relocate my portable stand on the opposite side of the trail, 30 yards to the northwest.

If the particular two-stand situation described above happens to be in a low elevation area, I'd use those stands only during the hours of dawn and dusk. By midday, I'd be on much higher ground along a ridge or at the head of a hollow, to avoid being detected, and again, at that general location I'd probably have two or more stand sites readied. The reason is that thermals drift upslope to higher and higher elevations during the midday hours, then reverse themselves and drift downslope during the night and early morning hours. In flatland areas, shifting between various stands is done at different times in accordance with cover density in the region. During the morning and early afternoon hours, the direction of thermal drift is from open places toward thick cover, but during the evening the wafting air currents travel from dense cover to the fields and meadows.

There are a couple of other instances in which I do not hesitate to move my stand. If a buck has obviously seen, heard, or smelled me and ran away, I will not use that particular stand again for at least one full week. And if I shoot at a deer and miss, I won't use that stand again for the remainder of the season because I've learned from past experience the chances are slim of getting another poke at the same buck at that very same location. In either of the above cases, the distance I move my stand may, if the cover and terrain allows for it, be as little as 50 yards. The critical thing is that it *must* be moved!

There are a few exceptions to the general rule. If I know of a particular food plot such as a meadow or cornfield that is being visited by numerous deer and there are several good bucks in the area, I may continue to sit in the very same stand after muffing an opportunity at one of the deer. Similarly, during the rutting period, if all indications point to several bucks sharing an overlapping breeding territory and my stand happens to overlook a so-called "community scrape," as described earlier, I may stay put at least a short while longer if one of the deer happens to approach from an unexpected direction and then bolts after catching my scent.

There are a few other points that can make a given stand more productive. If I'm considering several specific trees for installing a stand, I like to pick the particular one that is a gnarled, sorry-looking excuse for a tree. Com-

Although this stand is elevated and overlooks a worn trail, it's a poor choice because the hunter stands out boldly and his slightest movement is sure to be detected by a passing deer.

Yet notice how this hunter has almost melted into his surroundings by selecting this scraggly-looking tree with many limbs and branches to absorb his body outline.

pared to straight-trunked trees that are symmetrical and well-shaped, those which are twisted, contorted and scraggly-looking have many more forked limbs and such to better break up the outline of your body.

Once your stand is installed, it's then wise to go to extra pains to make it as noiseless as possible. Wearing thick leather gloves, I first run the palms of my hands up and down the tree trunk itself and any nearby limbs to remove loose bark particles. If you don't do this, the slightest contact of your clothing against the tree will create an audible rasping noise; the worst culprits are the shagbark hickory and various evergreen species, including cedars.

I have also cemented a square piece of indoor/outdoor carpeting to my stand platform, which quiets the otherwise scuffling noise created when you occasionally reposition your feet. This is especially important in cold weather when frost forms on your stand platform and crunches noisily underfoot.

In the case of ground-level blinds, be sure to scrape away dry leaves and brittle twigs, leaving only bare soil.

Finally, although serious deer hunters may know what hypothetically constitutes an ideal stand according to the time of year, existing weather conditions, rutting behavior, and other factors, little will be gained by becoming so obsessed with the word "perfect" that anything less is discouraging and reduces your confidence. Many of the deer I've collected over the years were taken from stands where, given the supreme power, I would have placed a bush here or there, altered the growth of a particular branch, or done something else to change the picture. But I still was successful.

This doesn't mean I'll ever stop searching for perfect stands. But if you know what attributes and features comprise a perfect stand, and do your best to find them or incorporate them into your hunting strategy, you'll be far ahead of the game and well on your way to securing your winter cache of deer meat.

23

The Vigil

◆◆◆

It's only the first hour of shooting light and already you're almost frozen and can't stop shivering.

Your hunt began with a bone-chilling predawn hike to your stand, with only the dim glow of a narrow flashlight beam pointing the way. As the dry snow crunched underfoot, you knew the day was sure to remain miserably cold.

Now you're perched 10 feet above the ground on a tiny square of plywood and your enthusiasm is steadily diminishing. Each new gust of biting wind somehow manages to rake through your clothing and gnaw at your soul.

Nothing is moving. At least, not here. But shots continue to ring out in the distance with exasperating frequency, allowing gremlins of doubt to erode the high level of confidence you once had in your choice of stand. With each additional burst of gunfire, it is clear to you that in this oasis of deer country, you alone have chosen to hunt the desert.

Finally, you climb down out of that blasted tree and try to restore some semblance of circulation to your numb feet and hope that maybe you'll see something by prowling around a bit.

In another state, another deer hunter's vigil and the climate are entirely different. The weather is torrid and the hunter's clothing is sopping wet from perspiration. Beads of sweat dribble annoyingly down his forehead and sting his eyes. Mosquitos are performing the worst bloodletting he's ever experienced, and that, apparently, is the only animal activity in the vicinity. Eventually, he abandons his ground-level blind.

What both hunters have in common is they did not remain on stand long enough—understandably so—to allow the odds to build in their favor. The modern, fast-paced lives we lead tend to make many of us feel restless and uncomfortable when things don't take place on schedule, and we forget that deer don't follow timetables. If we're to become consistently successful, therefore, it's necessary to become less regimented during the deer season and learn to slow down.

Agreed, it's incredibly difficult to sit down in a stand, relax, and do absolutely nothing but wait hour after hour . . . it is simply alien to the routines we pursue the remainder of the year. It's also discouraging and depressing when you're not seeing anything. But there's a little mental exercise I developed years ago which you can perform to bolster your enthusiasm. I call it, "a deer hunter's understanding of reverse geometric progression."

All it means is this: If you've done a thorough job of scouting and are sitting on a stand overlooking trails, scrapes, feeding areas, or bedding areas that you positively know deer are regularly using, because of recent droppings, tracks, or other fresh sign you have discovered, then the longer you sit there without seeing anything the increasingly better your chances become. Keeping this in mind gives you that extra spark of optimism that's needed to stick it out until the very last minute.

Of course, it's no simple matter to wait patiently for long hours, all the while remaining keenly alert. If you intend to do so, you'll need basic creature comforts plus a generous dose of mental discipline. These things are as essential to the end reward as being able to proficiently handle a firearm or bow.

Let's first cover the subject of staying warm. Most seasoned hunters have long since settled upon their own favorite combination of shirts, trousers, longjohns, boots, gloves, hats, and some type of outer coat. Some hunters prefer cotton clothing underneath, to absorb body moisture, followed by wool on top, while others like some type of super-insulating fabric underneath such as Thinsulate or thermolactyl, followed by goosedown on top. But all agree that numerous, moderately thin layers of garments do a much better job of trapping dead air and retaining body heat than one very heavy layer.

But some hunters, even veterans, are not aware there are still other methods of producing body heat, such as eating certain foods and doing isometric exercises. And regarding dress, I've found a few methods useful in staying warm no matter what type of clothing you may prefer.

When the weather is extremely cold, it's important to reduce your body surface exposure to the cold as much as possible. Protect your head, because this area of the anatomy is where a good deal of body heat is lost. Most have heard the saying, "to keep your feet warm, put on your hat," and although this is quite true you can do more than just that. Keep your ears flattened against your head and simultaneously keep your face and neck covered by wearing a combination watchcap-type of hat in conjunction with a knitted face mask. When sitting on stand or in a blind, try to keep your upper arms and forearms tucked against your body trunk, and try to keep your knees together so your thighs and lower legs are touching; if your legs are spread and your elbows are away from your body trunk, more body surface is exposed to the cold and this means you'll chill more quickly. By the same token, wear mittens (there are modifications for both gun hunters and bowhunters) instead of fingered gloves, and inside those mittens make your hands into fists instead of spreading and extending your fingers.

The bane of many stand hunters is having a long trek to their stand sites and, upon arriving, find they've been perspiring heavily and their undergarments are a bit moist. When this happens, and you next sit down to maintain a long, motionless vigil, you chill-off twice as quickly. Eliminating this problem is no more complicated than stowing your outer jacket, hat, and gloves in a daypack, or unbuttoning your shirt collar, then walking slowly to your stand to avoid exerting yourself. After you've climbed your tree or settled down into your blind, put your heavy outer clothing back on again.

Staying warm calls for not only suitable clothing but also preparing your body for the task at hand. If you're tired from lack of rest, unaccustomed to physical exercise, or on a diet, you can expect to freeze-out in short order. Your metabolism isn't ready for the assault of cold weather.

The right approach is to get into shape gradually before the season, even if this entails doing no more than taking a leisurely, one-mile walk around the block every evening and at work climbing the stairs rather than riding the elevator. Then, during the season, go to bed early rather than playing poker until 2 A.M.

Also, temporarily forget about your diet. A high-protein regimen is strongly recommended. A primary function of proteins is the production of body heat; this is the fuel that keeps your furnace going long and strong. Consequently, having a steak dinner the night before you take up your vigil the following morning is a wise decision, especially if it's followed by a hearty breakfast of sausage and eggs. Other high-protein foods include milk, cheese, cereals, legumes such as peas and beans, peanuts, and especially other meats and fish.

Significantly increasing your salt intake will also help you stay warmer. According to the famous explorer, mountain climber, and expedition leader Paul Petzold, "Lack of salt tends to dehydrate the body and draw blood away from the extremities toward the body's core, thereby increasing the chances of hypothermia or frostbite of the fingers, toes, and ears." Conversely, additional salt intake keeps blood volume up and flowing to all parts of the body.

In cold weather, bring a thermos bottle containing a hot beverage to your stand to help you stay warm. If it's not bitter cold, I prefer to drink coffee or tea; these are no-calorie beverages that provide temporary body warmth simply through transference. But if the temperature dips below zero, I switch to a hearty, high-protein soup such as beef broth, split pea, or ham and bean soup. These provide both immediate warmth through transference and sustained warmth through the heat generated by the digestion process.

Doing isometric exercises while sitting on stand helps your system liberate heat more quickly than simply waiting for the effects of the digestive process. In addition, the benefit of doing isometrics requires minimum movement because instead of moving arms and legs individually you are straining them against each other. While all body muscles can be exercised isometrically, greater heat-producing results are achieved when you work primarily with your arms, legs, and back.

I like to push and pull with my hands and arms on the side struts of my portable tree stand, or on nearby branches or limbs. Also, I push on the stand platform with my feet and legs. Another common isometric exercise is to clasp your hands together and push and pull; this contracts the arm and back muscles. In any case, the goal is to flex, contract, and stretch your larger muscle groups so they will burn more calories within them. The produced heat will then be carried by the blood to your other body parts.

And finally, when you sit down on your tree stand platform or in your blind, you compress the insulation covering your posterior, allowing coldness to quickly seep in. Remedy this problem in advance by cementing a square of thick-pile carpeting to the tree-stand seat. In a blind, do not sit directly on the cold ground. Instead, use a boat cushion or Hot Seat placed on a folding campstool. Another combination that many hunters use to ease the long hours of waiting is a lightweight aluminum lawn chair plus a padded cushion. It may look ridiculous as hell to carry a lawn chair into the woods, but if it helps you stay warm and allows you to patiently wait longer hours, do it!

Now, what about sticking it out in hot weather? That also requires physical comfort if you're to remain alert and prepared for action. Porous, open-weave clothing will give perspiration a chance to evaporate, thereby rendering a cooling effect. On sunny days, keep your eyes shaded because squinting in bright light makes you fatigued. Of course, the warm-weather hunter will want to use liberal applications of insect repellent to keep pesky bugs at bay, but he should hide its odor with a good masking scent.

What you eat in warm weather is again the yardstick by which eventual success often can be measured.

When it comes to planning meals, it should be obvious that high-protein, heat-producing foods should be reduced to a bare minimum. And because heat is a by-product of any digestion process, even that involving fats and to some extent carbohydrates, reducing one's overall food intake is wise.

As in cold weather, additional salt intake is likewise important in warm weather. In this case, however, you need the salt not simply in sodium form

In cold weather, some type of hot beverage will help you stay warm. Also, increase your salt intake to keep blood volume flowing to your extremities. This is outdoor writer Mark Hicks, toughing it out on stand in southern Ohio.

as is customarily found in foods for the purpose of generating body heat, but in dissolved mineral form—including sodium, potassium, and calcium—to maintain a desirable electrolyte balance. If these salts are lost during the normal course of perspiration and not immediately replaced, a stand hunter is far more prone to fatigue and muscle cramps. So while you may be tempted to take a canteen of water with you to your stand, much better would be any number of fruit drinks which are high in mineral salts; popular examples include orange juice, grapefruit juice, Gatorade, and Tang.

Now we come to the subject of mental conditioning required by any persistent stand hunter. If you expect to wait patiently and enthusiastically for long hours under any conditions, you must be able to maintain the utmost confidence in your chosen hunting area. Keep telling yourself over and over again that your buck is likely to come slinking along at any moment.

It's extremely important that you ignore shots that ring out in the distance. The great majority of these, especially lengthy barrages, do not signify a trophy buck meeting its maker. Sometimes they're fired by hunters checking the accuracy of their rifles before leaving camp. Other times they're often wasted, hurried, desperate, and perhaps even irresponsible attempts at deer hightailing it over distant ridges hundreds of yards away.

Once, over a period of an hour, I heard more than fifty shots in a long hollow about half a mile away. I hadn't seen a thing in hours and began thinking maybe I'd missed some crucial element in my scouting that other local hunters were aware of, like the location of some type of food they were being drawn to. I left my stand to investigate, certain that I'd discover deer stampeding all over and that I would finally get to enjoy some shooting action, too.

Imagine my disgust when I determined the source of the shooting. A gang of hunters had decided to stage a big drive down the hollow. And some dimwit in the group reasoned that if the traditional shouting among drivers would push deer from their beds, that even more effective would be for the drivers to occasionally fire their rifles into the air. Everyone else in the group went along with the idea and I was gullibly victimized as well. (One doe was indeed taken on this particular drive and I, red-faced with embarrassment, slinked back to the stand that I never should have left).

As has already been noted several times, prime times to see deer are the first three hours after daybreak and the last three hours before dark. But few hunters know that deer also feed and drink around the time period of 11 A.M. until noon. Another factor to consider is that sometime during mid-morning, most other stand hunters either freeze-out or become restless and begin walking around. Their action greatly increases the chances that they'll push bedded deer in your direction. During the breeding season, keep in mind that amorous bucks—and does in estrus—may be on the move almost anytime.

So if weather and other conditions warrant sitting on stand or in a blind in the first place, try to stick it out as long as possible. If the temperature is bitter cold or scorching hot, or you're simply tired, at least stay put until 1 P.M. Then return to your camp or your car for a nap during the least favorable afternoon hours. Resume your watch later in the day.

Here are a couple of other insights worth noting. Force yourself not to think about the long hours of waiting ahead of you. Instead, if a glance at your watch tells you it's 9 A.M., mentally concentrate upon waiting until 10 A.M. When 10 A.M. finally arrives, begin thinking about 11 A.M. In this manner, time seems to slip by rather easily, compared to the discouraging feeling that arrives when you begin wondering how you can possibly tough it out another four or five hours.

In other instances, it may not be wise to stay on stand for extended periods, particularly when you're bowhunting. During the archery season, there just aren't enough other hunters afield to keep deer stirring around. This means you're most likely to see them early and late in the day, and if you didn't see a buck at dawn you might have a better chance of success later at dusk—if you've napped during the day. Here's why. Bowhunting means close-in shooting, in which meticulous attention must be paid to details. You must be keenly alert and have all your senses operating at peak capacity. You also must feel well physically. Yet if a buck comes to your stand at 5 P.M., after you've already been sitting on stand for nearly ten hours, chances are you'll be feeling lethargic, listless, and just plain tired. Moreover, you'll be stiff and have muscle cramps. In short, there's a splendid chance you'll inadvertently blow your only chance of the day, by not being aware of the deer's presence until it has almost passed you, by moving at the wrong time, by creating noise, or committing some other error.

Contrary to popular belief, you need not remain so continually motionless on stand that you seem to have been carved from granite. In fact, trying to maintain such a statue-like stance greatly contributes to drowsiness.

To stretch and relieve cramped muscles, I frequently alternate between sitting, standing, kneeling, and squatting positions. Make these movements in very slow motion and only after you've thoroughly panned the surrounding terrain and have assured yourself that there are no deer in the immediate vicinity.

As was described earlier, doing isometric exercises also is helpful. By tensing opposing muscles you can, in effect, stretch them without actually moving them. Begin with your toes and gradually work all the way up to your head, but in warm weather do not engage in these exercises for prolonged periods or you'll begin feeling over-heated and uncomfortable.

Another method of staying alert is occasionally to do some deep-breathing exercises. By inhaling large volumes of air, you flood your circulatory system with oxygen, which is the tonic that revitalizes tired muscles by removing the lactic acid that has built up in them and made them feel stiff and sluggish. When you feel fatigued, try the long-haul-trucker's trick of exercising your eyes. Without moving your head, strain to look way up and to the left, then far down diagonally to the lower right, and vice-versa.

Every stand hunter should have a quart-size plastic bottle for urinating. That way, he doesn't saturate his area with human scent. He also should have various food items. In addition to a thermos bottle filled with broth or soup in cold weather, or fruit juice in warm weather, sandwiches and snacks help to lift one's spirits and disconnect the tedious hours dragging along. I stay away from pungent, spicy lunchmeats such as salami, pastrami, and corned beef. Cheese or peanut-butter sandwiches are high in protein and help generate body heat in cold weather. For snacks, I rely upon peanuts and granola bars for the same reasons. In warm weather, jelly or jam sandwiches are ideal because they are low in protein content. For snacks, hard candies, chocolate bars, raisins, dates, and figs are low in proteins yet high in calories (to increase stamina and alertness).

Another way to remain alert is to think about almost anything other than the slow hours plodding along. Teachers can mentally plan classroom lectures. Businessmen can think about sales techniques or upcoming board meetings. And factory workers can think about tips they'd like to put in the company suggestion box to improve production efficiency and maybe win a cash bonus. And everyone can ponder the holiday shopping they'll have to contend with when the deer season is over. Many times during the day, wildlife species such as squirrels or songbirds are sure to happen by, providing intermittent entertainment.

But what if other hunters occasionally pass by as you maintain your vigil? Just acknowledge their presence with a slight nod or wave and let them go about their business. You needn't begin feeling pessimistic, because far from hindering your chances of success, they may actually help. They'll keep deer circulating that otherwise might remain bedded. And the deer, in skirting these moving hunters, may very well use one of the trails you're watching.

All in all, waiting on stand or in a blind is one of deer hunting's greatest paradoxes. Sitting still seems to require no skill at all, but in reality it calls for plenty. First, the stand hunter must consider the weighty decision of *where* to sit. Then, to ensure that this preliminary effort eventually pays off, he must know *how* to sit patiently and comfortably.

If you're lucky, your buck will come along early on the very first morning. But perhaps you won't see that buck for several days. Sooner or later, though, it *will* come along. And when that handsome deer materializes, you will know that your wait has been worthwhile.

24

Whitetail Drives
That Work

◆◆

If I had read the anecdote in a book or magazine article, I wouldn't have believed it for a minute. But recently I had the rare opportunity of watching a sequence of events unravel that gave me a much fuller appreciation of the evasive capabilities of whitetails.

This was on my farm in southern Ohio where I had already filled my own deer tag and now, carrying only a camera, had organized a drive and was trying to help some friends get their deer.

From an elevated bench I could look down and occasionally see my partners on the drive line as flashes of bright orange through a dense screen of hawthorne and locust saplings. Suddenly, just ahead and to the left, there was a brief white flash that was entirely out of place!

Peering through my telephoto lens to have a better look, the "flash" became the tail of a six-point buck that apparently had been routed from his bed by Bill Matthews, who was the driver to my immediate left. Matthews didn't see the deer get up and move out, and the buck had no intentions of leaving his little chunk of security cover. He simply side-stepped a dozen yards to get out of Bill's line of travel and then quickly laid back down again, his nose held high to test the wind and his ears simultaneously swiveling in all directions.

I began hollering my partner's name and pointing toward the buck, but from his vantage point Bill couldn't see a thing. As Matthews continued along his intended route and drew closer and closer, the buck then began belly-crawling still another dozen yards, now with his head held low and his tail tucked between his legs.

I shouted again, but Matthews still could see nothing and pressed onward, one cautious step at a time. Then the buck, apparently feeling his disclosure was imminent, pulled one last stunt. With his belly still tight to the ground, the deer scrabbled backward like a crawfish until he was fully hidden underneath a thick multiflora rose bush.

Ingenious, I thought! If the deer had tried to go in frontwards, he surely would have entangled his antlers in the umbrella-like thorns and vines drooping low to the ground. So he simply backed in and the concealing cover easily slid right over the natural curvature of his rack.

Still again I hollered Bill's name and at this the buck lowered his head until his chin was flat on the ground. Matthews closed the distance, still, unaware of the deer's location. He now was within 15 yards of the bedded buck and for me the mounting tension was almost becoming unbearable. It was like watching a piano wire being stretched, not knowing when it eventually would snap.

When Bill was only 5 yards away, the buck finally could stand it no longer and exploded almost straight up through the multiflora and began bounding away with gobs of thorny vines trailing behind. This is when Matthews saw the deer for the very first time and, with a perfect neck shot, sent it into a cartwheeling spin to the ground.

My partner later admitted he "might" have been just a bit lucky with his shot. But moreover, the incident reaffirmed many basic principles of deer hunting, not the least of which is the whitetail's tenacity for sticking like glue to the home-range cover with which it is so intimately familiar. Another is the species sometimes uncanny abilities when it comes to playing hide-and-seek with hunters, because as Bill Matthews learned first-hand, "A deer you can't see isn't necessarily a deer that isn't there." Another tenet that is particularly relevant here is that when knowledgeable hunters plan drives, the drivers themselves often have as good a chance of scoring as those hunters stationed farther ahead on stand.

But why make drives, anyway? Don't most expert hunters agree the odds distinctly favor those who play the waiting game by sitting in blinds or perching themselves off the ground in tree stands?

Well, yes, sometimes, but then again, maybe no, which is a mouthful of gobbledygook in need of explanation.

If a hunter has thoroughly scouted the terrain and studied the available sign, he stands an excellent chance of waylaying an unalarmed buck engaging in its normal pattern of behavior.

However, *unalarmed* is the key word here. Every year, deer hunting grows in popularity. Combine this with the fact that most deer seasons are relatively brief and one very important point emerges: Every year, deer populations in almost any given state suddenly come under intense pressure by throngs of hunters. This typically brings about an abrupt change in the complexion of what may constitute the most effective deer hunting tactics shortly after the gun sounds of opening day.

In other words, it doesn't take the deer very long to realize that their habitat, which has remained largely unmolested in previous months, suddenly has been infiltrated overnight by legions of hunters intent upon eating tenderloin. When this happens, the personalities of the animals can be expected to radically change. Often, the deer no longer will continue to use their customary trails, visit their regular feeding sites, or engage in other normal behavior. Indeed, they may dive into the heaviest cover they can find and entertain no thoughts whatsoever about even blinking until after full dark.

Facing these circumstances, hunters who begin organizing drives unquestionably can expect to see far more action than those stalwart diehards who insist upon continuing their vigils on stands.

These days, driving deer is far different than it used to be. The drives our fathers and grandfathers staged generations ago generally were often disorganized and confused. Sometimes 30 or more hunters participated, half of them spread out in a lengthy procession that shouted, whistled, and stomped their way through the woodlands, hoping to push deer to the remaining half of their army situated randomly in the distance.

This isn't to say such mob-hunting efforts always were dismal failures, because an occasional sag in the camp game pole provided evidence to the contrary. But compared to the sophisticated, well oiled drive strategies an increasing number of today's hunters are using, those of the bygone era were inefficient. Without a doubt, only a fraction of the bucks living in any given area were ever seen, much less tagged.

One of the most notable features of the modern drive party is its much smaller size. In the drive I described at the beginning of this chapter, there were only four drivers and two standers. Sometimes, depending upon the nature of the terrain to be worked, as few as only two hunters may be required, but a good rule of thumb is ensuring the maximum number doesn't exceed eight.

Small drive parties have a lot going for them. In these troubled times of increasingly posted lands, a small group of courteous, clean-cut hunters stands a far greater chance of gaining access to private property than is the case when a veritable caravan of vehicles suddenly appears in the driveway of a predictably reluctant farmer. Even in the case of state and federal lands open to public hunting, a small group of hunters is easier to organize, position on stand, and keep track of on the drive line, and this means efficiency skyrockets.

As when hunting alone and reconnoitering the terrain in search of a suitable location to sneak-hunt or build a stand, the annual drive party will likewise want to familiarize themselves with the area they'll be working.

Topographical maps can play a valuable role because in addition to showing land contours, forests, and cleared ground, they reveal the presence of major landmarks such as trails, access roads, powerline right-of-ways, bodies of water, and other natural and man-made features. They can even be marked with felt-tipped pens to show property boundaries.

Although the acquisition process requires a bit of time and money, each member of the hunting party should have his own map that he can keep with him at all times. This way, he'll always have an instant, visual reference as to how each drive is engineered, the line of travel he is to take as a driver, or the best way to reach a specific location when he is designated to be a stander.

The enterprising drive party's next order of business prior to opening day is actually scouting the landscape and laying out the logistics of the drives. From my experience, it is always best for the members of the group to elect a drivemaster. In keeping with the old adage that "too many cooks spoil the broth," the same can be said of the drive party in which everyone voices differing opinions as to how the drives should be executed. Much wiser is to nominate one person to be the leader, and this may not necessarily be the hunter who has taken the greatest number of bucks over the years. Rather, it should be the member of the group who is the most familiar with the terrain to be hunted and who knows, from past experience, the best places to situate standers in anticipation of shooting action. Regardless of what may be ascertained as the behavior patterns of the deer before opening day, the primary goal of the drive party should be to guess where the animals will later be going as they begin seeking refuge from hunters. If one member of the group has that aforehand knowledge, is duly designated to be in charge of all decision-making, and everyone follows his instructions to the letter, each individual will stand a much better chance of success.

Of course, if no one in the group is familiar with the terrain, there is no alternative but for each member to study his map and then all have a powwow until some type of concensus is arrived at.

Just a few of the more common types of cover the deer can be expected to retreat into include dense stands of pines, conifers, or cedars where the lowest branches are close to the ground. Another prime location for enacting a drive is a thick grove of thornapple and hawthorne trees, or where there is a steep hollow or ravine filled to the brim with brush and downed, jackstrawed timber. Find junglelike stands of honeysuckle, laurel, or rhododendron. In low-lying areas, particularly along stream bottoms, look for nearly impenetrable willow thickets, especially those found in conjunction with tall vegetation or dead brush.

In conducting these reconnaissance missions, a crucial element for the drive party to keep in mind is that they'll enjoy far greater success if they entirely avoid large tracts of land. Such places take an eternity to drive. Furthermore, a small group of hunters simply cannot do justice in properly

In this aerial photo, the best possibilities for staging drives are shown, as well as the worst. Deer are not likely to be in the pole timber in the upper left corner because there are no places to hide. Deer are likely to be in the endless tract of pines in the upper right corner, but a drive would prove futile because the animals have countless escape options for dodging hunters. The aisles of pines in the center offer near-perfect drive conditions. Whitetails would be reluctant to expose themselves in open areas, so drivers can move deer through an aisle to standers positioned at the other end.

pushing the cover or guarding all possible exists, and this allows the deer far too many escape options. With so much room to roam, a crafty buck will find it remarkably easy to elude the hunters by remaining bedded, skirting the standers, slipping back through the drive line, or dodging the hunters in innumerable other ways.

So, much wiser is for the drive party to select well defined segments of terrain no more than 10 acres in size, heavily saturated with cover, and, just as important, bordered on two or more sides by natural or man-made boundaries the deer will be reluctant to cross.

This last consideration allows hunters to capitalize upon the fact that whitetails will do almost anything to avoid exposing themselves in open places for prolonged periods. For example, if there is a rectangular-shaped, 5-acre pine plantation that is surrounded on all sides by hay meadows and plowed fields, it's almost a certainty that deer moved from their beds will elect to travel the entire length of the pines instead of spurting out one of the sides and bolting across open ground. Hunters stationed at the far end of the pines can likely expect to have their hands full at almost the very moment their partners begin entering the opposite end of the cover.

This is, of course, the classic drive situation. It's a time-proven technique, but there are many ways to improve it for even more consistent results.

I'm thinking, for one, of the so-called "funnel drive" like the kind we work whenever I hunt with friends near Hinckley, Minnesota. There have been times when we've failed to take a buck on this type of maneuver, but never a time when deer did not move exactly the way we wanted them to right past our standers.

The cover in this particular situation happens to consist of a triangular-shaped plot of mixed pines, birch whips, and blowdowns bordered on two sides by alfalfa fields. At the apex of the triangle is a long, narrow aisle of thin brush that gradually joins with a stand of red maple saplings that, in turn, butt up against a large birch forest. When drivers begin approaching the far side of the pines, it is as predictable as the sun rising tomorrow that any deer bedded in the cover will travel all the way to the opposite end, and then slip out into the forest while using the aisle of brush to conceal their movements.

Last year I was the hunter assigned to take a stand overlooking the escape corridor, and what happened was eye-opening to say the least. At almost the very instant the drivers began moving, I heard a pounding of hooves and three does came through the brushy aisle like they had been shot from a cannon. Less than a minute later, two more does catapulted out of the cover, followed by still another that had her transmission in sneak-gear. My nerves were becoming frazzled when yet another deer came skulking along and I quickly spotted forked horns. I was just about to level my sights on the young buck when my peripheral vision caught a flash of tawny hide far to the left. It was an eight-pointer!

There had been six does and two bucks hiding in that small swatch of security cover. But even more significant, when the drive began, every one of the deer quickly riveted their full attention upon the single escape route leading to the forest. I was lucky and collected the big buck, whose head now hangs on my office wall as a constant reminder that funnel drives are perhaps the most lethal strategies a group of hunters can enact.

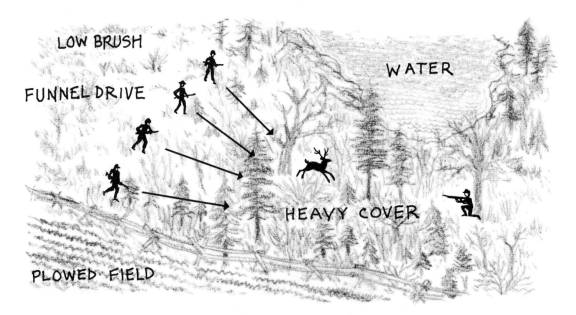

The funnel drive offers hunters one of the highest success rates because the animals'
intended escape route is so predictable.

Just keep in mind that regardless of the specific type of heavy cover that exists, there must be some location where it necks down into a narrow passage through which the deer must travel if they are to gain access to some connecting cover during the course of their attempted escape.

A slight variation of the funnel drive can be used whenever the hunting party finds a long, narrow ravine or hollow choked with dense undergrowth or felled timber. Although the topography of the terrain dictates placement of standers and how the drivers will move, it's generally best to make the push in a downhill direction. Landforms such as hollows usually begin to narrow at some lower elevation and therefore standers can be most strategically placed.

Another logical move in setting up such a drive is to concentrate mainly upon those particular ravines that have steep sidewalls, which encourage the deer to travel the entire length of the ravine in negotiating their escapes rather than attempting to go up and over one of the hillsides.

In any type of drive, hunters who are to be positioned on stand should bear in mind a cardinal rule of whitetail behavior. When deer are pushed from their beds, a buck almost always allows does to travel ahead of him to serve as advance guards, while he follows behind on a parallel course of travel. So it is imperative that a stand hunter not allow the initial wave of does passing through to detect his presence and warn the buck of impending danger. Moreover, be especially alert *not* to the does' immediate back-trail but to the right or left of their line of travel, as that is where you're most likely to spot a buck slinking along quietly while it keeps tabs on the does ahead of him.

But let's say it's only a two-man deer camp, yet you and your partner would like to help each other score by staging some type of drive. Is there any way only two hunters can effectively move deer in the direction of each other? Yes! And one maneuver that readily comes to mind is the type of strategy my friend Joe Cobb and I use whenever we hunt the Chippewa River drainage region near Eau Claire, Wisconsin. The countryside here is riddled with endless numbers of steep ridges that possess terraced hillside benches where wary bucks like to lie up in dense pole timber and evergreens. It's not only a perfect set-up for a two-man drive, but also will work anywhere else that similar terrain conditions prevail.

The gist of this drive is for one hunter to take one side of the ridge while his partner is on the other. Both hunters should be just below the crest of the hill, traveling parallel to each other as they hike along their own respective benches. Actually, what each hunter should try to do is not really drive the deer, but merely begin quietly stillhunting along the length of the ridge. Because the very spine of the ridge separates the two hunters from view, shots can safely be taken in any direction.

A two-man drive is ideal when you encounter a wooded ridge. When a deer is routed from its bed, it usually won't run very far straightaway. More likely, it will go up and over the crest and blunder into the hunter on the other side.

When a hunter jumps a buck from his bed, the deer will invariably line-out straightaway for a short distance and then cut sharply to the right or left and go up and over the crest of the ridge to the other side. I think bucks do this because they instinctively know that traveling the entire length of the bench will eventually bring them to the end of the ridge. And then they'll have no choice but go downhill, which they'd prefer not to do, especially during midday. That would mean sacrificing both their visual advantage and their ability to test the thermal air currents with their sense of smell. Yet by going up and over the ridge crest to the other side, the buck can then reverse his line of travel so he can remain on the same high ground. But, in this case, when the deer comes over the crest of the ridge, there is a hunter waiting for him.

Two years ago Joe Cobb and I were making one of these two-man drives and I jumped a very large deer from a spruce copse. I could only briefly see the deer's waving white banner in the distance before it disappeared from sight. About fifteen seconds after that I heard a single shot and knew exactly what happened.

"When the buck came over the ridge," saw me standing right there," Joe later explained, "he was so dumbfounded he just stood there and gawked. I dropped him right where he stood."

A drive party may consistently succeed in moving does in the right direction, but occasionally there will seem to be an apparent absence of any male deer. When this happens, it's a good bet the bucks simply are outsmarting the hunters and there's no law that says the hunters can't become just as conniving. At least, that's the concensus of one drive party I occasionally hunt with near Springfield, Illinois.

Bob Becker is the respectable drivemaster of the group, but some of the ploys he engineers are downright ungentlemanly. One of them he calls the "buttonhook drive" and it's used anytime there is extremely dense cover and bucks are suspected to be filtering back through the drive line.

Bob places two hunters on stand, then disperses five others in a spread-out drive line and has them begin pushing through the cover. However, two of the hunters on the drive line have instructions to go only about two-thirds of the way through the cover. Then they are supposed to about-face and begin stillhunting back in the opposite direction.

Frequently, these are the two hunters that get all the shooting because they see the very bucks that have managed to slip back through the drive line.

Over a decade ago, I developed a drive technique that entails the use of "flankers." If you know football, you know what flankers are and how they move. The system works great in a fairly large tract of mixed cover with some small clearings here and there. Flankers are the two drivers at each end of the drive line, but they don't travel a straightaway course through the cover with the other drivers. Instead, they flare out widely, one to the left

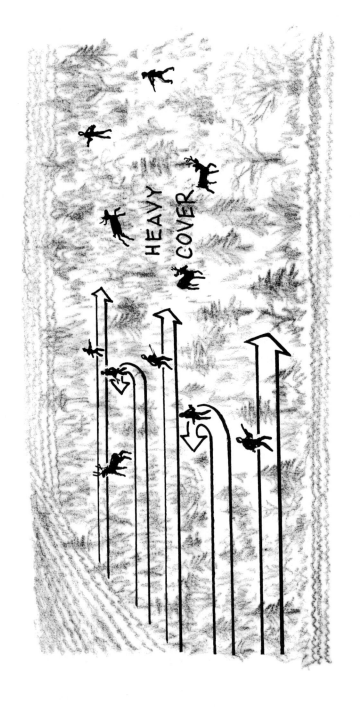

Use the buttonhook drive when cover is extremely thick and deer are suspected to be sneaking back through the drive line.

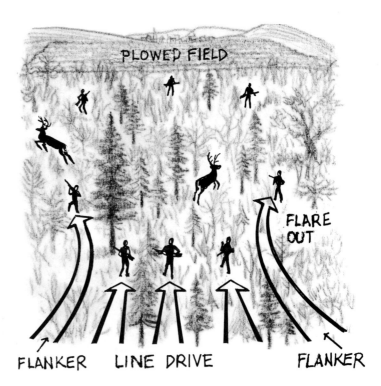

PLOWED FIELD

FLARE OUT

FLANKER LINE DRIVE FLANKER

Employing flankers on a drive line will tend to keep deer contained within the cover being driven rather than to spurt out the sides. But if they do try to sneak out a side door, there will be hunters in position to intercept them.

and the other to the right, moving in an arc away from the drive line to intercept deer that refuse to travel straight through the cover to the standers but have the unnerving habit of cutting left or right.

If your party consists of only a few hunters and you'd still like to make drives, try the "line drive," which does not require the placement of standers.

A four or five-man line drive works best in a rectangular chunk of terrain with two long sides, where clumps of very heavy cover are interspersed with clearings. The hunters start out on one of the long sides. They are quite far apart so that each hunter can just barely see an occasional flash of orange from his partners on either side. They move very slowly, and each hunter stillhunts on his own.

When a buck spooks, he is usually afraid to run toward the other long side of the cover because he will come to the open field beyond in a very short time. Instead, the buck will usually run a short distance ahead of the line and then turn to run across the face of the drive in order to stay in the woods. Eventually, he should expose himself to one of the other drivers on the line and present a relatively easy shot.

The "one-man drive" is just the ticket when all members of the hunting party prefer to wait on stands, but one man has already taken his buck and wants to help his partners fill their tags.

If this one-man drive is to succeed, the terrain must be scouted thoroughly or known in advance. The cover may be heavy, only moderately

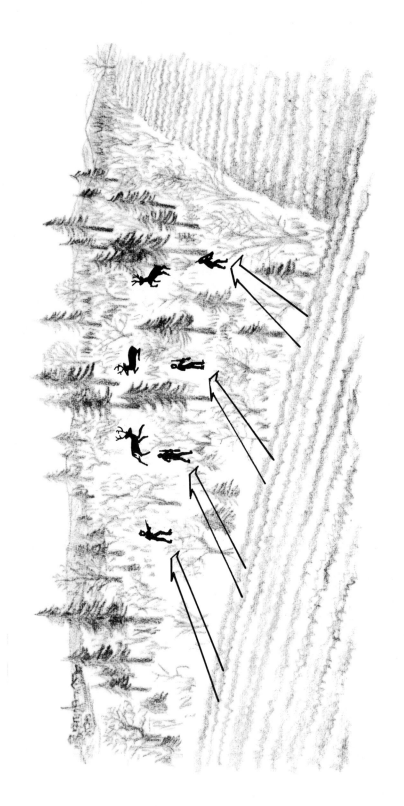

In the line drive, hunters are not placed on stands. This drive is most suited to long, rectangular strips of cover.

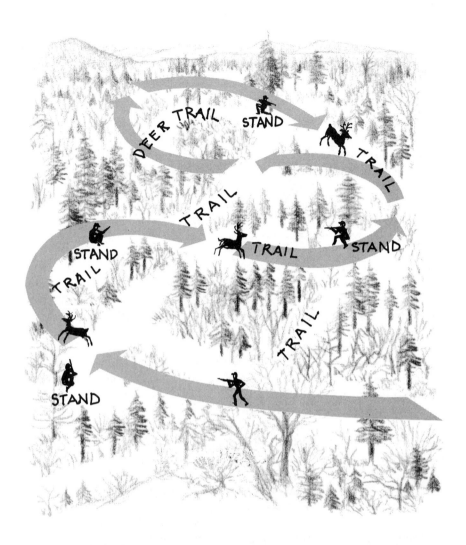

It's entirely possible for one hunter to stage a drive on behalf of his partners. The basic intent is simply to keep the animals circulating on their familiar trails where other hunters are waiting.

dense, or punctuated with many clearings, but the important thing is to be well aware of all the deer trails. Stands should be taken or blinds constructed at places where two or more trails cross or come together to form a major runway. The stands should not be so widely spaced that the lone driver is faced with seemingly endless miles of walking. If there are four stands, for example, they should preferably be within 600 yards of each other.

Standers take their positions, and the lone driver begins hiking a methodical pattern. He doesn't make a lot of noise, but he isn't entirely silent, and for safety reasons he should wear blaze orange. I often whistle softly as I go along, as though I'm on a routine summer hike. I know the deer trails, but I deviate from them now and then to push through heavy cover. Deer commonly see farmers, utility line workers, and others afield, and so a single driver not making an attempt to be too "sneaky" doesn't usually alarm them too much. They simply get up and move out of the approaching person's way before he gets too close, following one of their established trails. One driver can keep deer moving all day, and eventually the various standers should have shooting opportunities.

Regardless of the type of drive you choose in accordance with the topography of the terrain and how many hunters are available to participate, there are specific techniques that both standers and drivers should follow. First the standers.

Initially, a stander should move as quietly as possible to his stand area. But the exact place in which he waits probably is more important than anything else. If possible, he should have a good view of the landscape with at least several unobstructed shooting lanes. In nearly all cases, the stander's best vantage point will be on higher ground than the area where he is watching for deer to appear. This might be a steep hillside, rock outcropping, or a raised hummock or knoll. It also might be wise to use a portable, climbing-type tree stand. From a quickly installed, elevated platform, a stand hunter can more easily spot deer that are trying to sneak through cover, and approaching deer are less likely to spot him.

If the stand is at ground level, the hunter should use available cover to conceal his outline. Hiding behind a boulder, log, stump, bush, or tree trunk may be adequate in many instances. Take along a boat cushion or campstool that will enable you to sit quietly without moving, and be sure to clear the ground around you of brittle twigs and crunchy leaves that may betray your location. Try to avoid smoking until after the drive is over, and if the wind is not in your favor use a deer scent to mask your odor.

When deer begin passing through your area, they may be moving slowly but purposefully with their attention focused upon their backtrails and the drivers. They should have no idea *you* are there, so take your time and pick your best shot when the animals are motionless and looking over their shoulders in the opposite direction. Be alert for the buck that may suddenly appear after a bevy of does has passed by.

If the only shot you have is at a running buck, remember to calculate the necessary lead because a deer bounding along at 25 miles an hour is moving approximately 9 feet per second.

If a drivemaster posts you on a specific stand, don't wander off! The drivers are trying to push deer toward you, and if you're not there when the deer come through, you'll be unpopular. Additionally, any change of location on your part, after the drive has begun, constitutes movement that approaching deer may detect. Standers who wander also make life very dangerous for themselves. The drivers know where the standers are posted and do not shoot in their direction. It should not be necessary to say—but I'll say it anyway—that a stander should not fire in the direction of the drivers or to his left or right if other standers are posted there. In deer driving, as in all other forms of hunting, never fire unless your shot will be safely backstopped by a rise in the ground. If you are on an elevated stand, of course, the bullet is directed at the ground and most shots are therefore perfectly safe.

Now, tips for drivers.

There is a good deal of debate over whether drivers should yell and whistle or move silently. On one hand, noisy drivers usually succeed in moving deer that otherwise might remain bedded. But the deer often streak out so far ahead of the drive line that the drivers themselves seldom have shooting opportunities and those on stand are rewarded with only fleeting chances at fast-moving animals. When drivers move quietly, the deer are not as likely to panic and jackrabbit through the cover, which means both standers and drivers often have easy shots. But a quietly moving drive line encourages deer to remain bedded or attempt to circle and double back.

It is imperative for all drivers to synchronize their watches. A single .timepiece that is only one minute fast will cause a driver to begin too soon and quickly find himself far ahead of his partners. Aside from being dangerous, this may also push the deer in the wrong direction.

The spacing of the drivers is likewise important. As the cover opens up, hunters can expand the length of their drive line to push a wider swath. They'll want to close ranks when the cover becomes thick, to prevent deer from remaining bedded or slipping back between them. Each driver should make a point of investigating any particularly heavy cover in his immediate path to ensure bedded deer are duly rousted from their hideouts. Don't avoid thorny tangles; bull your way right on through them.

When a deer is killed, the lucky hunter should mark its exact location. I carry strips of fluorescent orange fabric cut from a discarded hunting vest and tie one of these on a nearby bush or tree branch. After marking the place, continue through the remainder of the drive as planned. There may be other bucks farther ahead that someone else may have a chance to collect. When the drive is completed, all members of the party can then return to dress the deer and take it to camp before the next drive.

No matter what the temptation, never fire in the direction of the standers unless there is intervening high ground to backstop your bullet. Keep track of the exact locations of other drivers as well, so you won't fire in their direction. This is one reason why some hunters who prefer silent drives nevertheless softly whistle now and then, to keep track of each other's progress as they move through the cover.

Finally, keep in mind the need to remain flexible. There is no single type of drive that is best, but rather drive concepts that can and must be tailored to the topography of the terrain, type of cover that exists there, number of hunters available and so on. Often, minor adjustments or adaptations in the way a drive is executed can spell a world of difference in the outcome.

For example, on one hunt in Michigan it seemed like there was virtually nothing we could do to push deer down a long hollow to our standers. We knew deer were in there, but for some reason they refused to head in a northerly direction, even though it would have meant being able to quarter into a crosswind. As a final desperation measure, we lined up and drove the cover still again, but this time in the opposite direction, toward the south. It worked like a charm and thirty minutes later we were field dressing a doe and two bucks!

Color some type of drive into your deer hunting picture this year. Especially in regions where deer are subjected to intense hunting pressure, drives can put bucks on the game pole when all else fails.

25

Hunting Spooked Deer

◆◆

Where the bucks go after opening day, and how they manage to evade throngs of hunters prowling the woodlands, remains a mystery to many. But sometimes small fragments of the puzzle fall into place, enabling smart hunters to take very nice bucks—even on the last day of the season.

My friend Clyde Beltner had one of these eye-opening experiences about six years ago. On his small farm in Morgan County, Ohio, well before opening day, he had pegged the routine of a handsome six-point whitetail using a trail through a narrow hollow choked with greenbrier. But after Beltner patiently waited on stand the entire season, the deer never showed, and Beltner's license went unfilled that year. Because guns had been hammering all around and a local newspaper reported that 24,000 hunters had infiltrated tiny Morgan County that year, Clyde was certain ''his'' deer had been taken by another hunter on a neighboring farm.

Two days after the season closed, Beltner grabbed a handsaw and hiked to the very center of an old meadow to cut down a Christmas tree. A raised patch of ground no larger than a front porch stood there, almost entirely shale and not capable of growing anything except a few evergreens that Clyde had planted years before as seedlings. Only one of those pines took root and survived. The lone pine, its branches drooping low to the ground, stood like a sentinel watching over acres and acres of open meadowland.

Beltner's mind was on unfinished holiday shopping, and so he wasn't prepared for what happened next. Suddenly, the same six-point buck he'd been hoping to collect days earlier jumped up from beneath the low pine boughs and bounded away, its hooves going like steam pistons. For a long moment, Clyde just stood there shaking his head in disbelief: That sneaky devil had probably been holed up right there for the entire season.

Understandably, Clyde later bought his Christmas tree in town. He also saw his buck many more times as the months passed. The following autumn, the deer was sporting a still larger rack—and still used the same trail through the same nearby hollow.

At the onset of the hunting season, Clyde went to his favorite stand, and gunshots predictably rang out in all directions all day. After two days of not even catching a glimpse of his buck, however, Clyde knew exactly where to go, and this time he was armed for the task at hand. After hiking halfway across the expansive meadow, he stopped and took a brief peek through his binoculars. Sure enough, the buck was bedded beneath the branches of the lone pine tree, his chin flat against the ground. Beltner quickly assumed a steady kneeling position, and with a single shot from 85 yards, collected his winter supply of venison.

Clyde now realizes, along with many other veteran hunters, that the complexion of pre-season scouting in states with short firearm deer seasons must necessarily take a different form than when pursuing deer in wilderness regions or during the bowhunting season, when one's strategies are seldom interfered with.

In many states, particularly those east of the Mississippi and especially on land such as state and national forests, timber company holdings, mining leases, and utility company property, hunting areas remain relatively fixed in number. But each year they must somehow accommodate more hunters than the season before. The net result is akin to cramming 6 pounds of apples into a 5-pound bag. Something, obviously, has to give, and in a vast majority of states, that "something" is a steadily diminishing hunter-success rate.

A good deal of research has attempted to explain how whitetails react to mounting hunting pressure. One of the most revealing studies was conducted by Illinois biologist Don Autry. In his report, titled *Movements of Whitetailed Deer in Response to Hunting Pressure on Crab Orchard National Wildlife Refuge,* tagged deer were described as having been monitored every day for seven months, including during the hunting season.

Interestingly, Autry noted that whitetails seldom leave their home ranges, no matter how high the hunting pressure. There are two instances in which they may indeed leave, the first being when they are chased by dogs. One study deer traveled 13 miles in an attempt to evade its canine pursuers. Yet shortly after the hounds were called off, the deer quickly returned to its home range. The other instance in which a deer was likely to evacuate was when it incurred an ultimately fatal wound during the hunting season. Shock was believed to account for the animal's unusual behavior.

It stands to reason that deer spooked by hunting pressure would elect to cling to that particular turf where they feel safest, which instinctively causes them to remain in places intimately familiar to them rather than venturing into distant and unfamiliar regions.

Many hunters believe trophy bucks are so intelligent they know in advance when the hunting season is about to open, and take evasive action before the inevitable fusilade of shots ever begins. In my opinion, this gives white-tails too much credit. I think, they are simply very cognizant of goings-on in their habitat. And in adapting to living close to mankind, they soon realize what does and doesn't constitute normal human activity within their home ranges. The survival strategy adopted by each buck certainly is unique, but each tries to be where the hunter is not. Once deer relocate themselves in "safety zones" within their home ranges, it's quite common for them to then sharply decrease their daytime activity. In Don Autry's research, the first and second days of the hunting season resulted in deer sightings decreasing by 42 percent.

Of course, when one intends to pursue deer on a relatively small tract of public hunting land, he'll want to begin enacting his scouting in the usual manner. This means acquiring maps and/or aerial photos of the terrain and then exploring the region to determine if huntable numbers of animals are present. Of course, it's also wise to locate bedding areas, feeding sites, breeding sign, and major trails the deer have been using.

However, one great shortcoming of most hunters is next failing to plug still another crucial element into the scouting equation: the sudden presence of countless other hunters that very shortly will also be in the immediate vicinity.

In whitetail habitat that has been relatively quiet and undisturbed for the previous eleven months, save the occasional hiker or bird hunter, suddenly convoys of vehicles are traveling seldom-used trails and back roads. Hunters themselves are tramping around in full force, saturating the woodlands with man scent, climbing trees, cutting brush for ground-level blinds, cutting firewood for camp, hollering while making drives, sending out barrages of shots, and chasing the animals back and forth through the woods.

Obviously, only one or two days of such blatant intrusion is more than enough to alter their normal behavior patterns and force them into hiding. Survival now becomes their foremost concern. Feeding and other activities become secondary and largely nocturnal.

One locale that hard-hunted whitetails frequently retreat into is any kind of marshy lowland, swale, or swamp containing at least several inches of standing water. Before wolves and big cats disappeared from the eastern and midwestern United States, whitetails instinctively knew to take to water to avoid predators hot on their scent. Hence, they ran into swamps or other boggy areas in low elevations. Today, the "predators" are hunters with guns and this keeps the deer's swamp-loving instinct alive.

Not many deer hunters dress appropriately for gunning in swamps. Fewer still have the desire to go sloshing through sometimes knee-deep water, muck, and mire because it's cold and wet, it stinks, and it is difficult to negotiate on foot. As a result, most hunters elect to bypass such hellish places altogether, or at least widely skirt their perimeters to stay on high and dry ground. Yet the bold, willing hunter will discover that shortly after opening-day rifles begin cracking, junglelike marshland may act as a magnet to deer inhabiting the immediate region.

I discovered last year in South Carolina's Francis Marion National Forest just how many deer seek refuge in swamplands. Due to prior commitments, Benny Wilson and I were unable to join forces until the fourth day of the deer season. We didn't even bother to scout or install portable tree stands in our usual places, as that was strictly the strategy we reserved for the opening two days of the season. Instead, we decided upon the belated tactic of donning chest waders and slowly sneak-hunting through flooded black-oak timber and cypress bogs.

During the early morning and late afternoon hours we saw dozens of browsing deer, standing hock-deep in the tannin-stained water. We discov-

Whitetails often like to hide in marshy lowlands or swamps. Hunters usually skirt these places because of the mud and sometimes waist-deep water.

When you wade in swamps, your approach is often so noiseless you may have point-blank shots. Look for deer bedding on slightly elevated hummocks and ridges where there's dry ground. I photographed this buck rising from his bed only 20 feet away.

ered that during the midday hours, these deer like to find small, dry, slightly elevated hummocks and ridges where they can bed down.

Because there are no brittle twigs or dry leaves to betray his location, a stealthy swamp hunter can often approach feeding or bedded deer quite easily. A hunter who wades slowly, hunts into the wind, and uses intervening cover to conceal each advance forward can move along as silently and inconspicuously as a wisp of woodsmoke.

On this particular hunt, Benny and I picked off bucks right in their beds and in both cases the shooting distance was less than 50 yards. If you miss your opportunity and the deer bound away, splashing through water as they make their escapes, don't despair. They won't leave the swamp but simply retreat into its farther reaches. Come back the next day, this time entering the swamp on the opposite side, and you can expect a repeat performance that this time may result in success.

If swamps are the premier locations for finding hard-hunted whitetails, second place must go to pine forests and plantations, which speckle the whitetail's habitat from coast to coast.

Another place spooked deer like to retreat into are thick pine plantations where immature trees still have dense whorls of branches close to the ground to afford concealment.

Whitetails have a distinct preference for long-needle species such as white pine and red pine, but the real key is to find the immature, closely planted trees no taller than 8 or 10 feet. These young trees generally have dense whorls of branches close to the ground, which create a thick understory that whitetails find ideal to hide under. Conversely, stands of older, towering pines block sunlight penetration, causing the lower branches to die and self-prune themselves, leaving little if any understory.

One pine plantation near Eau Claire, Wisconsin, contains such a density of young trees that a walking hunter could not see 6 feet in any direction. After several days of unsuccessfully hunting nearby birch ridges where tracks pockmarked almost every square yard of ground, our party eventually realized that the pressured deer just had to be hiding in the pines. To overcome the difficulty of not being able to see any appreciable distance from ground level, we hung portable stands high in trees surrounding the perimeter of the plantation and posted ourselves during the hours of dawn and dusk. From elevated vantage points, we could easily see long distances down and through the aisles of pines. By the end of the next day, four additional bucks were hanging from our camp game pole, every one of them having been taken from deep within the interior of the plantation.

However, security cover doesn't necessarily have to mean large tracts of impregnable terrain, as Clyde Beltner discovered. It only needs to consist of enough cover to conceal a deer, be situated so it won't arouse the interest of most hunters, and all the while give a crafty buck the self-assurance that he is safe from whizzing bullets. A classic illustration of this whitetail trait occurred once in Iowa.

Anyone who has ever visited the Hawkeye State knows the soil consists mainly of rich, black loam. Consequently, almost every square inch not used for houses, barns, or grain elevators is diligently plowed and planted. Many hunters still manage to take fine bucks every year, but usually from the most unsuspecting places.

Throughout most of the year, the deer cling to the very few woodlots and thickets that separate wide tracts of croplands. Yet when hunters begin swarming through these places on opening day, the deer seem to vanish. The woodlots and thickets are now barren of whitetail activity. All the terrain that surrounds them is flat and open, but that's exactly where the deer are!

One fall, our group found deer in unbelievable places. They would belly down in small depressions and drainage ditches, lie in the shade of a rock pile, or hunker down near a stack of old fence posts. Much hiking was

Whitetails don't always hide in large patches of thick cover. In many states, especially in the farm belt, where such cover doesn't exist, look for deer in small thickets and gullies.

needed to check each isolated feature, and we had to be prepared for quick action when a deer finally bolted from its hideout and began streaking away across the flats. Invariably, when the deer took off after being routed from their beds, they didn't head back to the woodlots or brushy thickets, undoubtedly knowing those would be unsafe places to be. Instead, they headed intently for the nearest still-standing cropland, which in this particular case usually meant corn.

Hunting in standing corn provides excellent lessons in humility, frustration, and exasperation because once deer have spooked and decided to hide in corn, they will refuse to leave. The only way to drive them to standers placed along the opposite edge is by having dozens of drivers spaced mere yards apart. Because this isn't practical, the deer will succeed in thwarting every drive by circling and dodging the hunters who are participating, giving each a monumental case of the vapors.

Sitting on a stand is probably the best way to hunt spooked deer hiding in corn. I like to station myself at a corner of the cornfield, which allows me to watch two long sides for a considerable distance, for maybe as much as

In agricultural regions, standing corn offers deer perfect hiding, and hunters acquire excellent lessons in humility and frustration.

700 yards of total coverage. In this manner, any deer that happens to peek out along the edge should present a clear shot, but this is likely to happen only during the first hour of dawn and the last hour of dusk.

In Louisiana a similar situation exists. For many years, when hunting pressure intensified in woodlots and brushy ravines, the deer commonly retreated from all the commotion, leaving local hunters baffled. Then the lid blew off the kettle, so to speak, when in the early 1980s a cropduster being interviewed by a television station reported that one of the most intriguing sidelights to his work occurred during hunting season, when he always saw a high number of big bucks lounging around in the middle of expansive cotton fields.

"I saw one enormous buck more than a half mile from the edge of the nearest woodlot," the pilot said. "He was just laying there without a care in the world, with just his eyes, ears, and antlers visible above the cotton plants."

The word spread like wildfire through hunting-oriented communities and it should not be difficult to guess what happened during upcoming seasons. Hunters began invading cotton fields full force. They stillhunted around the perimeters, staged massive drives right through the middles of the fields, and took many splendid bucks. Then the action began to taper off and, as this is being written, cotton fields no longer are so productive in large parts of Louisiana. Just as earlier generations of deer learned the woodlots and brushy ravines were not safe places to be during hunting season, more recent generations of whitetails have received a like education regarding cotton fields.

Today, the hotspots for finding spooked Louisiana whitetails include swamps, timbered riverbottoms, and other thick cover found in association with water. But the point to be made is that whitetails won't hesitate to give up heavy cover for sparse cover if they've learned from prior experiences that such decisions will allow them to avoid hunters.

Dr. Keith Causey, a professor of wildlife science at Alabama's Auburn University, who has also studied the evasive responses of spooked deer during the hunting season, spoke of one curious trait. "In our radio-telemetry studies, we discovered that one of the spots a mature deer will go to avoid hunting pressure is beside a rural residence that has much human activity and even barking dogs in the yard, provided they are kenneled or chained to their doghouses. Usually, the deer will bed in thick brush or tall grass sometimes within 30 or 40 yards of the house, with nobody ever being the wiser."

Causey's finding reminds me of two incidents I've personally witnessed in the last five years, but could never explain.

Behind our southern Ohio farmhouse there is a long, open-air shed where we house a tractor and other miscellaneous machinery. It's also where we hang any deer taken during the season, to protect the carcases from the

According to a radio-telemetry study conducted by Dr. Keith Causey of Auburn University, "one place mature bucks will go to avoid hunting pressure is beside a rural residence that has much human activity and even barking dogs in the yard."

weather as they properly age. Immediately behind the shed is a half-acre of tangled blackberry and raspberry bushes, and a long, narrow corridor separating the two. Maybe once every other week, I hike down through that corridor to an open hillside beyond to check on the operation of our developed spring, which supplies our home with water.

One afternoon, my father and I were skinning the hide off a buck I had taken that morning. It was the third day of the deer season. It also was a time for celebration and as we worked inside the shed we were each drinking a beer and laughing as we recounted the excitement that had taken place earlier that day.

About a half-hour into our work, my wife Marianne called out the back door that our water pressure had gone way down, and asked that we hike down to the spring to see if the pump was still running. As dad and I made our way through the corridor between the large stands of berry bushes, two large does suddenly leapt to their feet and bounded away. They had been bedded in the tangled briers all the while, not more than 20 feet behind the shed where we had been working and talking loudly!

Another time, during hunting season, I was standing at the edge of our backyard by a trash-burning barrel, dutifully stirring the flames with a poker and thinking about which of my several stands I'd return to later that afternoon. Because of the large pile of bags filled with stuff to be burned, I'd been there about fifteen minutes, and I'm one of those people who always seems to be talking to himself whenever alone.

Suddenly, from maybe 25 yards away, I heard a faint rustling in the dry leaves where several old trees had died and were blown down by the wind. I looked up just in time to see a young six-point buck unceremoniously rise to his feet and slink away. Like the does described above, that rascal had been there all the time. I sometimes wonder how many other times he had watched me burn trash. In any event, the atmosphere of the situation never posed any threat, so it suited him just fine during this brief frenetic week when redcoats were prowling around in nearby woodlands.

Of course, prior to Dr. Causey's research findings pertaining to deer seeking hideouts close to human habitation, I merely chalked up the two experiences as oddities. But now, I realize this actually is quite common behavior among whitetails. I've even attempted to put this insight to good hunting use.

Whenever hunting pressure seems unusually intense some year or another, and I'm not having much success seeing deer in their usual haunts, I check the unusual places. As often as not, these are the narrow and otherwise uninteresting looking drainage culverts descending downhill from our ridgetop farmhouse, the hillside choked with berry bushes behind our shed, or even the acre of dense honeysuckle that has grown out of control behind our barn.

This is *not* meant to condone hunting close to places of human habitation or anywhere that pets, livestock, or personal property may be endangered by shooting action. In fact, engaging in this type of irresponsible behavior is one of the best ways I know of to ensure your hunting permission on a private farm is revoked forever. What I'm saying is that, on your own private land, or on an abandoned homestead, or even on an occupied farm, there are certain to be places where deer elect to hole up because they have learned they are not likely to be disturbed there. When you're a guest on someone else's property and suspect deer may be hiding in similar circumstances, invite the landowner or a member of his family to hunt with you. Under his supervision, you can rest assured any shooting action will be safe and in accord with what he deems permissible.

In many regions of the country, growing numbers of deer-hunting parties are pursuing their quarry in yet another way, and they're enjoying notable success. The first day or two of the season, everyone in the group waits on his chosen stand, consistent with what has been learned during previous scouting missions. The deer have yet to be overly pressured, so watching well used trails, breeding scrapes, and feeding sites is likely to yield at least a couple of handsome racks.

But beginning about the third day, these hunters cloak themselves in fluorescent orange, spread out in a drive line, and begin marching cross-country. No standers are placed as in a conventional drive, though, because hard-hunted whitetails simply will not allow themselves to be pushed any significant distance. Instead, they merely run short distances away from the drivers. The drive line must maintain quite close ranks or the deer won't run at all but hunker down and not budge an inch unless they're almost stepped upon.

I recently participated in one of these "rabbit hunts" for whitetails in Kentucky and was amazed with the results. Five of us spread out about 15 yards from each other and began tramping the length of a stream bottom, where thick clumps of willows and goldenrod stalks offered perfect midseason hiding conditions for deer.

First a doe bounded out in front of us. She ran no more than 30 yards, quickly came to a stop, and then ducked back down again. Several minutes later a forkhorn buck popped up, which I brought down with an easy, close-in shot. As we approached the buck, the same doe we'd previously flushed got up again, ran another 30 yards, and spooked a six-pointer farther ahead. That buck scurried along belly-tight to the ground for only a short distance before hitting the deck. Later, Bob Wilson tagged the buck by simply walking him up and kicking him out of hiding.

Deer biologist Larry Marchington tells of having similar experiences during the course of his research work. "I've tracked radio-collared deer, knowing exactly where they were bedded. In walking toward them, they've often let me get so close I could see them breathing. There was one buck that allowed me to walk right up to within 3 feet of his hiding place and he never moved a muscle. I slowly circled him and he continued to just hug the ground. The only way I could get that deer to react to my presence was to make eye contact with him, and then he flew out of there!"

Any hunter should be able to use this knowledge in any region where hard-hunted deer simply cease engaging in normal daily behavior. It may sound contradictory to all the usual deer hunting lore, but in a case like this it's not necessary to be quiet, walk slowly, or worry about which direction the wind may be carrying your scent. Just find brier patches, stands of alders, swatches of tall buffalo grass, ravines choked with blowdowns, or other typical security cover. Then bull your way right on through, knowing that spooked whitetails are reluctant to move from their hiding spots until a hunter is so close he almost trips over them. It is necessary, however, to stop frequently and peer deep into dark tangles and other foreboding places, because if you move too fast, a deer's natural camouflage coloring works in his favor to help him go undetected. Obviously, don't expect to see a "whole" deer because they'll be laying down and your visual exploration should therefore be trained upon ground level.

In those particular regions of the country where there's no way to avoid crowded hunting conditions early in the season, and where deer are so subjected to pressure they are temporarily no longer adhering to routine lifestyles, wisdom may dictate that you not even go hunting at all, at least not right off. Many advanced deer hunters nowadays prefer to shun the clamor and din of opening day, reserving their most serious efforts for later in the season.

Hunting statistics compiled by numerous state game departments have repeatedly shown that hunting pressure is the most intense during the first three days of the season. During the first and second days is when upwards of 60 percent of that year's deer harvest is predictably recorded. Moreover, while some very nice bucks are taken during these early days, the statistics also reveal a majority are young deer, 1½ and 2-year-olds, that don't know the tricks of surviving the hunting season. From this point on, both hunting pressure and harvest figures dramatically decline.

By the time the final days of the season are beginning to draw to a close, hunter enthusiasm has so sharply waned you may even have certain regions entirely to yourself. But as this hunting pressure markedly decreases, there is a slow resurgence of "normal" deer activity. Many of the larger deer that instantly went into hiding when opening-day guns began booming are now coming out of hiding and gradually reverting back to their previous feeding and travel tendencies.

Consequently, after any hunter has stacked up a number of hunting seasons under his belt and had many accumulated experiences and successes, he may come to an intriguing conclusion. If he widens his perspective and looks back upon the largest bucks he has collected over the years, he'll undoubtedly find a majority were harvested on either the first day of the season, or during the concluding days.

Index